THE CANADIAN DON QUIXOTE:
the life and works of Major John Richardson,
Canada's first novelist.

THE CANADIAN DON QUIXOTE:

the life and works of Major John Richardson, Canada's first novelist.

DAVID R. BEASLEY

This edition is published by The Porcupine's Quill, Inc., 68 Main Street, Erin, Ontario N0B 1T0. Orders, be they trade or institutional, may be directed to Mosaic Press, po box 1032 Oakville, Ontario L6J 5E9.

American orders may be directed to Leonard Smuckler, po box 1051, Laguna Beach, California 92652.

Second printing, 1978.

This edition has been designed by Tim Inkster, and was printed & bound into books with the assistance of Elke Inkster and Peter Taylor in July of 1977. The type is Andover and the stock is Zephyr Antique Laid.

The cover is after an engraving by Cruikshank entitled, "The Point of Honour".

ISBN 0-88984-022-9 (cloth)
      0-88984-020-2 (wrappers)

Contents

Richardson's bibliographer, for his encouragement and interest throughout these years. And finally I acknowledge my debt to the Canadian people whose Canada Council helped me to research in England in the summer of 1971. To Professor Gerald Lahey and Mr E.C. Beer my thanks for reading the manuscript and for useful suggestions.

This book has been published with the help of a grant from the Humanities Research Council of Canada, using funds provided by the Canada Council.

Acknowledgements

IN THE EARLY SIXTIES I came upon a footnote in the John Askin *Papers* referring to a Canadian novelist named John Richardson who died as a result of starvation in New York City. Aside from the fact that I could see myself in a similar circumstance as I was writing novels unsuccessfully in New York City at that time, I was attracted to this unknown author because like most Canadians I had been educated to believe there were only some few poets who could be said to represent the Canadian literary heritage. Richardson's novels, when I located them, surprised me by their power of expression and originality. For some years I pieced together scraps of information with the aid of scores of librarians, archivists and many others for which I now thank them en masse. I remember, too, many kindnesses such as that of Premier Jean Lesage of Quebec who made possible my reaching old Montreal police records and that of Mr. Laurence French of London, England who photostated coded diary entries so that I might take them with me to decode. I thank Mrs Marilan Lund of The New York Public Library for editorial help on the first chapters, and with respect to editing I am particularly grateful to H. Pearson Gundy of Kingston, Ontario who patiently and encouragingly showed me how to thrash the wheat from the chaff (some of which settled into footnotes). Also I thank W.F.E. Morley,

For my dearest *Viola*,
companion in the search,
encourager of the nearly-defeated,
with much love.

... it will neither be wise nor prudent in you, having been received into a British regiment, to become the Don Quixote of your countrymen.

The Canadian Brothers, I, 23.

Incentive

Old Fort Erie and Windmill where Richardson lived as a small boy. City of Buffalo visible across river.

JOHN RICHARDSON was born on October 4, 1796. His birth may have taken place in the officer's quarters in Fort George which guarded the Upper Canadian capital, Newark, now called Niagara-on-the-Lake where the Niagara River flows into Lake Ontario. A plaque commemorating his birth stands a few miles upstream at Queenston village because it is thought that his mother, Madeleine, was staying in the Queenston home of her elder sister, Catharine Hamilton, wife of the fur-trading scion, Robert Hamilton. The Hamilton mansion could have accomodated Madeleine, especially since the older Hamilton children were away at school in Scotland, but Catharine — "dear Kitty" — was ailing with consumption, and Madeleine may have been sensitive about imposing herself on the household. It seems probable, therefore, that Madeleine was with her husband, Robert, the surgeon at Fort George.

Richardson's immediate ancestry was meaningful enough to him to figure in his writings, such as the novels *Wacousta* and *The Canadian Brothers*, and deserves a brief examination here. His mother's family had the greater significance for him. Madeleine Richardson's father was the fur-trader John Askin. Her mother was an Indian of the Ottawa tribe. Madeleine was the youngest of three children — born, perhaps, like the eldest, John Askin Jr., in the central Ottawa town of Arbre Croche on Lake Michigan. Nothing of her mother has been recorded; it seems, however, that, since John Askin married again in 1772, her mother died before that date.[1]

Many were the stories about her father, John Askin.[2] The patriarch of his family was John Erskine, the Earl of Mar, who led the Scottish uprising of 1715 and whose failure forced the clan to scatter to escape reprisal. John Askin's father fled to county Tyrone in

[1] John Askin Jr. was born in Arbre Croche (now Cross Village on the east coast of Lake Michigan near the Straits of Mackinac) in 1762, Catharine in 1763 and Madeleine probably in 1770. There is no evidence that Askin's wife was from the Ottawa Nation save that she would have had her children only amongst her own people, thus accounting for the births in the central Ottawa town. A.C. Casselman was told by descendants of the Askins in 1900 that she was a French lady! An affidavit of Askin's marriage to Archange Barth on June 21, 1772 is in the Ontario Archives.

[2] A short biography of John Askin is found in *Burton Historical Collection Leaflet* No. 4 (March 1925). A letter from Askin's daughter, Archange, to her nephew, Pattinson (May

Ireland and changed his name to Askin. Young John Askin, however, was raised by his grandfather in Dumbartonshire, Scotland. His grandfather left him money which Askin used to travel from court to court in Europe and finally to America where he invested in a general store in Albany with Robert Rogers, the backwoods hero of the French and Indian War. Askin, trading far into the North-West, lived for some years at Fort Michillimackinac on Lake Michigan. His land holdings were extensive. On settling at Detroit he owned a thousand-acre farm, a general store from which he conducted a thriving fur-trading business, shipyards, brickyards, a race-course and stables within the boundaries of the present-day city. Also a land speculator, he held title to millions of acres south of Lake Erie.[3] Then in 1802, when the American government was finally able to administer Detroit which had been ceded to it in 1783, he forsook it all rather than take an oath of loyalty to the United States, and he moved to the Canadian shore of the Detroit River. Here he built a mansion called "Strabane" after his birthplace in northern Ireland.

Askin's second wife, Marie Archange, was of French descent. She had been a small girl in Fort De-

troit in 1763 when Askin, at great risk, led an expedition bringing food supplies to the inhabitants beseiged by the Indian tribes under Pontiac. She sent Askin's two daughters, Catharine and Madeleine, to be educated at the Congregation de Notre Dame in Montreal where the girls became bilingual. Catharine returned to the West first and married a rich trading partner of her father's, Robert Hamilton. When Madeleine finished her schooling, she visited with her sister in Queenston for the winter months of 1793. Among the officers whom the Hamilton's entertained she met and married Robert Richardson.[4] He had come from Allandale, Scotland as a surgeon with the Queen's Rangers whose business was to hack the beginnings of a civilization out of the Canadian wilderness. His family also had tasted reprisal; it had taken part in the Jacobite rebellion of 1745. John Richardson, their second child, born into these romantic British memories, never lost the mark of their stamp.

When John was almost two, the Richardson family was sent to Fort Erie. Madeleine wrote to her parents: "John walks everywhere and is as fat as ever. He is fond of sleigh-riding for he loves a horse."[5] In 1800 the family moved to the new capital, York, where Dr. Richardson helped to choose the location for the Governor's residence.[6] The Doctor's transfer to Fort Joseph in the remote northlands the following year was not a pleasant prospect, especially as John Richardson was ready for school. Fortunately, John and Marie Askin offered to care for John in Detroit, where he could attend a school. His parents missed the little boy in the dreary winter months: "Madeleine and myself are extremely anxious to hear of little John. We trust him in good health and a good boy. We

11, 1847) in the Ontario Archives gives a romanticized version of Askin's background. It is interesting that she mentions the drowning of Askin's aunt and her husband in a sea squall when returning to England from the West Indies; Richardson used this incident in his *Canadian Brothers*, II, chap. 3 and cast the drowned couple in the role of Mrs Grantham's parents.

   [3] Askin purchased 20,000 acres from Moravian Indians on Mount Clemens, one million acres on the Miami River including present day Toledo and the Sandusky peninsula, land along Lake Erie from Cuyahoga River to Sandusky Lake including present-day Cleveland, 5,294,120 acres in Ohio, and the 20,000,000 acres of the entire lower peninsula of Michigan. (*Burton Historical Collection Leaflet* No. 4 (March 1925). Detroit Public Library.

[4] *John Askin Papers*, I, 441.

[5] *Ibid.*, II, 131.

[6] ALS, Robert Richardson *et al.* to Governor Simcoe (York, Aug. 24, 1799) Public Archives of Canada RG1 E3/47.94.

are perfectly convinced he is in good hands."[7]

He was in loving hands. John Askin, whose children by his second marriage were in their teens, had the time to give much affection and attention to his grandchild. John was sent to school with his older cousins, and taught to read by a Detroit clergyman at ten shillings a month.[8] In the evenings, perhaps to keep him from missing his mother as well as out of affection for him, Marie Askin told him stories of the history of the early French settlement, including the seige of Fort Detroit. Years later he wrote that her stories, by stirring his imagination, had given him the incentive to become a writer.

He must have been fascinated as well by the comings and goings of traders and Indians in his grandfather's trading business. His uncle, John Askin Jr., who was half-Indian, carried on his father's trade in the Indian country. Askin's agent to the Indian nations along the far reaches of the Miami River was a tall athletic Scot, John Norton,[9] whom young Richardson saw in his grandfather's store and heard referred to as the man from the territory of West Augusta, shortened to Wagousta.[10] The name "Wagousta" and Norton's adoption of Indian ways and dress were to provide the inspiration for the character of Wacousta in Richardson's most popular novel, *Wacousta*.

Richardson's separation from his parents ended the following year when the Queen's Rangers were disbanded and Robert Richardson became surgeon to the garrison at the newly-constructed Fort Malden on the Detroit River. His family, to which had been added two younger brothers, lived in the town of Amherstburg which grew up about the fort. Besides the garrison soldiers and the townspeople, Dr. Richardson cared for settlers and Indians in the surrounding wilderness. He innoculated hundreds of Indians against smallpox annually when they canoed from the Upper Lakes to Fort Malden to receive government presents.[11] The sight of these wild tribesmen descending on the village and setting up camp around it thrilled young John Richardson. Of course Indians stopped at Bois Blanc Island in front of the village throughout the year. There Richardson watched them as they silently fished in the evenings, the prows of their canoes lightened with birchbark to attract the fish and the spearsman standing poised to strike. In the gloom under a moonless sky, these wild visitors were like phantoms engaged in nightly warfare. But the fall visitation which brought hundreds of proud and fierce-looking braves moving through the streets of Amherstburg was the climax of excitement.

Richardson spent his boyhood in Amherstburg. The fort on the west side with the Indian council house near it, the dock and the painted wooden houses of the settlement cut out of the wilderness, and the high bank on the east which curved out toward the island leaving passage for ships coming into harbour, created a memorable scene. There were moments of rare beauty such as the setting sun winking and flashing behind the trees on the island which cast the village into shadow, and at twilight the song

[7] *John Askin Papers*, II, 368.

[8] *John Askin Papers*, II, 368 "For instructing John Richardson in reading from the 17th of July to the 25th Augt. (1801) at 10/- per month. 12/6." A description of the rapid construction of the schoolroom is given in F. Clever Bald, *Detroit's First American Decade, 1796 to 1805* (Ann Arbor: University of Michigan Press, 1948), pp.182-3. Reverend David Bacon taught reading, writing, arithmetic, English grammar and geography.

[9] J. McE. Murray, "John Norton," Ontario Historical Society, *Papers and Records*, 27 (1945), 7-16.

[10] *Western Virginia Historical Magazine*, III, 147. The western boundary between West Virginia and Pennsylvania on the Ohio River.

[11] ALS, Billy Caldwell to William Claus (1816), Public Archives of Canada.

View of Amherstburg, Summer 1813, by M. Reynolds. Foreground is Elliott's Point; on the left is Bois Blanc Island; on the right is the mainland and town.

of the whippoorwill.[12] John's closest friend was his younger brother, Robert. They played marbles in front of the general store, fished from the wharf, rode along the beaches, canoed to the islands, hunted in all seasons, and attended school or "college" as it was called. Richardson hated school — he was frequently beaten for no reason apparent to him. Often he planned to run away from home to escape the daily dosage of Latin and Euclid but the thought of being apprehended by his father prevented him.[13]

Dr. Richardson brought his family up frugally. In spite of working as District Judge and in other capacities he could barely make ends meet. "Austere in manner, severe in his administration of justice, he might have been considered a harsh man, had not

these qualities been tempered by his well known benevolence to the poor, and his staunch, yet unostentatious support for the deserving and well intentioned."[14] Richardson wrote later that it was his father's integrity and sense of duty which he emulated.[15] The father was proud of his sons and took them on trips to the back country where they learned to respect nature and hunt for their food. To catch a pheasant on the wing took a good eye and steady hand — training which was to become invaluable to Richardson when he was later confronted with the best duellists in Europe. In spite of the need for food, though, Richardson learned from his father to leave untouched the masses of migrating passenger pigeons which flew so low they could be killed just by knocking them down with a stick.

His mother's affectionate nature contrasted with the reserve of his father. Although Askin respected Dr. Richardson greatly, making him executor of his will, it was Madeleine who kept up a close relationship with the Askins by canoeing or sleighing or riding the twenty miles to see her relatives. At times moody and despondent, she would burst forth with enthusiasm for a sleigh-ride and picnic or for a dance in Detroit, even if there was a thaw which meant having the sleigh pulled by a Canadian from ice floe to ice floe across the river.[16] Richardson seemed to inherit her love for social intercourse and his father's reserve — a combination of traits which made him difficult to understand by those who did not know him well. His love for literature was given to him by his foster grandmother, Marie, whom he continued to visit at Strabane. He spent hours in his grandfather's library, and, of course, his many older cousins bought the latest books from New York and Albany. The Hamil-

[12] The whippoorwill's song has a nostalgic quality which haunted Richardson's dreams in Europe; see his "Notes" to *Tecumseh*, p.121.
[13] *Eight Years in Canada*, p.87.

[14] *The Canadian Brothers*, II, 33.
[15] *Ibid.*, II, 34.
[16] *Ibid*, II, 46.

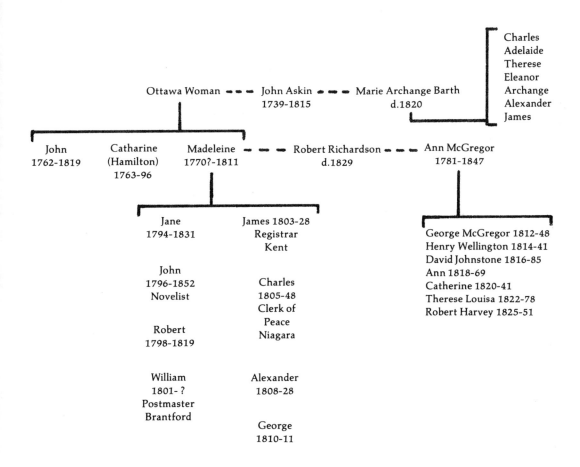

Ottawa Woman --- John Askin --- Marie Archange Barth
                   1739-1815   d.1820

Charles
Adelaide
Therese
Eleanor
Archange
Alexander
James

John   Catharine   Madeleine --- Robert Richardson --- Ann McGregor
1762-1819   (Hamilton)   1770?-1811   d.1829   1781-1847
                1763-96

Jane   James 1803-28
1794-1831   Registrar
                        Kent

John   Charles
1796-1852   1805-48
Novelist   Clerk of
                        Peace
                        Niagara
Robert
1798-1819

William   Alexander
1801- ?   1808-28
Postmaster
Brantford
                        George
                        1810-11

George McGregor 1812-48
Henry Wellington 1814-41
David Johnstone 1816-85
Ann 1818-69
Catherine 1820-41
Therese Louisa 1822-78
Robert Harvey 1825-51

13

ton boys, sons of his Aunt Catharine, returned from school in Scotland and fired the imaginations of the Askin and Richardson children with thoughts of Europe. Walter Scott's poems about chivalry in the Middle Ages, revered by these Scottish-Canadians, were basic reading for Richardson. Indeed, the infatuation of the English for stories of historical romance extended even to Amherstburg. The far-away world of Walter Scott was brought closer by the simple fact that the mysterious John Norton, or Chief Teyoninhokorawen (he had become the leader of the Six Nations), had made friends with the novelist on a trip to the British Isles.[17] Norton belonged to the Canadian wilderness; he rarely made an appearance among his white friends, as old John Askin noted laconically in his diary: "New Moon. John Norton came in the forenoon and stayed to dinner."[18]

Askin himself added reality to the chivalric romance: he, like most of the leaders of the pioneer communities, was a mason — his illustrious ancestor, the Earl of Mar, had introduced the masonic order of Knight Templars into Scotland, given new life to the Order of St. John of Jerusalem, and transplanted it from its last Mediterranean refuge.[19]

Yet the strongest influence came from Richardson's favourite book, Cervantes' *Don Quixote*, which was popular throughout the North American backwoods. The impracticability of the would-be knight amused the practical-minded settlers. At the same time, these struggling people sympathised with the errant knight who yearned to right wrong and bring some kind of moral order to the chaos of human nature. Did not every settler at some time feel that he was facing the unruly elements alone? The popularity of Hugh Brackenridge's *Modern Chivalry*, the first literary work published west of the Alleghanies, about an American knight, Captain Ferrago and his servant, Teague O'Regan, in the frontier communities, seems to corroborate the supposition that the settlers felt a bond with the Quixotic struggle. Richardson then had ample fuel for his imagination, and most likely, in make-believe games his brother played Sancho to his own Don Quixote de la Mancha.

Richardson's childhood ended abruptly in January 1811 when his mother died of tuberculosis. Unexpectly called home with his brothers from school, Richardson later described the scene:

Propped on pillows that supported her feeble head — her beautiful black hair streaming across her pallid brow, and her countenance wearing a holy and religious calm, she presented an image of resignation, so perfect, so superhuman, that the disposition to a violent ebullition of grief, which at first manifested itself in the youths, gave place to a certain mysterious awe, that chained them almost spell-bound at the foot of her bed.[20]

Her ninth child, still a baby, died soon afterwards of the same disease.

Warmth and affection went out of Richardson's life. His father, struggling in near-poverty, struck hard by Madeleine's death, became less communicative with his children. When he had to go away for days at a time to visit patients, he left the eldest girl, just seventeen, in charge of the family of boys. That summer he married again.[21] Richardson became res-

[17] ALS, A. Wilson to J. Norton (Edinburgh, April 30, 1820), Ontario Archives.

[18] John Askin, "Diary" (Sept. 9, 1809) Ontario Archives.

[19] William James Hughan, *Masonic Knight Templary in the United Kingdom*, Ars Quaturo Coronatorum, XVIII (Margate: Freemasons, London, Quator Coronati Lodge, 1905); Rylands, *Order of St John of Jerusalem*, Ars Quaturo Coronatorum, XVI (Margate: 1903).

[20] *The Canadian Brothers*, II, 39.

tive — neither the beatings at school nor his father's canings could curb his rambunctious spirit. He wanted to break away and lose himself in the world beyond Amherstburg. Appropriately this world came crashing down upon him. For years the Loyalists had harboured a fear that the Americans would declare war, and in June 1812 the inevitable happened. To Richardson's relief, school closed down as the thinly defended frontier prepared for the onslaught. "The transition was indeed glorious," he recalled, "and in my joy at the change which had been wrought in my position, I felt disposed to bless the Americans for the bold step that they had taken."[22] At fifteen Richardson joined the 41st Regiment, stationed at Fort Malden, as a Gentleman Volunteer, and shouldering a heavy musket he prepared for war.

War

OWING TO Dr. Richardson's position as surgeon to the British regiment at Fort Malden, John was accepted into the regular forces instead of into the Canadian militia.[1] His brother Robert became a midshipman in the tiny Royal Navy on Lake Erie.

Richardson drilled with his regiment and furiously studied the military orders in the few weeks left to him before the first active engagement.[2] The dilatory advance of the American Army, under General Hull, out of Detroit was held up at the Tarontee River by two privates of the 41st regiment — a great morale booster for the outnumbered British force.[3] Askin, who knew Hull personally, paid him two visits and won his promise to leave Strabane unmolested.[4] Nev-

[1] *War of 1812*, p.21. Richardson mentions in *The Canadian Brothers*, II, 42, that Henry Grantham's father (i.e. Dr Richardson) was an old friend of General Brock who secured an ensigncy for Henry Grantham (i.e. John Richardson).

[2] *Eight Years in Canada*, p.87.

[3] *War of 1812*, p.21.

[4] Robert Fuller, "John Askin and his associates; June 20, 1947," Essex County (Ont.) tourist association, *Radio Sketches of periods, events, personalities, from the history of the Essex-County-Detroit area* (Essex County historical association, 1963).

[21] *John Askin Papers*, II, 685.
[22] *Eight Years in Canada*, p.87.

ertheless, Askin and his family spent the night in the woods when the invading forces took over the area.[5] The great British General Isaac Brock, whom Richardson idolized,[6] had just issued a counter-proclamation to Hull's invitation to the Canadians to surrender, and was on his way from York to Fort Malden in August 1812. The confidence engendered by this tall, full and handsome figure preceded him, giving heart to the citizens of Amherstburg. The appearance of many Indian tribes coming from the West was reassuring to the Canadian defenders — since the Americans were terrified of Indians, their psychological value alone was inestimable. Throughout the campaigns of the Right Division, Richardson was affected deeply by what he saw of the Indian "savages."[7]

Before Brock arrived at Malden, a small group of Indians ambushed two hundred Ohio Riflemen carrying dispatches from General Hull on the American side of Lake Erie. The Riflemen were slaughtered, yet only one Indian brave was killed — a popular young Chief named Logan. Richardson was in the detachment sent to sort the dispatches. He watched the braves emerge singly and in groups from scouring the woods for Americans who had escaped. Occasionally they brought prisoners to their tents. One young despairing prisoner suddenly brightened with hope when he saw the British officers. But as he approached them, an aunt of Logan stole behind and struck him with a tomahawk. Richardson, shocked and helpless to intervene, saw the Indians dispatch the writhing man in fulfillment of their custom of an eye for an eye.[8] Still shaking from the scene, he heard the "yip-yip" of the Indian news cry as braves brought word of

an advancing American force. Immediately his detachment was sent with the Indians in an attempt to repulse them.

The road passed the spot where the Riflemen had been ambushed. Death lay everywhere in the hot August day.

The road was ankle-deep with mud, and the dark forest waving its close branches over our heads, left no egress to the pestilential exhalations arising from the naked and putrid bodies of horses and men, which had been suffered to lie unburied beneath our feet. No other sound than the measured step of the troops interrupted the solitude of the scene, rendered more imposing by the wild appearance of the warriors, whose bodies glided by us with almost noiseless velocity, without order, and without a chief: some painted white, some black, others half black half red, half black half white, all with their hair plastered in such a way as to resemble the bristling quills of the porcupine with no other covering than a cloth around their loins yet armed to the teeth with rifles, tomahawks, war-clubs, spears, bows, arrows and scalping knives. Uttering no sound and intent only on reaching the enemy unperceived, they might have passed for the spectres of those wilds, of those ruthless demons which war had unchained for the punishment and oppression of man.[9]

This detachment encountered about seven hundred Americans and attacked their centre. In the heat of the engagement in a woods, the British mistook the Indians for the enemy and opened fire on them. In spite of the ensuing confusion the British rallied on a hill and brought about an orderly retreat to the boats.

---

[5] *Ibid.*
[6] *Eight Years in Canada*, p.21.
[7] This becomes apparent to one reading "A Canadian Campaign."
[8] *War of 1812*, p.29.

[9] *Ibid.*, p.34.

No glory was won in this first engagement, but Richardson by his steadfastness under fire had won the right to wear his redcoat.

When he returned to Malden, he was probably a hero to his younger comrades. His brother Robert yearned to see action,[10] but would have no opportunity until both the American and British fleets were constructed. Robert's leader, Captain Barclay, a one-armed veteran of the Nelson sea-campaigns, was expected to arrive shortly. A chipper and ruddy-faced man of great spirit, in the early days of the war he became as heroic a figure as Brock. The third great hero whom all the citizens respected and the boys looked upon with awe was, of course, Tecumseh, the leader of the Indians.

With a white plume of ostrich feathers in his black hair and wearing his deerskin frock ornamented with porcupine quills, the bronze-skinned Tecumseh was a handsome, majestic figure. Looking younger than his forty-some years, he radiated confidence much as the youthful Brock. Lightly-built, finely proportioned with an oval face and bright hazel eyes, he had a magnetic personality. With him in Amherstburg to meet Brock were bands of Indians from the West: the fearless, cannibalistic Pottowatomies and others who joined the Chippewas and Mohawks. Amherstburg was ringed with Indian encampments.

Tecumseh knew the Askins. John Askin had given him the ostrich feather he proudly wore.[11] Richardson became acquainted with the great chief who seemed to take a special interest in this young, red-coated soldier, whose tanned skin marked his descent from the Indian race.[12] Although Tecumseh spent his

life fighting to preserve the Indian identity, he may have had premonitions of the hopelessness of his cause. Richardson, whose energy, intelligence, and bravery made him quickly noticed, was a product of the mingling of the two races which could not have failed to interest Tecumseh. In later life, Richardson remembered Tecumseh's considerate attentions with gratitude[13] and attempted to defend his noble character against calumny.

The bold advance on Detroit planned by Brock and Tecumseh brought about Hull's quick surrender of the fort. When describing the event years later, Richardson recorded his admiration for their unflinching courage,[14] a trait which Brock exemplified when he lined up his troops for the charge under the very mouths of the Detroit cannon. A proud moment for Richardson came when he mounted guard at the flag-staff; as he strutted back and forth with a musket taller than himself, he looked down at the American troops on the esplanade and knew the elation of victory.[15] Brock, pleased with the boy's courage, furthered his cause significantly by commissioning him an ensign in his own regiment, the 8th or King's, stationed in Fort George at Niagara. Richardson, however, could not take up his new posting until his commission was processed. He fought the entire war with the 41st on the Right Division, but not under Brock, who returned to the Centre Division and was killed at Queenston Heights.

It was not only through his valour in battle that Richardson became aware of his manhood; he was awakened to the charms of the opposite sex, in particular to women of strong and full contour, of sensuous "embonpoint" as he phrased it.[16] Just prior to the

[10] *Ibid.*, p.137.

[11] *Ibid.*, p.212. In *The Canadian Brothers*, I, 173, Richardson names Mrs D'Egville (Mrs Askin) as the donor.

[12] *Eight Years in Canada*, p.18. "This (Negro) absolutely seemed pleased when he saw me with a countenance not many shades lighter than his own."

[13] *Eight Years in Canada*, p.130.

[14] *War of 1812*, p.53.

[15] *Ibid.*, p.58.

[16] *Wau-nan-gee*, p.125.

The Massacre at Fort Dearborn, August 15, 1812.

siege of Detroit, General Hull entrusted his private papers to his daughter Betsey, and sent her from the fort by ship down Lake Erie.[17] A Canadian merchant brig chased the ship and brought it back to Detroit; the fort had been captured in the meantime. The full-figured Betsey attracted Richardson. Later he used her image in creating Matilda Montgomery, one of the most strong-willed women in literature. Betsey was gallantly set ashore by the British at Buffalo, and it was some time before Richardson met her again,

under totally different circumstances.

Several weeks later he saw what he conceived of as the prototype for his ideal of the desirable woman. She was Mrs. Heald, who with her husband, the Commander of Fort Dearborn (near present-day Chicago), escaped the Indian massacre of the inhabitants and, guided over three hundred miles by an Indian friend, reached the protection of the British lines. Near the end of his life Richardson made her one of the heroines in his novel, *Wau-nan-gee*, depicting that massacre, and wrote in his postscript:

> Little did we at the time, as we shared in the general and sincere homage to her magnificence of person and brilliancy of character, dream that a day would arrive when we should be the chronicler of Mrs. Headley's glory, or have the pleasing task imposed upon us of re-embodying after death, the inimitable grace and fulness of contour that then fired the glowing heart of the unformed boy of fifteen for the ripened and heroic, although by no means bold or masculine woman of forty.[18]

However strong his desire to play the gallant knight to the female heart, the boy was called to the grim task of keeping the American armies from forming a concerted attack. Under General Procter the British Right Division fought a negative delaying action out of Amherstburg, a tactic which disgusted Tecumseh and often dismayed Canadians like the Richardsons[19] who could not understand Procter's slowness to capitalize upon an advantage. The Battle of the Raisin underscored Procter's indecisiveness. Leaving a small guard at Malden, Procter set off with a force of regulars and Indians. Richardson described

[17] *Report of the Trial of Brig. General William Hull* ... By a Court Martial held at Albany... (New York: Eastburn, Kirk, 1814), p.41.

[18] *Wau-nan-gee*, p.125. Rebekah Heald ("Headley") was really 23 years old.

[19] *War of 1812*, p.134.

18

their departure:

It was the depth of winter; and the river at the point we crossed being four miles in breadth, the deep rumbling noise of the guns prolonging their reverberations like the roar of distant thunder as they moved along the ice, mingled with the loud cries of the Indians, seemed to threaten some convulsion of nature; while the appearance of the troops winding along the road, now lost behind some cliff of rugged ice, now emerging into view, their polished arms glittering in the sunbeams, gave an air of romantic grandeur to the scene.[20]

Since the ships were laid up for the winter, their crews accompanied the expedition. Fourteen-year-old Robert Richardson, forbidden by his father to go, had slipped out of Amherstburg in the evening and on the first night caught up with the troops in their camp. Excitedly, perhaps naively, the brothers prepared for their first campaign together.

On the second night someone took Richardson's firelock and left an ill-used one in its place. As the troops started out in pre-dawn darkness he did not notice the exchange at first, and when he did, he inquired after his own in vain. The musket was much heavier; when the troops drew up in the field, he was ready to drop with fatigue. The balls flew about his head, yet he could barely keep his eyes open. When preparing to fire, he discovered that the powder flashed in the pan so that he could not discharge his gun. Later he wrote to a relative: "I never was so vexed — to think that I was exposed to the torrent of fire from the enemy without having the power to return a single

Battlefields of the War of 1812-14.

shot quite disconcerted the economy of my pericranium."[21]

Thinking the snow and ice prohibited the approach of an enemy, the Americans had not posted sentinels. Richardson was puzzled when Procter, instead of rushing the first line, fired the cannon and awakened the defenders—with the result that twenty-four British soldiers were killed taking the line. Richardson, who was preparing to charge with a useless musket, felt foolish: "if I had fired fifty rounds not one of them would have had any effect except upon the pickets, which I was not at all ambitious of assailing like another Don Quixote."[22]

He was called away to aid his brother, who had been struck in the leg by a shell. In great pain Robert was borne from the field—not to the staff section where Dr. Richardson was caring for the wounded—but to a remote part of the field where he begged the

[20] *Ibid.*, p.134.
[21] ALS, John Richardson to Charles Askin (Amherstburg, Feb. 4, 1813). Reproduced in *War of 1812.*

[22] *Ibid.*

41st regimental doctor to tend him. The pain of being carried the extra distance was preferable to his father's wrath.[23]

The second line broke and the Americans were pursued along the ice of the river where, if not captured by the British, they were killed by the Indians. The Saukies or Sacs from Missouri, a noble race whose men of towering height Richardson admired most,[24] and the Minoumini or "devoted men" who could be likened to suicide squads, swelled the Indian ranks to three thousand. Protection for the wounded prisoners in the midst of so many savage warriors should have been Procter's first concern but, promising to send sleighs for the wounded, he retreated with his army back across Lake Erie. Both Richardson and his father were appalled at the slaughter which followed, for the Indians doubled back, killing the helpless men and burning the houses. The Richardsons' letters condemning Procter on this occasion survive: sent to John Askin they testify to the humanity of the doctor and his son and their disgust for their commander.[25]

The story of the Frenchtown massacre horrified both sides and sharpened the antagonism between the opposing camps. Captain Paschal Hickman, Betsey Hull's husband, was killed there. But the death which sickened and infuriated the Americans above any other was the killing of one of their most popular officers, Captain Nathaniel Hart.[26] Hart had given money to some Indians to set him on a horse and lead him out of the burning village. But as they were about to reach the safety of the woods, a small group of Indians accosted them, took the money, and slew Hart. The man

whom the Americans chiefly blamed for the killings was Tecumseh, who, with Procter, became the most hated of the enemy. Tecumseh, however, was unaware of the Frenchtown massacre. A few weeks before, he had left for the West country to recruit Indian tribes.[27]

Tecumseh returned in the early spring with more Indians from the West. The lakes and rivers were open to canoes and the snows had melted in the forests, permitting the transport of heavy cannon. The Americans sent another army under the now famous Indian fighter, General Harrison, to take over Fort Meigs on the Miami River.

Richardson, like his fellow officers, recognized the importance the Americans were placing on the western front and was extremely glad to see Indian reinforcements.[28] His family remained in Amherstburg so he was able to visit his wounded brother. If he were frightened of death and of the agonies of being wounded, the good humour of the other officers reassured him, and the heroic examples of some inspired him.[29]

In late April, when the ground was soft from the rains, Richardson was serving with the force with which Procter attacked Fort Meigs. The troops encamped a mile downstream from the fort and then dragged heavy cannons through mud as high as the axles to the banks opposite the fort. Procter's scheme was to bombard the fort to make a breach. The artillery was deadly accurate, and fired continuously for four days. Indian snipers picked off those who tried to fetch water from the river. Contact with the wet mud put out the fuses of many shells, but the British, un-

[23] *Ibid.*, p.138.

[24] Major Richardson, "The Sunflower," *Graham's*, 37, No. 5 (Nov. 1850).

[25] ALS, R. Richardson to J. Askin (Amherstburg, Feb. 7, 1813) Burton Collection.

[26] Letter to the Editor, *New Monthly Magazine* (1828), pt.I, 179.

[27] *War of 1812*, p.134; "Incidents of the War of 1812..." as reported in *The Literary World* (May 3, 1851).

[28] *Ibid.*

[29] Gwell augau neu Chuwilydd, "Major-General Sir Isaac Brock, and the 41st Regiment," *Albion* (New York, March 28, 1846). Richardson mentions his fellow officers after whom he patterned his fictional characters.

Siege of Fort Miegs.

daunted, set up another battery on the same bank as the fort to catch it in a devastating crossfire.

Unknown to the British, a large American relief force was coming down the Miami River in boats. General Harrison got word to its commander to attack the British artillery on the opposite bank while he, Harrison, led a sally to take the battery near the fort. The relief force took the batteries across the river, and spiked the guns as ordered, but instead of retiring to the fort, the force was decoyed into the woods by the Indians. The British infantry came up quickly from the encampment and supported the Indians who, in the woods, turned on the Americans and forced them into a sprinting retreat.

Richardson with the smaller section of the force came up on the American right. This was his fifth engagement. For a sixteen-year-old boy, his achievement was outstanding: he went into action as fearlessly as those veterans of the Napoleonic wars fighting beside him; he paid such keen attention to the regiment's strategic movements that he was able to record them with exactitude many years later; he adopted the comportment of an officer with ease; but beneath this show of maturity were the high spirits and recklessness of youth. His immediate superior, indignant that the Americans had taken the batteries, threw down his sword, picked up a musket from the grasp of one of his men who had been shot dead a minute before, and called out, "Who'll follow me and retake that battery?" Richardson, standing beside him, enthusiastically cried, "I will."[30] Both of them, followed by several others, dashed toward what might have been sudden death. Luckily the Americans were being hard pressed by the Indians on the other wing, and confusion and panic swept through the whole position. Richardson and his group took the batteries and miraculously routed the defenders.

For this act of bravery his superior officer cited him in his dispatch to Procter. But the General, in his official dispatch to Headquarters, did not distinguish Richardson from the other three Gentlemen Volunteers. Two of them had been taken prisoner by Harrison and the third, Procter's son, was forbidden to leave their encampment and never saw action in battle.[31]

Harrison, successful in his enterprise on the right bank, took his British prisoners to the fort. He was infuriated by the chaos on the opposite bank. He arranged for an exchange of prisoners and used the temporary cease-fire to fetch supplies from the newly arrived gunboats. The Indians had captured the last section of the boat-train carrying the baggage and private stores of the troops. Meanwhile the British discovered that their batteries had been improperly spiked and could be fired with their usual precision. Hostilities were reopened.

Richardson had an opportunity to observe the In-

30 *War of 1812*, p.150.
31 *Ibid.*, p.167.

dians closely. With a fellow officer he wandered through the neighbouring Indian camp, belonging to the Minoumini braves, who fought heedless of pain or death. These Indians were boiling pieces of flesh which they claimed were the enemy.

Several were decked out in the uniforms of the officers; and though embarassed to the last degree in their movements, and dragging with difficulty the heavy military boots with which their legs were for the first time covered, strutted forth much to the admiration of their less fortunate comrades. Some were habited in plain clothes; others had their bodies clad in clean white shirts, contrasting in no ordinary manner with the swarthiness of their skins; all wore some article of decoration, and their tents were ornamented with saddles, bridles, rifles, daggers, swords, and pistols, many of which were mounted and of curious workmanship. Such was the ridiculous part of the picture; but mingled with these and in various directions, were to be seen the scalps of the slain drying in the sun, stained on the fleshy side with vermillion dyes, and dangling in air, as they hung suspended from the poles to which they were attached; together with loops of various sizes, on which were stretched portions of human skin taken from various parts of the body, principally the hand and foot, and yet covered with the nails of those parts while scattered along the ground, were visible the members from which they had been separated, and serving as nutriment to the wolfdogs by which the Indians were accompanied.[32]

The battle slackened. Many Indians, content to have booty, drifted into the forest, leaving only Tec-

[32] *Ibid.*, p.159.

22

umseh and his faithful tribe of Shawnees. The militia returned to do spring planting. The British lifted the siege in mid-May and fell back to Lake Erie, which was controlled by a British fleet of six ships.

The rigours of an American campaign were also a factor in breaking off the siege. Dysentry, ague fever, and other ills brought on by wet and unhealthy weather plagued the troops. Richardson had had his fill of sickness throughout the campaign; he learned that a protracted siege could be as dangerous to the health and morale of the attackers as to the defenders.[33]

The officers of the regiment liked and respected Richardson as a plucky and intelligent youngster. Because of his junior position he was last in line at the cooking pot; this disadvantage and his constant hunger (he was still a teenager) afforded his comrades some humour.[34] The Indians he knew were fond of him; some had watched him grow up and spoke with him in the Indian languages which he had learned after a fashion.[35] The authorization of his commission to the 8th Regiment had been processed, yet Procter refused to let him take up his new post. He said that he needed every available man for his own force.[36] The decision disappointed Richardson, who had to remain a Gentleman Volunteer for the time being.[37]

[33] *Ibid.*, p.160.
[34] *Eight Years in Canada*, p.137.
[35] When he wished to purchase some of the Indians' plunder he could strike bargains more easily, no doubt, than his fellow officers who knew no Indian tongue. Over thirty-five years later on a visit to the Indians at Walpole Island he spoke in the Pottawattomie tongue which he had not used since the War.
[36] *War of 1812*, p.188. Procter could not afford to lose a man because his force was very low in numbers.
[37] Richardson became an Ensign in the 8th Regiment on Aug. 4, 1813 (*Army Lists 1814*, p.159). He did not take up his new post until he returned from imprisonment in Kentucky on Oct. 4, 1814.

Tecumseh prompted the next engagement with Harrison in June. A ruse to lure the defenders of Fort Meigs into the open failed. Anxious to satisfy his impatient Indians, Tecumseh taunted Procter with cowardice and thereby won his consent to attack a smaller Fort where the Sandusky River flowed into Lake Erie.

In Richardson's description of the British siege of this fort, which he wrote in his *War of 1812*, he accused Procter of virtually wasting the lives of his soldiers by sending them into a galling fire with ladders too short to scale the walls of the fort and axes too blunt to cut through the pickets.[38] When night fell those soldiers who had survived were pressed to the ground in the ravine. The order to retreat was whispered softly from company to company in the Indian language.

Richardson and his company were separated from the others by brushwood. The passage describing his predicament illustrates not only his reckless bravery but also his pique at the men under his command for refusing to follow his leadership:

It was now half-past nine o'clock. We had continued since half-past five lying extended on the wet ground, where the mud was ankle deep, and most of the men chilled with cold. At this moment we heard, though indistinctly, various orders given in the direction of our encampment, and then only did we surmise the fact of the troops having been withdrawn. In this belief we were speedily confirmed by hearing a command issued to open the sallyports. Perceiving that no time was to be lost, I proposed in a whisper which the rising ground prevented from being overheard by the enemy, that we should brave every risk and attempt our immediate retreat. The men, however, refused to move, until the moon, which was then in the first quarter, and reflecting its

[38] *War of 1812*, p.182.

beams everywhere but in the bed of the ravine, was set, or should be obscured by some passing cloud. Leaving them to their fate, I therefore prepared to effect my escape alone, and immediately in front of the fortress, but notwithstanding all my caution, I had not advanced many paces, when I stumbled over the dead body of a soldier, who, after having received a mortal wound, had evidently crawled on his hands and knees to rest his bleeding form against a clump of bushes, and had died in that singular position. The noise occasioned by my fall put the enemy once more on the alert and as the moonbeams reflected on my arms and regimentals, I had no sooner ascended the opposite side of the ravine, than the whole front of the fort was lighted up with their fire. Not an individual, save myself, was exposed to their aim, and the distance did not exceed fifty paces: yet, although the balls whistled round my ears in every direction, and hissed through the long grass with which the plain was covered, I did not sustain the slightest injury, even though a second volley was fired after the interval of half a minute. On reaching the spot where the columns had been originally formed for the assault, I found that my retreat had been well-timed, for the troops were already in motion towards the boats, the guns having previously embarked. In that which contained my provision basket, I discovered a few bottles of port wine, which had arrived that very morning from Amherstburg. This was indeed a luxury that I would not at the moment have exchanged for a throne; and so thoroughly exhausted was I with hunger, thirst and fatigue, that placing a bottle to my parched lips, I did not abandon it until the whole of its contents had been emptied at a draught. The effect was instantaneous, and I lay in the bottom of the boat all night enjoying the most delicious moments of repose I recollect ever having experienced. When I awoke at a late hour on the following morning, a mild September sun was glancing its golden rays along the tranquil bosom of Lake Erie, in the centre of which our boats were all assembled, and gliding along its surface with a speed proportioned to the vigorous efforts of the rowers, the men alternately singing and indulging in rude jests, reckless of the comrades whose dying groans had assailed their ears a few hours before, and evidently without care or thought for the future. Every individual of those who refused to accompany me were made prisoners by the American party despatched through the sallyport.[39]

He expressed no sense of guilt at leaving his men behind; on the contrary, he blamed them for remaining. This attitude belied an egotism, which perhaps at this time was excusable because of his youth, but which remained characteristic of him throughout his life. It is interesting to note, also, that his men would disregard his command, and that Richardson would write that he "proposed" rather than "ordered" a retreat. Evidently he was having trouble persuading the men to respect his authority.

Richardson had lent his brace of pistols to a fellow officer who was killed in the siege. Because by their artistry they seemed to be family heirlooms, the young American commander of the fort returned the pistols during a prisoner exchange. Richardson expressed a boundless admiration for such a chivalrous act.[40]

General Harrison's army was fast growing to overwhelming proportions. Procter decided that further attack upon the American forts was futile and preferred to leave the Canadian line of defense to Captain Barclay's ill-equipped little fleet on Lake Erie. The American fleet, built quickly under the direction of Captains Oliver Perry and Jesse Elliott, closed with Barclay's ships in the famous bloody battle of September 10, 1813.

From the heights of Amherstburg Richardson and the other citizens watched the start of the fight, but soon the smoke from the guns obscured the action. Some time after the artillery ceased, the smoke rose and the British ships could be seen drawn in tow by the American fleet. The way was clear for invasion.

Dr. Richardson, as naval surgeon, tended the wounded Captain Barclay and laboured to save the lives of officers and crewmen on the captured, battered ships.

Mrs. Richardson, with her two baby children and her young stepsons, took shelter at Strabane under the care of John Askin, who, with his wife, was too old to flee.[41] Luckily, the Askins were left unmolested owing to the marriage of one of their daughters to an American, Elijah Brush, Captain of the Detroit Militia, who interceded with General Harrison on their behalf. Their daughter embodied the neutral spirit.

My dear mother [she wrote], I am with my American friends here and have asked about your fleet. They say that many were killed on both sides but that Richardson and Commodore Barclay were both taken prisoners and that it was aboard the *Queen Charlotte* that the Commodore received the broken arm, and that the others were quite comfortable. I am leaving now to cross over.[42]

---

[39] "A Canadian Campaign," (1827) pt.I, 451-2.
[40] *Ibid.*, p.182.

[41] *John Askin Papers*, II, 769. (Letter, T. McKee to J. Askin, Oct. 10, 1813).
[42] *John Askin Papers*, II, 769.

Presently Brush wrote Askin to tell Mrs Richardson that the doctor was well and that he had asked Perry to release him along with Captain Barclay.

The only member of the family far out of the trouble was Robert Richardson, who had been sent to Quebec to work at Army Staff Headquarters.

Invasion was imminent; the American troops lined the opposite shore. Tecumseh urged Procter to make the lake his battle-front, but the General insisted on retreat, though he made the concession, half-heartedly, to form a line of defense at the Moraviantown plain on the banks of the River Thames. When the Indians heard this, the Pottowatomies, Miamis, Chippewas, and some of the Ottawa left in disillusion and disgust to care for their families who would be left at the mercy of the rampaging army. Of the three thousand warriors only one thousand joined in the retreat.[43]

The Canadian families fled Amherstburg and the border settlements for inland towns. The younger Askins took their children and the daughters of relatives and friends, including Richardson's older sister, over the Thames River route to the Head-of-the-Lake, a long and difficult journey.[44]

Before starting their retreat in the last week of September, the British troops spent some days demolishing the stores and fortifications of Forts Malden and Detroit. Richardson marched through the autumn woods while Detroit and Malden blazed behind him. The conveyance of baggage and the blowing of bridges made the retreat slow, but the news that Harrison had landed with five thousand men on the Canadian shore kept the British constantly at the task.

Richardson, like the rest of his regiment, was bewildered by the retreat.[45] The lay of the land at Moravian village was perfect for confronting an American army twice their size. The British guns could be trained over a ravine, and the Indians had the thick woods in which to fight on one flank while the river bounded the other. Procter ordered the regiment to draw back, however, so that they were already in the woods when they were hastily ordered to form their line. The British in their redcoats made a fine target. Because the woods were thin enough to allow the men to ride through, the American cavalry was ordered to rush the enemy.

Before the battle Tecumseh walked the line and shook every officer by the hand. Richardson was to remember the moment proudly as the Chief looked deeply into his eyes and wished him well.[46] Whereas Procter dismayed the men, Tecumseh gave them confidence.

The Americans overran the position quickly. The British Right Wing and Centre had time to fire only two volleys. Richardson, on the Left Wing next to the Indians, was able to put up a stiffer fight. The Americans, under Harrison, were a mixture of regulars and backwoodsmen from Ohio and Kentucky. The backwoodsmen fought from behind trees like Indians, leaving hardly an inch of skin visible.

The Indians fought valiantly. Richardson happened to see a chief, whom he knew well, scalp one of the enemy with dexterity and finesse, which he recorded later.

A Kentucky rifleman who had been dismounted within a few yards of the spot where I stood...was fired at by three warriors of the Delaware tribe. The unfortunate man received their several balls in the body yet although faint from loss of blood, he made every exertion to save himself. Never

[43] *War of 1812*, p.209.
[44] Robert Fuller, "John Askin and his associates..." *op. cit.*
[45] *War of 1812*, p.225.

[46] *Ibid.*, p.212.

Battle of the Thames. The Death of Tecumseh.

done, he grasped the bloody instrument between his teeth, and placing his knees on the back of his victim, while at the same time he fastened his fingers in the hair, the scalp was torn off without much apparent difficulty and thrust, still bleeding, into his bosom. The warrior then arose, and after having wiped his knife on the clothes of the unhappy man, returned it to its sheath, grasping at the same time the arms he had abandoned, and hastening to rejoin his comrades. All this was the work of a few minutes.[47]

Tecumseh was killed. The question as to who killed him has remained a bone of contention to this day. At the time it was believed that it was Colonel R.M. Johnson who led the Kentucky cavalry against the Indians.[48] But the Colonel had been badly wounded at the first charge and taken from the field. Another claimant for the honour was backwoodsman David King. The latest research on the subject suggests that the wounded chieftain was shot by an old Indian fighter, Colonel Whitely, at the same instant as he shot his assailant.[49]

The American troops cut off pieces of Tecumseh's skin for souvenirs. It is now believed, however, that the Indians succeeded in stealing away and burying the true body, as they later claimed, and that the Americans mutilated the body of another chief.[50] Richardson denied that the mutilated body was that

was fear so strongly depicted on the human countenance, and the man's hair (for he was uncovered) absolutely seemed to me to stand on end, as he attempted to double a large fallen tree, in order to elude the weapons of his enemies. The foremost of his pursuers was a tall powerful man. . . . When within twelve or fifteen paces of the rifleman, he raised and threw his tomahawk, and with such precision and force, that it immediately opened the skull, and extended him motionless on the earth. Laying down his rifle, he drew forth his knife, and after having removed the hatchet from the brain, proceeded to make a circular incision in the scalp. This

26

47 *Ibid.*, p.209.
48 *Ibid.*, p.212.
49 Glenn Tucker, *Tecumseh: Vision of Glory* (Indianapolis: Bobbs-Merrill, 1956), p.321.
50 Captain Billy Caldwell, who was alongside Tecumseh when struck down, directed Tecumseh's son to the body because it was important for the son's health and happiness that the father receive a decent burial. D.P. Botsford, "The Caldwell Family..., July 30, 1960," Essex County (Ont.) tourist association, *Radio Sketches.... op. cit.*

of another chief, because officers of the 41st Regiment had identified it as the dead Tecumseh.[51] He was equally certain that Johnson was Tecumseh's killer. The facts of Tecumseh's death were to become a matter for debate late in Richardson's own life.

After twenty minutes of fighting Richardson and his companions heard no shooting on their right and decided to escape into the forest. But instead of going deeper in the woods, they came onto the road and found their comrades being disarmed. A body of cavalry rode upon them from the other side.

> At the head of these, and dressed like his men, in Kentucky hunting frocks, was a stout elderly officer whom we subsequently knew to be Governor Shelby (of Kentucky) and who the moment he beheld us emerging from the wood, galloped forward and brandishing his sword over his head, cried out with stentorian lungs: "Surrender, surrender, it's no use resisting, all your people are taken, and you had better surrender."[52]

Thus Richardson became a prisoner. Exhausted from lack of sleep, in fear of being murdered, he walked dejectedly in the rain, his feet swollen in his boots. The captives had to pass through a gauntlet of Indians who had fought with the Americans. He was surprised to find that the warriors were sympathetic.

> Several who had been at Amherstburg previous to the war, and had had daily opportunities, at the period, of seeing both officers and men, smiled and nodded their heads in token of recognition as we passed, and the general conduct of the whole, as they stood calmly leaning on their

rifles, was confirmatory of the fact long since conveyed to us, that the services of these men, under the American banners, were entirely compulsory; they having been reduced to the necessity of preserving the lives of their women and children, detained as hostages in the United States by an appearance of devotedness to the cause of a people for whom the natives have ever entertained the most rooted and unqualified aversion.[53]

Meanwhile Procter, who had stood behind the second line and fled at the first appearance of the cavalry, was galloping with forty dragoons and mounted Indians to the Head-of-the-Lake. Many of the Indians fighting with the British were still at large in the forests about the American camp. As the Americans retreated to Erie, they picked off stragglers and from the woods attacked in small bands all night.

Richardson and his fellow officers were received by General Harrison and Captain Perry at a large central fire which was surrounded by many smaller ones. Bullocks were killed and butchered. Young aides-de-camp served as chefs and handed the warmed pieces of meat to the famished prisoners. When Harrison was told of the manner of Tecumseh's death, he was furious with his men for degrading the body and saddened that the great warrior had met his end. These two who had been enemies for some years, had come to respect each other's generalship. Richardson was extremely unhappy, for Tecumseh had been a hero to him, and within the same year he had lost another hero, Brock.[54]

Lacking tents, both victor and vanquished slept in the open, except for Harrison and his senior officers

---

[51] *War of 1812*, p.213.
[52] *Ibid.*, p.211.

[53] "A Canadian Campaign," (1827) pt.I, 448.
[54] General Brock was killed at the Battle of Queenston Heights.

who stayed in an inn by the Pike River. Richardson sank into a deep sleep, but he could not escape from the horrors of war. The memory of one of his acts remained with him: while an American cavalryman aiming carefully at one of the British light company waited for a convenient moment to shoot, Richardson's immediate superior told him to fire at the cavalryman. Setting his musket against a tree, Richardson fired and watched the man's rifle tumble from his shoulder and the man sink over his horse's side.[55] The war had nurtured in Richardson a hardness, almost a casualness toward death that was to figure significantly in later years of his life.

Imprisonment

THE LONG MARCH back to the Detroit River was accomplished with dispatch. Both the Askin home and that of an influential neighbour had been spared destruction. The officers were taken to a public dinner in the neighbour's mansion, "Moy House", at which John Askin was present.[1] Richardson would not see his grandparents again; he was not to return to this part of the country for many years. Askin charged the American Colonel, Elijah Brush, with seeing that the boy was looked after, and he may also have approached General Harrison and Colonel R.M. Johnson, who were staying at Strabane, on the subject. The old man wrote in his diary: "Since Sunday the house full of American soldiers, who slept day and night to warm themselves, and take apples and killed some fowls."[2]

The influence of Elijah Brush made itself felt immediately. Richardson was not sent with the majority of army officers up the Miami River, but rather with a few prisoners by gunboat to Put-in-Bay Island on Lake Erie where the battered Canadian Fleet lay. He was allowed to go aboard the *Queen Charlotte* to

[1] "A Canadian Campaign," (1827) pt.I, 449; *Wacousta*, 2nd ed., pref.

[2] D.P. Botsford, "The Caldwell Family of Fort Malden, July 30, 1960," *op. cit.*

[55] *War of 1812*, p.223.

greet his father tending the wounded Barclay, and tell him the news of the family under Askin's guardianship. Captain Barclay beamed at Richardson, whom he called "my little warrior."[3] Richardson admired this man greatly,[4] and when he saw the chaos of damage to the ships — from splintered masts to bloodstained decks — he marvelled at the courage of the man who could greet him with such good spirits.[5] The reunion was short. On the second morning, Richardson's group, with those naval officers able to travel, was sent by ship to Sandusky Bay, the scene of that catastrophic seige. When Richardson found an opportunity to inspect the fort he reflected on the folly of trying to capture it.

Richardson and his fellow prisoners were given half-starved horses to ride on a long journey to imprisonment inland. One American officer accompanied them through late autumn rains and frosty nights over plains and through deep forests, ever onward in the gloomy state of captivity. Worn in body and spirit, Richardson turned to his comrades for stimulation.

Play was the occupation of several at night. . . I can never recall without a smile the picture of our party, seated often in the heart of a forest, where, in the absence of any human habitation, we were sometimes compelled to repose from the fatigues of our journey. A fallen tree, covered with a cloak or pockethandkerchief, constituted our table; and, squatted like savages on the ground, we usually played by the glaring light of the birch bark, supplying the absence of a candle, and falling on our harassed and anxious countenances, as we threw the cards successively

on the board; at a little distance, our more sensible companions, wrapped in their cloaks, enjoyed that unbroken slumber which awaits on bodily but is seldom the attendant of mental fatigue; and our horses stood quietly grazing in the background — all tending to fill up the measure of a scene which would not have disgraced the pencil of a Hogarth.[6]

It rained for weeks. The men, with neither sufficient clothes nor the opportunity to wash, were soon covered with vermin. The countless swollen streams, the wet nights in the open, and the occasional shabby habitations they chanced upon, demoralized them. Their horses sank down at every step and appeared likely to die. But the chill of late October and early November forced them to move onward. They finally reached Chillicothe, Ohio, where the other officers and troops of the 41st, who had taken the Miami route, awaited them.

The troops were kept in a stockade on the outskirts of the town, while the officers had apartments in town. Richardson, to his surprise,[7] was met by an influential man in the community, a close relative of Elijah Brush. This gentleman gave him an apartment, had a cover laid daily at his table for him, and put his horses at his command. Thanks to this treatment, Richardson rested and regained his strength, which was to be put to the test once more.

Among the American prisoners taken on the Canadian frontier, twenty-three were found to be deserters from British regiments. They were sent to England and put under sentence of death as traitors. The Americans in retaliation took twenty-three British prisoners and confined them in dungeons. In turn the British and the Americans each retaliated

---

[3] *Eight Years in Canada*, p.85.
[4] *Ibid.*
[5] *Ibid.*

[6] *Ecarté*, I, 32.
[7] "A Canadian Campaign," (1827) pt.I, 453.

by imprisoning an equal number, until, finally, nearly all the officers of both sides were imprisoned.

Instead of being sent with his fellow army officers to prison in Frankfort, Kentucky, Richardson was imprisoned with the naval officers in Chillicothe. He and nineteen companions were locked in two small, connecting rooms, heavily guarded. Execution appeared probable, for they would be hanged if the British hanged the convicted traitors in England. The unhealthy crowding, uncomfortable cold, and tyrannical fear of death the men experienced was exacerbated by a boorish gaoler who at one point showed his sadism by cracking open the head of one of the mildest of the prisoners.

As the weeks dragged by the men in the fortified camp on the outskirts could no longer tolerate this indignity to their officers. They communicated a plan to the officers to overpower their guards at midnight and divide into three groups, the first to release the officers, the second to seize the boats moored in the Scioto River, and the third to patrol the streets to prevent the citizens from assembling. They would take the boats downriver to the Ohio, on to the Mississippi, to the English fleet anchored off New Orleans. In order to obtain the necessary intelligence, the officers took two Federalists, opposed to the war, into their confidence.

The day set for their escape passed slowly. About four in the afternoon a tremendous racket burst out in the courtyard. A trampling of horses' feet, the sound of drums and voices brought the officers to their window. The Governor, armed to the teeth, and accompanied by a large staff, seemed in great agitation. The Federalist townsmen had panicked and revealed the escape plan. The general alarm was sounded, the guards were doubled, the militia was called in from the country, and all citizens were assembled. A rumour had spread that the prisoners had planned to set fire to the town.

All the officers, save Richardson, were put in irons. Richardson's angry insistence that he, too, be manacled was ignored. Thus free to move, he was able to perform services for his fellow prisoners with which the gaoler never concerned himself.

At first the officers tried to see the humour in their condition in the cell and the commotion outside, but after three days of painfully swollen hands when the ends of their fingers turned blue from numbness they again despaired. Richardson twice wrote letters of protest to the Commander, but to no avail.[8] A naval officer hit upon the idea of replacing the iron nails, which were riveted to the irons around their wrists, with some lead ones which he had in his knapsack. This would enable them to relieve their limbs whenever necessary to attend to their person. Richardson worked silently throughout the night splitting the nails with his penknife and blackening the lead to make it look like iron until the last man was free to restore the circulation to his hands. In the daylight, the officers' coatsleeves partially concealed the new nails.

Ten days later, orders came for the officers to be moved to Frankfort prison. They were marched out to the courtyard, informed of their destination, and led in a roundabout way through the town, so that the citizens could insult them. Richardson was appalled to see former hosts and friends glaring at them with hatred, because of the rumour that they intended to burn the town.

On the voyage downriver, when their boat hit a sawyer and almost overturned, the prisoners immediately withdrew the nails from their irons lest they had to swim for their lives. Their American guard offered to take off their manacles if they gave their word not to attempt an escape. They did so, and at the same time confessed to his astonishment

8 *Ibid.*, p.457.

that they were already able to escape.

Swiftly swept down to Cincinnati, the state capital, they experienced their first relative freedom in weeks. One officer had accused two others of cowardice during the Erie naval conflict. Borrowing duelling pistols from an American major who was staying at the same hotel, the challenger and one of the challenged, with their seconds, quietly went into the woods. A couple of hours later the other man challenged, with Richardson as his second, went to fight in his turn. Both times the challenger fired harmlessly into the air, and, luckily, each of his opponents missed him. They made up the quarrel, glad to be rid of their venom harmlessly. Richardson was impressed, thinking the duel was an effective way of resolving disagreements.[9]

Leaving Cincinnati at noon, they floated by beautiful wild country. Richardson later wrote about the trip:

Descending the full waters of the Ohio, we enjoyed the wild surrounding scenery, with additional and unbroken interest, while our guards amused themselves with firing at numerous flocks of wild turkeys which sprang up at every instant from either bank, and, winging their dull and fearless flight over our heads, presented in their vast bulk an unerring mark for the murderous lead.[10]

When they reached the prison in Frankfort, the officers who had preceded them waved in greeting through the tiny barred windows of their crowded cells.[11]

This period of confinement was brief. The news of Napoleon's reversal in Russia prompted the Americans to improve the prisoners' condition from that of hostages to parolees, because now that the British could spare more troops for the American campaign the Americans were expected to sue for peace.

The prisoners were removed to Weisinger's Inn on the outskirts of Frankfort. Some of the local citizenry stood outside the wall around the grounds of the Inn and watched the officers as if they were captured animals. A series of caustic remarks erupted in turn on each side. Dan Weisinger, the owner of the Inn, gave them comfortable rooms, excellent food (with decanters of whisky at the table) and slaves to do their washing and other chores. Since the American government paid each officer three shillings per day and six to the wounded, Weisinger was eager to please. But despite the more pleasant surroundings, the continued state of captivity accompanied by the settlers' insults weighed heavily on Richardson's spirit.[12]

Luckily not all the citizens goaded the officers. Close to the hotel, on the outskirts of town, was the mansion and estate of Betsey Hickman, the same fetching lady who had been caught escaping from Detroit with her father's papers and whose attractiveness Richardson had noticed. Betsey lived with three teenage daughters in wealthy circumstances. Her slaves and property were valued in 1813 at over $9,000.[13] She belonged to that type of woman who never seemed to lose her beauty.

9 *Ibid.*, p.540.

10 *Ibid.*

11 A.C. Whitehorn, *History of the Welch Regiment* (Cardiff: Western Mail and Echo, 1932) relates that thirty officers were crammed into two small cells and nine hundred other prisoners were in various parts of the building. Accounts from the Chillicothe and Frankfort papers of that day give the names of the officers.

12 "A Canadian Campaign," (1827) pt.I, 542.

13 G. Glenn Clift, *Remember the Raisin!* Kentucky and Kentuckians in the battles and massacres at Frenchtown, Michigan Territory in the War of 1812 (Frankfort: Kentucky Historical Society, 1961), p.126.

Richardson, now seventeen, felt less like the "unformed boy" of two years before.[14] He was naturally delighted to be included among the officers whom Betsey Hickman invited to her home for afternoon garden parties.[15] This unexpected hospitality shown to the prisoners by the more affluent Kentuckians was owing to the efforts of Major George Madison who had been a close friend of Betsey's husband.[16] Madison was taken prisoner in the Raisin battle and sent to Quebec. After he was released on a prisoner-exchange, he arranged for the British prisoners to travel within a twenty-mile radius of the town to visit the spas and private estates in the country, in return for the fair treatment he himself had received.[17] To show their appreciation, two of the British naval men carved facsimiles of warships for his daughter, Agatha.[18]

Agatha was sixteen and beautiful:

To a mind highly cultivated and a purity of feeling equalled only by the tenderness of a heart alive to every nobler and more generous impulse of humanity, she united those glowing and luxurious beauties of person which distinguish the

females of the American continent even at an age when in northern Europe they are regarded as mere children.[19]

Thus Richardson described her in his first novel, *Ecarté*, which depicted the romantic relationship between a young officer and an American girl, Agatha, in Frankfort. In the novel the couple took long walks in the hills about the town; among the glories of nature they fell in love. Undoubtedly Richardson strolled with the real-life Agatha about Frankfort, as did other young officers, but Agatha's "Aunt" Betsey may have held his primary interest.

Betsey was not only rich and desirable: she enjoyed a high social standing, which, in spite of three children, made her eligible for remarriage — especially in the mind of a tall and burly Kentuckian named James, who was courting her favour at the time. Richardson, whose background was already known to Betsey through the friendship of her family, the Hulls, with the Askins, was readily received by her. Sensing their attraction to be mutual, he felt bold enough to challenge his rival. At a party in Betsey's home Richardson deliberately remarked aloud on the bad manners of Mr. James for smoking his cigar in the drawing room regardless of the suffering ladies. James looked sullen, remained silent, and presently left the room.[20] With one sure step, the seventeen-year-old opportunist had cleared the field and stood ready to claim the spoils.

In his novel *The Canadian Brothers*, the fictional Matilda, who, like Betsey, was caught trying to flee Fort Detroit, and who also lived on the outskirts of Frankfort, influenced her young lover to assassinate a man whom she loathed. The theme of assassination was fashioned after a true event in Frankfort, but the insight and sensitivity of the story came largely from Richardson's experience with the mature and strong-

14 *Wau-nan-gee*, pref.

15 "A Canadian Campaign," (1827), pt.I, 543.

16 *Ibid.*, p.542.

17 Ibid.; also, in *Ecarté* Frederick Dormer when a prisoner in Frankfort gambles at the resort spas, to his detriment.

18 *Ibid.*, p.543; Major Madison becoming a widower just before the War, Betsey took the Madison children under her own roof when Madison and her husband, Paschal Hickman, left for the front with the regiment they had formed. Hickman was killed at the Raisin where Madison was captured. Madison became Governor of Kentucky in 1816 but died of tuberculosis after a few months in office. His daughter, Agatha, died of the same disease three years later and was buried near her father in the hills by Frankfort.

19 *Ecarté*, I, 33.

20 "A Canadian Campaign," (1827), pt.I, 543.

willed Betsey.[21]

Richardson could only have known Betsey furtively for a couple of months, as he left Frankfort in mid-July. He spent his last evening in Betsey's home and left at a late hour.

The house was situated in an unfrequented part of the town, and my path lay along a solitary declivity leading to the foot of our garden wall. I had not advanced more than a hundred yards when through the gloom I perceived a man stationary near the road. The unusual appearance of this person at such an hour somewhat startled me, yet I resolved to see who it was. My suspense was not of long duration. The figure proved to be Mr. James, who now placed himself in such a manner as to bar my passage. I endeavoured to avoid him, and demanded the motive of his conduct. This, he said, I should presently know, and, swearing a horrid oath, observed, "You have escaped me once, but I'll take good care you don't again." His right hand grasped a stiletto or dirk, which he held behind his back, and with the other he made a sudden movement to seize me by the collar. I felt all the danger of my situation, and found that, unarmed as I was, my only chance of safety was in flight. The thought was no sooner conceived than executed, and, eluding his touch, I ran with all the speed of one who perceives that life hangs on the fleetness of his steps. This unexpected movement rather discountenanced my enemy, but he speedily recovered from his surprise; and on his uttering a shrill whistle, several other persons sprang up from an ambuscade on either side of the road and joined in the pursuit. Not a cry was uttered—not a sound broke on the stillness of the night, save that of rapid and numerous footsteps; for I felt that any exclamation for assistance would be too late, and that one desperate attempt alone could save me. If fear sometimes deprives men of the power of action, it also sometimes urges them to undertake seeming impossibilities. The garden wall which I now rapidly approached was upwards of five feet in height, and the ground leading to it from the outside sloped rather abruptly off from its base. At any other moment I should not have thought of attempting it, but a successful leap was now my only hope of escape. Placing my hand on the wall, I made a desperate bound, and cleared it with an ease which surprised me even at that moment; as I was in the act of passing, I felt my coat glide from the uncertain grasp of one of my pursuers. Nor was this all the effect produced by a sense of danger. Impressed with an idea that my enemies were still in pursuit, I stopped not an instant in my flight, but advanced to the opposite extremity of the garden. The gate which opened into the court was firmly closed, but such was the violence with which I thrust my person against it that it fell as if entirely unsupported; nor did I discontinue my speed until I had finally gained my apartment.[22]

Since there was no lock on his door and he had no weapons, he stayed awake all night with fear. He wrote Betsey of the event the next morning. She replied that she had barred her door to James, who boasted of trailing Richardson a few days before to the exhibition

---

[21] Also, the strong will of Ann Cook undoubtedly stood as a model for Richardson (who mentioned the Beauchamp case in his "Letter to the Editor" of the *New Monthly*, (1828), pt.I, 183) but without his acquaintance with the remarkable Betsey whom he knew at an impressionable age, he would not have created Matilda. Betsey remarried as late as 1823 to a Kentucky judge to whom she bore a son in 1824.

[22] "A Canadian Campaign," (1827), pt.I, 543-4.

balloon flight in Lexington in order to shoot him in the crowd, but had lost sight of him. The majority of Kentuckians would have been indifferent to the murder of a British prisoner.[23] There was still the chance that James or one of his men would take a "long shot" at Richardson as he rode out of Frankfort.

In the exchange of prisoners, those officers who could afford to buy their own horses left for the border; the others were being sent on horses provided by the American government. Richardson, smartly dressed in Kentucky frocks with a broad red morocco belt, selected his American-provided horse and joined the file of his companions riding into the hills to the north. Watching the trees along the trail for a sign of James with a rifle, he did not breathe easily until well away from the town.[24] That evening at Cincinnati the officers were reunited with their men brought up from Chillicothe, and began the return in the long sultry days of July and August.

When they reached Sandusky, there were no ships to take them over Lake Erie. They were not allowed to camp in the fort, so with straw and blanket, they bedded down on a marshy plain at the foot of the hill on which the fort stood. They all became sick with the ague. Richardson sat with his friends day after day hoping for the appearance of a ship. When all their money had been spent on food, they bartered their clothes for milk and vegetables from the neighbouring farmers. At night they were threatened by wolves that came down from the hills. After a month, the prisoners pleaded to be removed to tents on the hill, but were firmly denied. Richardson was convinced that they had been left to die in the marshy hole.[25]

At the end of September, however, a gunboat slowly poked its nose around the bend of the creek. Richardson wrote:

Disease had worn away our persons and our minds were deeply tinged with that morbid melancholy which is a characteristic feature in the complaint. Existence itself had nearly lost its value with its charms; and in our then tone of feeling, liberty or captivity were situations of indifference.[26]

Soon after setting sail a sudden gale overturned them in shallow water. They managed to right the boat and drag it to a sandy beach. The American officers accompanying them were able to feed them only with potatoes and rancid butter procured from the local inhabitants. Ranting in fever and lying on the damp beach, a lieutenant, exhausted by this last catastrophe, died.

On reaching the present site of Cleveland (two miserable houses on a clifftop, at the time), they made a dash for the peaches growing near the beach. But the fruit worsened their fever and made them delirious. Herded into the hold of an old ship, they were transported from Erie to Long Point where they stumbled ashore hardly recognizable to the officer of the 41st Regiment who was waiting to receive them. This officer reported: "All the officers and almost all the men were ill when they arrived, and I fear a great number will never recover."[27]

In October 1814, after a year of imprisonment, Richardson stepped again onto Canadian soil. Burlington Heights was still the line of defense, although the 41st Regiment occupied Forts George and Niagara at the mouth of the Niagara River. Richardson and his fellow convalescents were carted over the rocky shore to Fort George where they rested for two weeks. Then on November 4 the whole regiment was shipped to York and thence to winter quarters in Kingston.[28]

[23] *Ibid.*, p.545.
[24] *Ibid.*
[25] *Ibid.*, p.550.

[26] *Ibid.*
[27] A.C. Whitehorn, *op. cit.*, p.95ff.
[28] *Ibid., passim.*

For five months, one of the worst winters in years, Richardson lay with fever in his barracks. Below-zero temperatures, huge banks of snow, bleak, sunless days — all nature seemed to reflect his misery. Those officers who had had money to leave their Frankfort imprisonment before him amused themselves in their quarters. The others groaned with the ague.

The cold fit generally commenced about four o'clock in the afternoon, and was preceded by excessive hunger, which it did not afford time to appease. It continued with dreadful shivering, accompanied by distortions of the features, until seven, at which hour fever and delirium resumed their empire, raging with intolerable violence, and causing the sufferer frequently to start in agony from his burning couch and rush into the open air. This usually lasted longer than the cold fit, and was succeeded by languor and a torpor of the senses amounting almost to imbecility. Arsenic was copiously administered to several, yet without effect; but large quantities of strong Peruvian bark infused in Port Wine proved an efficient remedy. The evil stopped not here. The disease was accompanied by dysentry and ended with many in an affection of the spleen.[29]

In February 1815, Richardson took up his ensignship with the 8th Regiment in Montreal. The mansions of the rich, the banking district, the busy port traffic, the numerous regiments in colourful dress uniform, the French-Canadian establishment, these novelties greeted the youth as he gradually recovered his strength, as the dire winter transformed itself into the long, green, and invigorating Canadian spring.

Orders arrived for the Headquarters staff of his regiment, of which he was a member, to sail im-

View from the Citadel overlooking the St. Lawrence.

mediately for Europe in a troop convoy of sixty ships. Overjoyed at the prospect of fighting Napoleon,[30] Richardson and his fellow staff officers embarked on a wonderful new invention, the steamer, for Quebec City. His excitement quickened at this walled bastion of memorable battle scenes,[31] where his brother Robert was serving at Army Headquarters. Robert's cleverness and dependability had elicited the highest praise from his senior officers.[32] Just before he welcomed John to Quebec he was able to

[29] "A Canadian Campaign," (1827), pt.I, 550-1.

[30] *War of 1812*, p.293.

[31] The military campaigns at Quebec no doubt were prominent among "the military exploits of the most renowned warriors of by-gone days" (*War of 1812*, p.3) which he studied in school.

[32] *Eight Years in Canada*, p.106.

throw away his crutches for good, though the pain in his leg still lingered on. He must have watched the great fleet bearing his brother down the St. Lawrence with infinite sadness. And Richardson might have looked back at the high cliffs with a momentary regret at leaving all that he had known, for a future that gave no promise of return.

Abroad

THE CONVOY set sail for Ostend in June. Among the young officers of the 8th Regiment, Richardson made a close friend of George Jarvis, son of William Jarvis, Superintendent of Indian Affairs and an old friend of Doctor Richardson from the days of Lieutenant-Governor Simcoe. The two had in common their rank and their Canadian birth, the latter circumstance drawing them together in the face of a certain condescension on the part of the English-born officers. Years later in one of his novels Richardson expressed his feelings about the English officers' prejudice towards colonials:

'True', quickly returned the youth, with a flushing cheek, 'Gerald is sufficiently avenged, but you forget the taunt he uttered against Canadians.'

'And if he did utter such taunt, why acknowledge it as such,' calmly rejoined Colonel d'Egville, 'are you ashamed of the name? I too am a Canadian, but so far from endeavouring to repudiate my country, I feel pride in having received my being in a land where everything attests the sublimity and magnificence of nature. Look around you, my nephew, and ask yourself, what there is in the wild grandeur of these scenes to disown?'[1]

Richardson's pride in his Canadian birth went very deep. He often referred to his "being" as springing from the land. Yet in the years ahead he would come to regard England as his home — its sophisticated society charmed him — and to regard Canada ambivalently — sometimes with a loathing for the backwardness of its people, and sometimes with a proprietary concern for its political and cultural development.

Richardson's convoy was half-way across the Atlantic when the Battle of Waterloo was fought. A frigate, dispatched from Ostend to redirect the fleet to Portsmouth, met it two weeks off the coast of Europe. In spite of the jubilation of victory, many young officers were disappointed at the news. And greater disappointment was to come.

Immediately after landing on July 27, Richardson was promoted from ensign to full lieutenant in the 2nd Battalion.[2] But he did not know that the 2nd Battalion of the 8th Regiment was scheduled to disband. As news of reductions in various regiments appeared in the newspapers, career officers began to worry. All through autumn the half-pay lists swelled with new names. Thirty thousand men were cut from the Foot and Dragoon regiments alone. When word reached Richardson on December 24 that his battalion was to cease to exist, he was desolate. On Christmas Day while taking their after-dinner wine, the officers fetched the colours of the regiment from the Commanding Officer's quarters and each cut off a relic as a memento. The remaining pieces they set on poles and held into the fire. They then

[1] *The Canadian Brothers*, I, 29.
[2] On July 27, 1815. John Davis, *History of the Second Queen's Royal Regiment* (London: Eyre and Spottiswoode, 1906).

held a funeral service for the ashes in the Portsmouth Barrack Square while their captain read the last rites.[3]

Richardson was placed officially on half-pay in February 1816, which meant retirement from active service. He was earning forty-two pounds as a half-pay lieutenant in a Foot Regiment — hardly sufficient for a young man who relished life and had an eye for adventure. With no idea of how he was to survive, and no hope of finding a way back to Canada, he travelled to London, a home for strays of all nations. Since it was assumed that officers were privately well-off, his pay was often regarded as a mere formality. He had no high family connections to turn to in England, no one to guide him in London. He tried, unsuccessfully, to exchange places with some of the more fortunate lieutenants who, though retained on active service, did not relish it. Nearing desperation, with all other avenues exhausted, he paid a visit to Norton in London.

Teyoninhokorawen, alias Colonel Norton, who had come to England with his Indian wife and son, was sitting for Phillips, the portraitist of the fashionable world. Norton presented his family to Queen Caroline who stood in for the aging George III at the royal court during his spells of insanity.[4] From this debut, the Gurneys, Wilberforce and their friends became his staunch friends. The British Army at headquarters also showed him respect, and it was Teyoninhokorawen's influence there which helped Richardson.

Norton had spent the war with the Centre Division of the army near Niagara, but he remembered Richardson as a school boy. Richardson had no trouble recognizing the grace and bearing of the tall muscular Indian agent from Wagousta in spite of his fashionable

Colonel John Norton, Chief Teyoninhokorawen of the Six Nations, by Phillips, London, 1815.

London clothes. Norton asked Richardson to send a memorandum of his services to him.

Richardson summarized his army career, devoting most of the description to his captivity; "So without the means of returning to his friends he would be happy if he could know whether or not he is to be brought on full pay in his turn. Begs leave to say that some officers of the Regiment are senior to him in the half-pay list who have on no occasion been on Service with their Regiment."[5] And in a note to Norton accompanying the memo, he wrote: "I only trust that your representation of my situation with the aid of this memorandum will have the effect of accomplishing something in my favour. I am certain you will do what you can for me, therefore will not despair."[6]

[3] *Eight Years in Canada*, p.116.
[4] "Tales of Haldimand — John Norton," *The Spectator*, Hamilton, Ontario (April 14, 1945).

[5] Memorandum, J. Richardson to J. Norton, n.d., n.p. Ontario Archives.
[6] ALS, J. Richardson to J. Norton, n.d., n.p. Ontario Archives.

On May 25, 1816, exactly three months after being put on half-pay, Richardson was brought back into full service and transferred to the Queen's or 2nd Regiment of Foot. His friend, Jarvis, was taken into the 104th Regiment at about the same time.

After Waterloo, the Queen's Regiment was stationed in central England and then shipped to the Newport Barracks on the Isle of Wight. The island, today dotted with large white Victorian houses, then had only a few buildings and was a popular haven for Englishmen who liked to camp out. The town of Cowes on the island was the site of a military prison; men were taken from the prison to fill the ranks of regiments destined for unhealthy climates. When the Queen's Regiment received orders to embark for Barbados at the end of April, it was swelled by three-hundred prisoners from Cowes sent to join the fleet at Spithead. To most it was as good as a death sentence.

Before joining his regiment, Richardson familiarized himself with London. The mansions in the West-End, the renowned houses of Tory and Whig families ran from Piccadilly to Park Lane; Chelsea was still a village to the West; and Westminster, a settlement of shopkeepers. London was on the threshold of the Regency period. Robber bands roamed the streets at night, terrifying the rich and keeping the Bow street runners busy. Richardson had not seen a city with such wretched poor on the one hand and such opulence on the other. But there were the Royal Academy paintings, the new public library at Kings Cross, the British Museum, and literary meetings open to the public. The experience of London struck at his heart so deeply that he was enthralled with the city for the rest of his life.[7] There was also a light side: such as Vauxhall Gardens, a mile and a half from London, with its music, its gaiety, and its intimate apartments adorned with Hogarth illustrations.

One incident during this London interlude illustrated Richardson's impetuousness and his predilection for gallantry. On leaving the King's theatre, entranced by the performance of Eliza Vestris, he was offended when one of the officers criticized her, and he challenged him to a duel. Eliza Vestris, at nineteen, had made her stage debut just the year before: within a few years she was to electrify England with her low sensuous voice, and her "breeches" role of Don Giovanni which inspired ballad writers to sing of the shape of her legs.

Richardson, a friend of Henry Cole, a half-pay captain who was Vestris's lover at the time, explained that he considered any disparagement of her acting a dishonour to his friend.

The opponents met in Hyde Park, distinctly separate from the city at that time; few paths crossed it, and cattle and deer grazed there. They exchanged shots off the mark, and thus, harmlessly, they vindicated their "honour." This, Richardson's first duel, gained him a reputation among the "fast set" he belonged to before he joined his new regiment.

At Newport, Lieutenant Richardson, assigned to handle incoming despatches, made friends with a superior officer who perhaps was something of a father substitute for him. Major James Connolly had come from half-pay to the Queen's at the same time as Richardson. Strict, but not harsh, with a fine sense of duty and utterly without pettiness, Connolly was described by Richardson as "a stern commander in the field but a perfect gentleman at the mess table."[8] Richardson worked under him throughout the summer months until ordered to join the regiment at Barbados.

Regiments serving in the West Indies had to

[7] *Eight Years in Canada*, p.159.

38

[8] "Recollections of the West Indies," *The New Era* (June 17, 1842).

have human reserves, held ready in the home country to be shipped out as replacements. The scourge of yellow fever constantly decreased the number of officers and men. The Queen's Regiment, which had landed in Barbados in early June, also inherited a tense political situation from the departing regiment, for a recent slave insurrection had put the country under martial law. At the close of September therefore, a detachment from the Queen's led by Richardson marched from Newport Barracks to Cowes where the troopship *Wilson* took it to the main fleet at Spithead.

While in the harbour the English officers were invited on board a Russian vessel which was bringing a gift of stallions from Tsar Alexander to the Prince Regent. Richardson was impressed by the Russian officers. The young noblemen attached to the imperial guard wore several decorations, spoke French perfectly, and had the best French manners. Richardson felt inferior "as in fact all Englishmen do when placed in competition with Russians of rank and acquirements."[9] He revealed his lack of sophistication when he took a large mouthful of caviar, an instant later realized what it was, and dashed from the room to spit it into the sea.

A strong breeze sent the fleet on its way, but it dropped when they reached the Bay of Biscay, a basin of torture for seafarers. Richardson described his state:

Who that has ever been in the Bay of Biscay during a calm, can recall without loathing the horrid nausea and wretched and comfortless state, both of mind and body, incident to such a situation — not to mention the crash and confusion occasioned in the cabin by the unceasing motion of the vessel, rolling her yards and some-

times even her gun-whales, into the troubled deep, while the loose and extended sails, striking with fury against the masts, seem like so many harpies flapping their wings in mockery of your misery and despair.[10]

The long ocean voyage was made bearable by adherence to discipline. On crossing the Equator, the men planned to observe the tradition of initiating first-crossers by shaving and washing them — despite Richardson's disapproval of the ceremony as a breach of discipline. The ship's carpenter, "Neptune", and his followers advanced towards Richardson. With another lieutenant from his regiment, Massie, who was his close friend, Richardson drew his pistol and threatened to kill the first man to approach him. He intended to protect his dignity and self-composure at any cost. Perhaps taken aback by Richardson's response, "Neptune" and his friends relented. The officers climbed to the highest part of the rigging to escape the deluge of water from the mainyard and watched the struggles of the men being shaved and splashed in riotous confusion.

In spite of his fears about lack of discipline, the *Wilson* continued with the fleet in good order and came within sight of Barbados at dawn on December 6. The Island "appeared to rise like a bed of emerald from the deep bosom of the waters."[11] It was about the size of the Isle of Wight, but more colourful. Bridgetown stretched like a crescent along the Bay shore and spread inland. White sands, foaming surf, and thick groves of trees first caught the eye, then the white-painted houses with green jalousies glimmering in the tradewinds under a slate-blue sky, and, last of all, the highlands in the interior wreathed in fog. The military fortification was situated on the

---

9 *Ibid.*, (March 2, 1842).

10 *Ibid.*
11 *Ibid.*

shoreline about a mile from town. On the surface, the tropics appeared beautiful, but under it, there was the ugliness of sickness and death.

Until this time love for action and glamour spurred Richardson's enthusiasm. The North American campaign set him wondering about war and the pointlessness of slaughter. Although England had awakened in him a desire for sophisticated society, his stay there was too fleeting, the impressions too many and too overwhelming to strike any thoughtful response in him. His stay in the West Indies was different: it provided a contrast to the staid Canadian society he had grown up with. The two years he was to spend here gave him an added perspective in judging man and the human condition.

The season for yellow fever began in September. Many officers and men had already died, including the Commander-in-Chief. Even men of Richardson's detachment died within a few days after their arrival. Victims of an unknown assailant, the soldiers drilled and paraded stoically until they were struck down. Since Barbados was the first posting for regiments stationed in the West Indies, there were continuous parades to maintain discipline. Richardson and his friend Massie took the first opportunity, ten days after arrival, to walk into Bridgetown. A few days later when he was about to be relieved from duty as the officer of the main guard, the blood rushed to his head and he felt intense pain. Leaning on his sword, he staggered the sixty yards to his cabin and collapsed on his bed. His servant called a surgeon and stretcher bearers.

His head shaved, his body showered in cold water, his temporal arteries opened to drain out blood, Richardson lay in the hospital; gaunt and unable to speak, he was capable of overhearing his fellow officers speak of him as dying. Miraculously he soon rallied to recover. From the next room he could hear the delirious cries of Massie, who died within a short

40

time. Richardson was surprised to see that the strong succumbed as quickly as the weak.[12] Nine officers from his regiment were attacked by yellow fever at this time; only he and one other survived.

The hospital was kept very clean. The native nurses looked after the sick conscientiously, and gave constant attention to the critically ill. Visits from his senior officers cheered Richardson, especially one from his Colonel who brought him Madeira wine and a refreshing fruit called watermelon, which he had never seen before.

The after-effects of the disease plunged him into deep melancholy. He looked sadly upon "the healthy forms of the yet unharmed, who trod as it were on a concealed fire, and might in the next hour be cut off from friends and from existence forever."[13] The best cure was duty. He was set to the task of guarding Negro insurrectionists.

The slave insurrection of the previous year began as a small disturbance among slaves on one plantation. Firing indiscriminately, the militia chased three slaves to other plantations and, in a show of fierce repression, burned all slaves' houses. Two white planters were killed, and one-thousand slaves were lost in the field or by summary military executions. The "insurrection" may have been created by the planters in an attempt to discourage the English parliament from passing a Bill for the registration of slaves which the planters claimed would weaken their control over the slave population.[14]

With a black kerchief about his brows and balancing his tall black shako, Richardson often leaned against the prison walls. He was gradually regaining

[12] *Ibid.*, (March 11, 1842).

[13] *Ibid.*

[14] *Remarks on the Insurrection in Barbadoes and the Bill for the Registration of Slaves* (London: Ellerton and Henderson, 1816), *passim.*

his strength. Rotting in the sun, the heads of many of the rebel slaves were displayed on poles throughout the countryside.

As soon as the prisoners were shipped off to Honduras, Richardson was sent on a tour of duty into the country. Although he found that the people in the country were more prosperous than those in the city, he was appalled at their ignorance and insensitivity. In his short essay *Recollections of the West Indies*, written about 1830,[15] he gave a stark picture of the brutality of the society and his reactions to it.

The colonial women, although handsome, were too limited in interests and conversation to attract the heart of a European, he wrote.[16] There was a dearth of intellectual stimulus in the colony. The white slave-owners were interested only in money matters, and having sent their wives and daughters to Europe, they were free to indulge their passions. The class system was utterly rigid. Social status was determined by the gradation of skin colour, the blackest being the lowest. The children with lighter skins than their parents often disdained them, and, if they became free, they behaved just as brutally towards the slaves as the worst European owners. "Removed by their birth from that complexion which is the symbol of slavery, they still feel that the remove in the link of connexion is not sufficiently distant, and appear as if desirous to visit the shame they secretly

experience at being compelled to trace their origin to such a source, on those who are the innocent cause."[17]

In wooden barracks, on the southern limits of Bridgetown, lived the rotund and stately mulatto women, who sent their slaves to sell fruits and vegetables at the fort. Their slaves stood motionless with their produce on their heads from dawn to evening under the hot sun. From time to time, the formidable female mulatto, wearing an immense turban with a hat over it and holding an umbrella over the hat, paid them a visit. Richardson asked "Is cruelty then, inseparable from power, and are the cravings after wealth and authority such as to stifle the sentiments of nature within our bosoms?...it cannot be denied that ignorance and brutality must ever complete what selfishness and avarice have suggested and begun."[18] His sympathy, however, was reserved for the poor unmarried women. He was touched by their simple faithfulness to their irresponsible mate and children.

But his sharpest attack was reserved for the system of slavery itself.

As for the wretched blacks sunk the lowest in this endless scale of colour and degree they are suffered to live even as the brutes of the field and scarcely possess a sentiment beyond that of promiscuous intercourse. Nor is this at all to be wondered at since the planter alive ever to his own interest, even at the expense and sacrifice of every better feeling, instead of repressing the profligacy likely to arise between the sexes, thrown together by the various duties of their labors, rather encourages an intercourse which, in according the prospect, seems the most likely means of feeding his wealth. With this

[15] We surmise 1830 from internal evidence. Richardson quoted from a speech made by Foreign Minister Canning on June 12, 1827 (*vide* Great Britain, Parliament, *Parliamentary Debates*, NS17 [1827], 1255) and refers to it as "at that period" ("Recollections.."May 25, 1842).Recommending emancipation it must have been written before the passing of the Emancipation Act in 1833. Casselman reported that it was published in England (*vide* War of 1812, xvii).

[16] "Recollections of the West Indies," *The New Era* (April 15, 1842).

[17] *Ibid.*, (May 25, 1842).

[18] *Ibid.*

view are dances at the termination of their labors frequently countenanced among the younger negroes. It is by no means uncommon for an unmarried planter or manager to have several mistresses at the same moment, and as these women reside on the same estate and are each aware of the affinity in which the others stand to their master, a thousand jealousies of course are the result. Should the proprietor or manager perceive and select any young female among his slaves whose ripening beauty serves to inflame and act upon his depraved imagination, there is no obstacle thrown in his way, since from herself alone opposition can arise, and that she is never disposed to put in force, not only because she is not taught to consider incontinence a vice but because she fears to irritate her tyrant, and to provoke punishment by resistance. I have several times been present at parties given to single men only, and after having partaken copiously of exhilarating wines, been introduced into the hall where the best looking of the young female slaves, with a few young men, have been assembled dancing to the discordant sounds produced by some old negro performer. Here the host, willing to extend the rites of hospitality to the utmost, has usually inquired of his guest if any particular female pleased his eye, and if answered in the affirmative, soon made a signal to the girl, which being understood, was instantly obeyed. Many of these young creatures did not exceed twelve or fourteen years of age. The immorality thus encouraged by these men ought in some measure, to be held responsible for the conduct of their slaves, is glaring in the extreme, but what must excite the deepest astonishment and disgust of the European, is the fact of their suffering their own children, by these young negresses, to be classed among their slaves, and to serve and toil for them as such.[19]

Wilberforce and his followers gave talks on the need for emancipation, but nothing would have aroused the indignation of the English as Richardson's first-hand description. "When are the sufferings of these wretched people to find a termination? and when will the Legislative authority of this country interpose between the tyrant and his victim?" he asked.[20] He proposed a plan for emancipation, which called for freeing the male slave at forty-five and the female at forty, and thus having little detrimental impact on the economy. In 1833, Britain passed the Emancipation Bill calling for the immediate freedom of slaves in the colonies.

Richardson disliked the tropical vegetation. The tall bare trunks and sickly-yellow leaves of the cocoanut tree made him melancholy, and he thought the ubiquitous palm trees made the countryside appear monotonous. He did not care for the animal life either. The wood-slave was an offensive-looking lizard. The land crabs frequently crawled noisily at night in regular files between the hills and sea, like armies on manoeuvres. On his morning guard duty, Richardson often observed these creatures labouring for cover as if caught by surprise by the dawn. Although the natives ate them, Richardson could never bring himself to do so, for he had seen them feed at the cemeteries and felt squeamish about eating an animal which had probably been eating the remains of his late comrades. One time he caught a chigger in his heel while swimming, but his native servant managed to cut it out before it could work itself into his foot. Large rats, which swarmed through the old wooden houses quartering the officers, scampered nightly

19 *Ibid.*, (May 20, 1842).
20 *Ibid.*, (May 25, 1842).

across his bed. Once, as he was falling asleep, he found a rat under his pillow.

It was, therefore, with pleasant surprise in July 1817 that he found himself one of a group of officers selected to go to Grenada to preside at a court martial for deserters. At the very least, Grenada would be a welcome change of scenery.

His selection had come about through Major Connolly, who had recently arrived from the Isle of Wight. Embarking in a gunship, the Major and his officers sailed the one-hundred and forty miles to Grenada swiftly. Their approach to the Island provided a beautiful sight: "Rich and flourishing vallies clothed in green and teeming with the various produce of the climate, were everywhere visible between the dark and frowning masses, whose summits lie buried in the dense clouds perpetually rolling along these ridges of mountain, while in the foreground, the town of St. George, built on a sloping ground, rose like an amphitheater before us..."[21] The architecture of St. George, with its lead-coloured houses and red-tiled roofs, was English in style. Richmond Hill barracks was situated on a lofty hill about a mile from the town.

Richardson listened to testimony during the day and partied in the houses of the distinguished residents by night. He and his fellow officers were quartered in a dilapidated barrack called Fort Adjutant. They travelled to and from Richmond Hill to judge six privates accused of desertion. These soldiers belonged to the York Rangers, a special regiment composed of men sentenced to serve the remainder of their lives in the West Indies. One man preferred to be whipped every six weeks and spend his days recuperating in the hospital rather than do his assigned duties. The regiment was virtually a prison.

The six men on trial were doomed. Three of them, who had attempted escape before, were given the death penalty. The remaining three were to be given eight-hundred lashes and to be branded with the letter "D". One of these was at first sentenced to death, but the court relented because he was a veteran of many years' standing and had two sons in another regiment.

Richardson, at 20, was the youngest on the panel of judges and totally inexperienced in such matters. He relied on his senior officers, and voted with them, an act he was to rue to the end of his days.[22]

At the end of the judging and the partying, the members of the tribunal re-embarked for Barbados. Major Connolly was struck down by fever on the voyage, lapsed into a coma and died at sea. The sailors wished to bury the body at sea, but the army officers, Richardson especially, insisted that they wait until reaching Barbados. The smell of the decomposing corpse fed the sailors' impatience but, fortunately, a good wind arose and bore them quickly to Barbados. A military funeral was immediately arranged. Richardson, saddened by the loss of another close friend, was relieved when his regiment received its marching orders. He was tired of Barbados and the strict military regimen in force there.[23]

The Right Wing of the regiment which included the Headquarters staff was posted to St. Vincent's Island, while the Left Wing (which included Richardson) was transported to Grenada in late August. Back to Grenada it was for Richardson, and back to the scene of the court-martial. Richardson was the only member of the tribunal to return; the others had been sent to St. Vincent. The sentences were carried out a few days after Richardson's arrival at Richmond Hill Barracks in a scene he could never forget:

[21] *Ibid.*, (June 9, 1842).

[22] *Ibid.* (April 1, 1842).
[23] *Ibid.*, (June 17, 1842).

Accordingly one morning, the whole of the garrison appeared under arms, drawn up in a low ground immediately beneath the barracks, which was used as a parade. The troops consisting of a few artillery, the York Rangers, and our Regiment, occupied three sides of a square, and on a fourth were placed three coffins at equal distances from each other. A clergyman in his robes of office was present, and the most impressive silence pervaded every rank. One settled look of serious melancholy was discernible in the features of both officers and men, and the words of command were even given in a lower tone of voice. Every individual seemed to find his situation painful, and the minutes which intervened until the arrival of the condemned were passed in anxiety and awe. It had been feared that an attempt at rescue would be made by their comrades and our corps had in consequence been secretly ordered to provide themselves with ammunition while care was taken by their own officers, that the Rangers should have none. At length the unfortunate men appeared slowly advancing surrounded by their guard, and as they entered the open space in front of the troops, I saw one of them point me out to one of his companions...I would have given anything to have been absent from this scene... The criminals moved toward their coffins, and kneeling on them with their faces turned towards the line, prayed separately, and for a few minutes with the minister of religion. This being ended the clergyman withdrew, when the fatal caps were drawn over their faces, and they remained motionless, with their hands tied across and suspended in front. Three sections consisting of men drafted for the occasion from their own corps, and commanded each by a corporal, were then silently drawn up in front

44

of the coffins. No command was delivered, everything was done by signal, and as their pieces were directed against the hearts of their companions, that which was to launch them into eternity was given, and one simultaneous blaze of light flashed along the line of sections — not a groan was uttered — one fell dead on his coffin — another bounded several feet from his knees in the air, and then sunk lifeless on his head — the third was the only one who suffered — the balls had not touched a vital part, and he lay writhing in agony on the ground — two of the reserve immediately advanced with a corporal, and approached so near that a part of the poor wretch's head was blown away, presenting a most cruel spectacle, and his struggles were at an end.[24]

Richardson continued the gruesome realism of his account with a description of the torture prepared for the remaining three prisoners. The troops marching in slow time past the bodies and coffins, and the branding irons heating in a furnace smoking in the distance, men prepared triangles on which the prisoners would be stretched for whipping. The lashings were interrupted periodically to allow the doctors to inspect the sufferers but the smell of burning flesh and the screams continued several hours. The troops watched the proceedings with horror; each knew that he could be the next victim on the morrow. Richardson thought that, unlike public executions when crowds came to be amused, military executions were grim reminders and hence made better soldiers of the men.[25]

In spite of his memories of the court martial, Richardson enjoyed the finer climate and freer mili-

[24] *Ibid.*, (June 24, 1842).
[25] *Ibid.*, (June 17, 1842).
[26] *Ibid.*, (June 17, 1842). "...eternal drills" comprised life on Barbados.

tary life on Grenada.[26] In October 1817, a general order was issued which stated that all troops in the West Indies were to be paid daily instead of monthly. As a lieutenant with under seven years of service, Richardson earned six shillings and sixpence per day — enough for him to indulge his interest in gaming at the many hot springs. Unfortunately, however, there is no further record of his experiences on Grenada, for after the execution of the deserters he cut short his *Recollections of the West Indies*.

Yellow fever swept the islands of St. Vincent and Grenada in the spring of 1818. Between April and June, thirty-eight men were invalided home. From July to September two more were sent back.[27]

Richardson is listed in the "Monthly Return of Officers for Windward and Leeward Islands" as obtaining a leave of absence on September 16, 1818 to return to England for the purposes of being placed on the inactive list. He seems to have made a last minute decision to ship out for England, for his name appears at the foot of the list of officers who had been granted permission during the preceding month to return. Ten years later when applying for a return to active service, Richardson gave his reason for retiring from the West Indies as "both private motives and from ill health, that is from the effect produced by a violent attack of yellow fever during which all hope of recovery had been abandoned by the medical staff of Barbados."[28] Since his illness had occurred two years before this request to leave, perhaps other, private motives were his true reason for desiring leave. He was bored with the regimental life, but it was unlikely that boredom would have decided him to return to England. Possibly having found time to write, he had sent articles to his friend Henry Cole. Intimately acquainted with the literary and journalistic circles of London, Cole may have encouraged him to return.[29]

Back in England, perhaps by the end of October 1818, Richardson was transferred on half-pay as of October 1 to the 92nd Regiment or Gordon Highlanders, which had been recently reduced and was preparing to sail for Jamaica in November.

At twenty-two, darkly handsome with a proud bearing, he faced the cosmopolitan world of London, and sought acceptance by the sybaritic Regency society.

[27] John Davis, *History of the Second Queen's Regiment. op. cit.,* passim.

[28] Return of Service, Dec. 2, 1828. Gt Brit. Public Record Office. WO25/772.

[29] Cole rented his house in London from Thomas Love Peacock who retained a couple of rooms in it. His son, later known as Sir Henry Cole, the founder of the Victoria and Albert Museum, was introduced to John Stuart Mill, Charles Buller and George Grote by Peacock and formed with them a discussion group in the 1820's.

Novelist

RICHARDSON found lodgings in the Hanover Square district and renewed his friendship with officers he had known in the 1812 War.[1] As a half-pay Lieutenant he had a problem of finances. Officers on half-pay without extra income usually lived in the cheaper towns outside London. Even hard-working journalists could barely afford the expense of the city. There was money to be picked up, however, in the many pamphleteer wars which called for sharp, satiric pieces to be turned out in quick order. Also, with the development in the early part of the century of new methods of making paper and better printing machines, newspapers proliferated, and many opportunities were in the offing for young men. Theodore Hook, the versifier and novelist who was welcomed into the best society for his wit, began the *John Bull* in 1820 in support of royalty and dismayed the political opposition. The *Morning Chronicle*, a Whig paper, was edited by John Black, whose defiant approach in his uncompromising editorials and pioneering criticisms of the law and English institutions, was adopted by Richardson when he edited newspapers in Canada years later. The *Times*, a Tory organ, was edited by Thomas Barnes; under him the paper became known as the "Thunderer."

The period was one of the most turbulent in English history. The changes wrought by the Industrial Revolution aroused the new proletariat to riot, which in turn led to the Peterloo massacres in 1819. The Cato Street Conspiracy of 1820 to assassinate the entire cabinet of George IV shocked the upper and middle classes who regarded it as a sign of the mental imbalance of the age. Richardson witnessed the public hanging of Thistlewood and his fellow conspirators. Thistlewood, a gentleman known for his keen intellect, had attracted wide-spread interest in his case. He was said to be a rebel seeking revenge on society for its inhumanity. Such a character, an outlaw championing the downtrodden against implacable authority, was becoming popular in the literature of the day.

Richardson was involved in the world of carefree Regency society where sparkling conversation, quick wit and impeccable dress were the most admired acquirements, and in which he came to excel. He joined in the crowd of half-pay officers and rich dandies who frequented the theatres and amused themselves with the actresses and demi-mondaines. Fabulously rich young men such as Joseph "Pea-Green" Hayne, a friend of Richardson's,[2] inherited fortunes and took in a steady income from plantations in the West Indies. One of Pea-Green's favourite enterprises was financing the pugilist "Whiteheaded Bob" Baldwin. Boxing matches were long and bloody contests of brute strength on which the dandies bet heavily. Pea-Green used to drive Baldwin about in his carriage with a negro boy as his "tiger" who, riding behind his master, would, at a signal, jump down to accost a pretty young woman for her name and address.

Aside from sponging off rich friends such as Pea-

---

[1] Richardson kept track of his officer friends for whom he retained a fondness throughout his life (*vide* "Major-General Sir Isaac Brock and the 41st Regiment," *Albion* (March 28, 1846).

[2] *Lola Montes*, p. 5.

Green Hayne, an English adventurer, as Richardson was called, sometimes made money at the gambling tables. Gambling at cards was a life-long habit with him, and he became known for his expertise in écarté. There is a parallel between the confrontation of two men over the game of écarté and the confrontation in duelling, for which he was also known: both gave him a vicarious pleasure attendant on risk. Gambling halls which sprang up in the vicinity of St. James' Street required only that a stranger be introduced to obtain admission. Richardson's fascination with écarté provided the inspiration for his novel, *Ecarté*. Like Dormer, a character in the novel, Richardson may have tried to escape the profligate life he was leading in London, and decided early in 1821, to spend a few years travelling on the continent.[3]

If Richardson left for the continent in 1821, there is little indication where he visited. In later years he implied that he had seen the four corners of the globe.[4] He wrote about the Alps of Switzerland as if he had seen them. It would be surprising, however, if he did

Gambling life in London in the 1820's by Cruikshank.

not travel through parts of Germany, Switzerland, northern Italy, and the South of France; the Wanderlust, engendered by the literature of the day, infected the young man. He was said to have "resided several years in Paris . . ."[5] In a return of Service to the British Army dated December 1828, Richardson replied to the query as to where he had spent the past five years — "Paris and London."[6] British half-pay officers flocked to Paris where the cost of living was much lower than in London.

In *Ecarté*, Dormer gambles at the Salons d'Ecarté, and when he cannot pay his creditors who descend upon him all at once, he is arrested and sent to a country prison for almost a year. While in prison he encounters a French Colonel who had served under Napoleon but who had been found guilty of theft and sentenced by the Bourbons. Because this episode bears no relation to the theme of the novel, except possibly as an illustration of the hypocrisy of the Bourbon regime during the Restoration, it seems to have been an experience of

---

[3] Both Dormer and Delmaine in the novel are drawn autobiographically, Dormer as a sort of alter-ego to Delmaine. The date 1821 when Dormer left England as the supposed date for Richardson's departure fits internal evidence in the novel, that is Delmaine's attendance at a Calais Theatre to see *Le Soldat Laboureur* (*Ecarté*, I, 19) a popular play of a military spirit protesting the state of peace which was first produced in Paris in September 1821. (Henri d'Almeras, *La vie parisienne sous la restauration* (Paris, 1910) pp. 159-160.

[4] Richardson wrote in his *Journal of the Movement of the British Legion in Spain*: ". . . recalling to memory some of the strongest outlines of Swiss scenery..." (p.58): "First Russia, and next Switzerland, suggested themselves to my imagination... But there was wanting the inspiriting air of liveliness, and vigourous action peculiar to the inhabitants of these climes as well as the internal comfort to be met with in their homes." (pp. 96-7). He wrote in "The Sunflower" (1850): "...in any quarter of the globe we have visited."

[5] *International Magazine*, 3 (July 1851), 37.

[6] Return of Service Dec. 2., 1828. *op. cit.*

Richardson's about which he felt so strongly that he made it part of his novel. Richardson probably spent some time in Saint-Pelagie, debtor's prison in Paris, which he described in *Ecarté*.

The gambling houses in Paris were encouraged by the government on account of the taxes they paid. Many Englishmen lost fortunes at the tables of Frascati's and the Palais Royal during the day, and at Astelli, Le Pain and Magnolli in the night. French noblemen acted as "touters" who befriended foreigners, borrowed from them, and introduced them to the gaming tables as well as to young ladies who encouraged the victims to gamble. Touters received a certain percentage from the salons. Beautiful women of hardened character appear in the background of Richardson's realistic description of the salons.

Yet the picture of gaming salons, money lenders, and debtor's prisons drawn by Richardson in *Ecarté* could have been only a part of his life there. English society in Paris was quite extensive. Galignani's, a house for foreign exchange, was the centre of tourist activity. An English-language newspaper, *Galignani's Messenger*, provided news from home and also reported events in the Parisian community. A literary magazine, *The Paris Monthly Review*, was published from Paris during the 1820's. Richardson may have written for one or both of these publications.[7] Paris was a centre of intellectual ferment. Literary salons flourished faithfully attended by such figures as the ageing Chateaubriand, Stendhal, and Victor Hugo. Lamartine lived in Paris at this time; he was translating Byron's *Childe Harold*.

The truly significant event of the decade, however, which appeared to have an effect on Richardson, was the propagation of the doctrine of Saint-Simonism. Its symbolic reversion to Christ and his disciples appealed to the young men for whom the old values had become shallow and hypocritical. Its idea about the nature of man — "the most ecstatic contemplation of God by man neither can nor must remove man from divine personality, for he is himself an integral part of that personality."[8] — remained a principle for Richardson throughout his life.

Years later he wrote:

I verily believe that the Deity, the great Creator of mind as well as of matter, looks with no extreme disfavor on the man who causes in his own person, and as far as his imperfect nature can attain that end, that high sense of individuality with which he has endowed the most intellectual of his creatures, to be respected by the stern assertion of its own dignity.[9]

Also the St. Simonist objective of equal rights for women appealed to Richardson, who had an almost mystical reverence for female beauty and love. He wrote:

As it is, what are women? Slaves, literally the slaves of men, and regarded principally because they are necessary to their own selfish ends. Few is the number of those, among the millions of the earth, who love woman for herself alone — the perfection of God's will, made manifest in her surpassing beauty — and who are willing to make all sacrifices of self, that not a wish of her soul should remain ungratified.[10]

[7] Cyrus Redding, sub-editor of the *New Monthly*, who accepted Richardson's "A Canadian Campaign" for publication, was an editor of *Galignani's Messenger*.

[8] Barthelemy Prosper Enfantin, *Life Eternal* (Chicago, Open Court, 1920), p. 108.

[9] *The Guards in Canada*, p. 43.

[10] *The Monk Knight of St. John*, p. 121.

On occasion his attention to women involved him in duels. According to Richardson, a duel in *Ecarté* initiated because of an unkind remark about a lady, was fashioned after an actual duel he had with a French Marquis.[11] His opponent, learning of Richardson's proficiency with the pistol, insisted on their shooting with unwieldy horse pistols.

The meeting took place in the Bois de Boulogne, then a few miles outside Paris. Richardson was accompanied by two Irish officers. From his description, Richardson's opponent seems to have been the Marquis du Hally who had killed several young English officers. The Marquis was accompanied by two officers from his corps, the Cuirassiers. An umpire for the early morning match was an Irishman in the Garde du Corps Roi, undoubtedly Captain Warren, noted for killing nine men by duel in one year. This bull-necked giant of a man with a fierce, unpredictable temper was given a minor role in *Ecarté*, in which Richardson described him as a bully yet a coward at heart.[12]

News of the impending duel spread through Paris in a matter of hours, and scores of observers positioned themselves behind the trees and bushes. Six pairs of horse pistols were tossed in a bag, and the opponents each reached in for one. Richardson's pistol had a stubborn trigger which swerved his aim. The Marquis hit Richardson over the Achilles tendon of the right ankle. Richardson tried to stand for a second shot but could not. The Marquis apologized for his offence and helped carry Richardson to his carriage, an act of gallantry which Richardson appreciated. Richardson was in bed for a week and on crutches for some time afterward. His courage in challenging the notorious Marquis brought him attention in the social circles of Paris. "C'est un Dom Quichotte," a hostess in *Ecarté* said of the hero, "donc il faut absolument corriger la manie d'aventures."[13]

11 *Personal Memoirs*, pp. 15-16.
12 *Ecarte*, I, 37.

Duelling in England, 1820's, by Cruikshank.

English journalists, especially those involved in the pamphlet wars, lived in Paris, out of reach of English libel laws, and sent their articles to London publishers. Harriette Wilson, the courtesan, used to send installments of her *Memoirs* by the mail pouch of the English Ambassador in Paris to her London publisher, J.J. Stockdale.[14] But before each installment went to the printer, she would send a copy of the pages describing her affair with a particular nobleman to that nobleman, and offer to suppress that section if he paid her. Those who refused were immortalized by the immense popularity of her book, which made ten thousand pounds in the few months after its publication in January 1825. Beginning in March 1825, *The Confessions of Julia Johnstone* was published serially, ostensibly to refute Harriette's assertions about one of her friends. Both Harriette and Stockdale believed that Julia had been dead for years; according to Stockdale *The Confessions* was written by either John Mitford or Captain Richardson in order to discredit him.[15]

13 *Ibid.*
14 *Stockdale's Budget* (London, Dec. 13 1826-1827), *passim.*
15 Angela Thirkell, *The Fortunes of Harriette: the surprising career of Harriette Wilson* (London, H. Hamilton, 1936), p. 275. Miss Thirkell, unfortunately, gave no source. Aside from Amy and Nicholas Bochsa, Richardson could have

Mitford was a likely suspect — he was a well-known underground writer whose light satirical style had been directed at Queen Caroline; by 1825 however, he was suffering from alcoholism, and it is questionable that he could have produced a book in just a few weeks. Richardson, who followed the custom of the day and called himself "Captain,"[16] could write in a light, satirical vein. Moreover, Richardson had been in London near the end of Harriette's heyday and was acquainted with her milieu.

Harriette attacked the establishment by ridiculing it, whereas *The Confessions* tried to discredit Harriette and singled out for attack her lawyer, Henry Brougham, the Whig politician who was becoming a thorn in the side of the establishment. Brougham defended Harriette's book in a few law suits, one of which was brought by Charles Nicholas Bochsa, the famous harpist, a friend of Richardson's. Wanted for forgery in Paris, Bochsa fled to London and married Harriette's sister, Amy Debouchette, who had been the mistress of several noblemen, including the Prince of Wales. When Harriette's *Memoirs* cast Bochsa in a questionable light, the newspapers wrote about his past, and his career was ruined. Perhaps as a favour to Amy, the

Prince of Wales made him supervisor of the musical department of *His Majesty's Theatre*. The intimate knowledge of Harriette's life at the time she knew Julia could have been passed on to Richardson by Amy Bochsa.

On August 12 1825, Richardson was married; perhaps with an increase in income and hopes for a literary career, he was optimistic about his future. Only the wedding certificate remains to identify his wife: "Jane Marsh of Leamington in the County of Warwick, Spinster."[17] They were married quietly in the dining room of the British Embassy, the only English Chapel in Paris, by a gentleman substituting for the regular chaplain. They were still married in December 1828 when Richardson applied to be taken on active military service. Richardson married again in April 1832. As divorce was not allowed, his first wife must have died in the interim. There are no records of her in Warwickshire.

His second wife, Maria Caroline Drayson, whom he loved deeply throughout their thirteen years of marriage, completely eclipsed his first wife. In none of his writings, much of it autobiographical, did Richardson refer to an earlier marriage. Only in his novel *Frascati's* (1830) is there the slightest indication of how he may have regarded this marriage. An Englishman is tricked into marrying an Englishwoman in Paris only to find that she is the mistress of his best friend. She pretended to love him in order to get his money for his false friend. Although it cannot be taken literally as Richardson's experience, Richardson reveals an attitude of mind, when describing the husband's disgust, that seems to indicate that he had had a similar experience. In the novel, the wife drowns herself in the Seine.

Could Richardson's sudden emergence into the

received information from Colonel Cotton whom Harriette named as Julia's seducer and keeper. He is mentioned in *The Confessions* as residing in Paris "not far from where Julia pretends to reside." Stockdale wrote that Cotton would not have been dismissed from the 10th Dragoons if he had seduced a poor girl rather than the Honourable Julia Storer, niece of the Earl of Corysfoot (*Stockdale's Budget, op. cit.*, p. 59). Therefore, Cotton must have been living in Paris on half-pay, possibly near Richardson. Also, Mitford's pirated edition of Harriette's *Memoirs* (referred to in *The Confessions*) establishes that he had a press and would have published *The Confessions* had he written it. But Benbow, a radical, anticlerical publisher (who issued some of Byron's works) published it.

16 *County Press* (Hertfordshire, Aug. 30, 1831).

50

17 Miscellaneous Foreign Records, Aug. 1825. General Register Office, Somerset House, London.

field of literature shortly after his marriage indicate that Jane Marsh brought him literary connections? There were booksellers named Marsh in London, one of whom, William Marsh, published a poem by Richardson. And there was the one-time parliamentarian, Charles Marsh, who from 1819 made a living by writing articles for periodicals, particularly for *The New Monthly Magazine*, which accepted Richardson's first long article.

In December of 1826, *The New Monthly Magazine* printed the first installment of Richardson's narrative of the War of 1812, "A Canadian Campaign." He returned to London in the spring of 1826. An undated note from Richardson in London to Cyrus Redding, the sub-editor of *The New Monthly Magazine*, states that the printer has not sent him the proof sheet of the "Campaign" and asks Redding to have it sent to him as he fears the need for many corrections.[18] The informality of the note and his warm salutation "Very faithfully yours" implies a friendship with Redding, as does his "kind compliments to Mrs. Reading."

In "A Canadian Campaign" Richardson strove for a sense of realism. Detailing the movement of the Right Division in the War of 1812 and writing in the first person, he was scrupulous to state only those facts that could be corroborated by his brother officers. His eye for detail, his ability to portray a scene, and his adherence to a formal style, combined to bring to the English a fascinating picture of guerrilla warfare in America and the character of the North American Indian. Alexander Henry, the good friend and business partner of his grandfather Askin, published his *Travels and Adventures in Canada and the Indian Territories* in 1809. Henry's style seems to have had an influence upon Richardson:

The dead were scalped and mangled; the dying were writhing and shrieking under the unsatiated knife and tomahawk; and, from the bodies of some, ripped open, their butchers were drinking the blood, scooped up in the hollow of joined hands, and quaffed amid shouts of rage and victory. I was shaken, not only with horror, but with fear.[19]

This was a description of the slaughter of the inhabitants of Fort Michillimackinac. "A Canadian Campaign" was written in the same bold manner; but there are two aspects in Richardson's writing which were unusual in this genre of narrative history. His treatment of the "savage" Indians revealed them as men coming from different cultures, and as peoples who were defending themselves against genocide; his picture of the American enemy showed them as individual men of good or of weak character. During his imprisonment in Kentucky, he portrayed the Americans in one circumstance as a mob ruled by prejudice and in others as friends from whom he had been temporarily divided by the politics of the day. This humanitarian trait was an essential ingredient in his development as a novelist. Richardson's criticism was sharpest against the British General Procter, whom he depicted as careless of the lives of his men and concerned only for his own welfare. His uncritical portrayal of the British soldier may be the major flaw in the essay. The narrative of the military campaign is interesting despite this flaw, which reflects the uncritical esteem of a boy soldier for a "glorious" institution, the British Army.

The poet Thomas Campbell, who was made editor of *The New Monthly Magazine* by the publisher, Colburn, because of his fame, left all of the actual work of editing to Redding. Campbell's poem "Gertrude of

---

[18] J. Richardson to C. Reading (*sic*) (Connaught Place, 1826?). Bodleian Library, Oxford.

[19] Alexander Henry, *Travels and Adventures in Canada and the Indian Territories* (New York: Riley, 1809), pp. 80-81.

Wyoming" which told of the massacre of settlers by Indians, had been popular in America for years. Richardson referred to it as "beautiful and affecting."[20] If anyone in England were to be receptive to a poem about North American Indians, it was Campbell. Campbell, then, may well have liked Richardson's next literary offering "Tecumseh" and sent Richardson to Colburn with it, as was his habit with promising young authors.[21] Colburn, anxious to please Campbell to the point of following his advice in all literary matters, directed James Moyes, one of the printers in his publishing empire, to print Richardson's poem.

Tecumseh or the Warrior of the West in four cantos with Notes came out in May 1828; it did not sell well. *The Literary Gazette* a weekly owned by Colburn, reported briefly upon it: "Of *Tecumseh* we can only say that the feeling which prompted it is better than the execution. The Notes are exceedingly interesting."[22] Many of the "Notes," Richardson explained in his preface, were taken from "A Canadian Campaign." Actually few of the notes were taken from the article; Richardson had signed both publications "By an English officer" and obviously wanted the public to recognize that they were by the same person. The literary game of guessing the identity of the author was common (it was exemplified by Walter Scott who would not admit even to the King that he was the author of the Waverley novels). *Tecumseh's* commercial failure was attributed to the Englishman's disinterest in the North American Indian. A better reason, however, would seem to be one based upon economics. In 1826 a commercial depression had hit England and bankrupted publishers and book-sellers, including James Moyes. By 1828 sales of poetry had virtually stopped. The irrepressible Henry Colburn took advantage of the commercial crisis to buy up well over half of the publishing business in London. Any serious writer, therefore, had to deal with Colburn and his partner, Richard Bentley, to see his works published; if he fell afoul of them, he had small hope of publication. Eventually, it happened to Richardson.

Tecumseh, opening with preparations for the naval battle on Lake Erie, describes the defeat of the British fleet, and the disastrous battle in which Tecumseh was killed. Richardson intended "to rescue the name of a hero from oblivion" and ended the poem with a reference to the Americans who degraded his corpse. "Oh! may he hear his offspring loud proclaim that Chieftain's worth, whose glory is his shame!" He dedicated the poem to Captain Barclay, then living in Edinburgh, who, flattered by the compliment, requested that Richardson praise the victor, Commodore Perry, for his humanity, which Richardson did in his preface. He suspected that the poem would enjoy more popularity in America than in England, for he knew that "A Canadian Campaign" had been reprinted in the *National Gazette and Literary Register* of Philadelphia in 1827, and had excited great interest there.[23] Intent on a realistic portrayal of an Indian, he thought "that a greater degree of interest would be executed by a strict adherence to the wild poetry of the character:"

The vivid lightnings of that eye where roll'd
Deep vengeance for the sufferings of a land

[20] *Tecumseh*, p. 122, n. 6.

[21] For example: "Permit me to introduce to you my friend Mr. Borrow. He is young — but a man of extraordinary promise — I wish you would talk to him about his being a correspondent for the New Monthly." Campbell to Colburn (London, April 24, 1825). Forster ms., Victoria and Albert Museum Library.

[22] *Literary Gazette*, No. 604 (Aug. 16. 1828). 519.

[23] *National Gazette and Literary Register* (Philadelphia), 7, No. 915 (Jan. 30, 1827): 7, No. 942 (April 3, 1827): 7, No. 992 (Aug. 2, 1827): 7, No. 993 (Aug. 4, 1827). A Kentucky resident wrote refuting Richardson's statements to which Richardson replied (*vide National Gazette* (March 24, 1828); *New Monthly* (1828), pt. I, 178).

Long doomed the partage of a numerous horde
Whom lawless rapine o'er its vallies pour'd.

At one point in *Tecumseh* he abruptly departed from his main theme to contrast the happy state of a youthful officer in the bonds of comradeship in America to the misery of European society where "man falls the victim by his fellow's wiles." The passage continues in a mixture of melancholy and bitterness:

Yet ah! how many o'er the wide world roam,
And curse the loneness of their rayless doom;
For them no friendship warms — no
                   smiling home
Lights the dark picture of their bosom's gloom;
For them the pathless wastes and wild wave's
                   foam
Are scenes more fitted than the crowded room,
Where social man scarce takes the pain to hide
His cold hypocrisy — his upstart pride.
Still there are those who, with indignant scorn,
Who, curs'd from birth, and to endurance born,
Drain to the dregs the bitter cup of Fate
And as they linger o'er the hopes they mourn,
And with the past compare their cheerless state,
Would fain renew, upon that savage soil,
Their first privations, and their youth's
                   sweet toil.

Interpreted in a personal way, these lines reveal Richardson's deep hurt at his social ostracism, evidently determined, he felt, by his birth. The intimation seems clear, and it is the only reference he ever made to it; he experienced some prejudice in English society owing to the colour of his skin. The "hopes" he "mourned" apparently refer to his stifled hopes for an army career. His Indian origins, which had cursed him to drink "the bitter cup of Fate," were, perhaps, the basis of his private motives for relinquishing this career. The hypocrisy in society, which he attacked throughout his writings, he felt keenly in his own experiences; he was not merely reflecting a contemporary theme of the romantic poets. This sensitivity to social prejudice probably made him unusually susceptible to insult and may help explain his issuing challenges to duels whenever he felt he had been slighted.

He had written the poem in 1823 when he was living in Paris. [24] Its rhyme scheme, ottava rima, was used by Lord Byron in his *Don Juan* published between 1819 and 1824. The poem's sombre emphasis on destruction and death, even to the lonely mourning by a chief over the body of his young son killed in battle, shows the literary influence of German Romanticism. [25]

Richardson naturally was attracted by the literary fashions of the day and the general fascination felt by the English for the German Romantics. Germans were also contributing greatly to the development of the writing of history in which there was a renewed interest owing to archaeological discoveries made in the ancient world. Richardson apparently was intrigued by the new emphasis on historical fact and tried to treat his experiences in a historical context.

His "Recollections of the West Indies" narrating his experiences as a lieutenant in Barbados and Grenada, is in the same genre as "A Canadian Campaign" but with a shift of emphasis from narration of events to social criticism. He wrote the essay before the enactment of emancipation in 1833 yet after a speech made

[24] *Tecumseh*, pref.
[25] Richardson was particularly interested in the works of the poet Edward Young, 1683-1765, whose "Conjectures on Original Composition" by spreading a doctrine of individuality and original genius as exemplified by Shakespeare had immense influence in Germany where it gave impetus to the development of German Romanticism. A pessimistic weariness of life expressed in Young's *Night Thoughts* is in evidence in Richardson's *Tecumseh*.

in June 1827 by Prime Minister Canning to which he referred in the text. Social criticism was very much in the atmosphere of course, and the literary men whom Richardson met through Thomas Campbell and Cyrus Redding were heatedly engaged in the effort to reform English institutions.

One of them, James Silk Buckingham, who had returned to England after a life of adventure in the Far East, founded a number of periodicals after 1827, notably *The Athenaeum* in which he was in partnership with Colburn. Buckingham through his writings and lectures against the monopolistic trading policies of the East India Company brought that Company to an end. *The Athenaeum* (which carried a pre-publication notice of *Ecarté*) absorbed *The London Weekly Review*, begun in 1827 by Lieutenant David Richardson. The two Lieutenant Richardsons — John and David — who were friends,[26] could have been mistaken for the same person. This kind of mistake was the occasion for a hostile review of Richardson's *Ecarté* by the most powerful critic of the time, William Jerdan.

Jerdan was hostile to David Richardson because he was the literary intelligence behind the new *London Weekly Review* which represented powerful competition to his prestigious *Literary Gazette*. The conflict between the two burst into print in 1827 when the poet Thomas Hood defected from *The London Weekly Review* to the *Gazette* and was suspected of writing a scathing notice of David Richardson's poems. Jerdan reported that another poet, G.F. Richardson, did not want to be confused with David Richardson because of the "notoriety" of his poetry, which caused G.F. Richardson to deny that he had implied anything of the sort.[27] That there was a third writer called Richardson would have

been too much for Jerdan to have suspected; when *Ecarté* appeared, and he learned that it was written by a Lieutenant Richardson, he released all his pent-up anger upon it:

> This is another of those detestable publications whose only tendency can be to deprave the minds of even the most superficial and thoughtless readers. It is not easy for us to describe, certainly not to expose it without polluting our paper with obscene extracts. Suffice it, therefore, to say, that if you suppose a coarse and vulgar writer attempting to paint with his utmost warmth and vividness the vice, and harlotry, and prostitution of the worst resorts of a dissolute city, you will have some idea of his noxious "fashionable novel." Unfit to be seen beyond the precincts of the stews, the profligate manners of which it describes, Ecarte is merely less pernicious in consequence of the contemptible talent of its would-be libertine and licentious author. The only public notice, indeed, that it deserves, is such as is bestowed by prosecution upon indecent prints, the class of productions of which it is the companion.[28]

The evening after the review appeared, Jerdan approached John Richardson at a literary party given by Cyrus Redding and, unaware of his identity, asked him to take some wine with him. When Richardson introduced himself as the author of *Ecarté*, Jerdan looked surprised and turned away with embarrassment. "Jerdan" wrote a memoirist,

> was the puppet of certain booksellers, and dispensed praise or blame at their bidding, and it may be feared "for a consideration"... *The Literary*

---

[26] *Vide*, letter from Isaac D'Israeli to David Richardson in David Lester Richardson, *Literary Chit-Chat* (London: J. Madden, 1848).

[27] *The London Weekly Review and Journal of Literature and the Fine Arts*, I (1827), 223.

[28] *Literary Gazette* (March 28, 1829), p. 208.

Gazette's conductors and writers spared no pains to attack, to vilipend, and to injure, so far as they could, anyone who had to do with a rising journal so merciless in its exposure of a false and demoralizing system.[29]

Jerdan employed the vindictively talented Letitia Landon whose stream of slickly written sentimental poetry and novels under the pseudonym of L.E.L. made her beloved to the generation of the 1820's. The review of *Ecarté* may have been written by her, for, according to the memoirist, she "gilt or blackened all writers of the time, as Jerdan ordained."

The *Gazette*'s review of *Ecarté* was said by Richardson to have hampered the sale of the novel in England and dissuaded Colburn from publishing anything else by John Richardson, though pirated editions sold well in America.

Actually Colburn published Richardson's sequel to *Ecarté*, entitled *Frascati's, or, Scenes in Paris*, and it was the failure of this sequel which caused Colburn's loss of confidence in Richardson. An illegitimate son of nobility, Henry Colburn manoeuvred himself to a position of a near monopoly in English publishing. Redding called him "a small man in a perpetual turmoil."[30] A procrastinater and evader of questions, Colburn "dealt in petty arts and small stratagems... He was of a fickle temper and loved trickery. His publishing arts were not always worthy arts, but he saw

[29] Henry Fothergill Chorley, *Autobiography* (London: R. Bentley and Son, 1873), p. 107.

[30] Cyrus Redding, *Yesterday and Today* (London: T. Cautley Newby, 1863), p. 80. Richardson attributed Jerdan's attack upon *Ecarté* to a disagreement Jerdan had with Colburn (*vide Eight Years in Canada*, p. 8n). But a real disagreement did not take place until 1832 when the juvenile library, which Jerdan was editing for Colburn and Bentley, failed miserably. Moreover, the attack upon the author of *Ecarté* is more severe than upon the book.

ECARTE;

OR,

THE SALONS OF PARIS.

BY MAJOR RICHARDSON,

AUTHOR OF "WACOUSTA," "HARDSCRABBLE," ETC.

Title page to Richardson's *Ecarté; or the Salons of Paris*, (New York: Dewitt & Davenport).

the gullibility of his "majesty," the public, and made a profit of it." His house in Bryanston Square was the meeting place for the literary notables of the day, such as Bulwer-Lytton, the Disraelis, Buckingham, Harrison Ainsworth.

The popular success of Bulwer-Lytton's *Pelham*, published by Colburn in 1828, which like *Ecarté* deals with a young Englishman in Restoration Paris, prompted Colburn to publish *Ecarté* in 1829. But Pelham, unlike Clifford Delmaine the hero in *Ecarté*, returned to London and set a sartorial example which prompted dandies to switch from coloured coats to black. *Ecarté* has a more serious purpose and owed more to Goethe's *Wilhelm Meister's Apprenticeship* and its message of learning through experience.

Delmaine, in debt through gambling and the dupe of his French mistress, betrays the trust and affection of his uncle and the love of a beautiful Englishwoman. When a money-lender puts him in prison, his French mistress pawns her jewels to help him. Delmaine spurns her, causing her death when the violence of her emotion ruptures a blood vessel. She represents the real tragedy in the novel because in spite of duping Delmaine she truly loved him.

She is described in one passage as reading Laclos's *Les Liaisons Dangereuses* which depicted women in French society as victims of the Machiavellian strategies that the male world employed against them. In some measure the cruelty of this society disappeared after the French Revolution; it is its residue that Richardson describes so well.

The meeting of the Parisian demi-monde with the upper class English society provides the learning ground for Delmaine in whom desire conflicts with conscience. Richardson's description of his hero seems to be an analysis of himself, such as "Endowed with a susceptibility which rendered him unable to endure even the shadow of slight or insult, he was equally incapable of conveying intentional offense to another; and the very sensitiveness of feeling for which he was remarkable, was in itself a certain pledge of the delicacy he observed in regard to others."[31] Other editorial comments in the guise of warnings to the young reinforce the impression of personal experience:

> If the exposition of hidden danger can possibly produce that effect which it is the almost exlusive province of experience to encompass, we may at least derive satisfaction from the conviction that a salutary lesson has not vainly been afforded by us to the young and inexperienced, the tendency of which will be to prevent the latent germs of evil from ripening into premature fullness by too close an approximation to these hot-beds of vice and immorality.[32]

Although ministers referred to the book from their pulpits because the vices of Paris were described by a repentant sinner, Richardson's objective was not to present a moral lesson, but rather to use his experience to give an impression of realism. He declared this ambition to his English readers inundated by romance novels, churned out for subscription libraries throughout the country: "We pretend not to enter the lists with those who have the happy art of divesting their heroes and heroines of all the weaknesses common to human nature, and clothing them in such brilliancy of wisdom and virtue as to render it a task of difficulty to determine whether they should belong to earth or heaven..."[33]

Richardson's English predecessor in literary realism was Theodore Hook whose *Sayings and Doings* began to appear in 1824. Richardson, though, was more successful in portraying the psychological complexities of his personages than Hook who manufactured his major characters out of conflicting and incongruous impulses. Also, Hook tended to push satirical comedy into farce whereas Richardson kept

[31] *Ecarté*, I, 97.

[32] *Ecarté*, I, 96.
[33] *Ibid*.

his comical scenes in check.

A more immediate influence upon the writing of *Ecarté* was a popular book, treating of contemporary courtesans, London dandies and London gaming tables with a central character named D'Almaine: *The English Spy* by Westmacott, a leading member of the underground press. Subtler influences which lasted throughout Richardson's writing career are more important, however.

When one recalls that Honoré de Balzac developed a similar psychological insight and sense of realism through detailed descriptions of scenes from all walks of life at the same time as Richardson, the decade of the twenties in Paris, one turns to the thought of the time for an explanation. The great suffering of the French people during the Revolution and the Napoleonic Wars and their disillusion as a conquered people had much to do with the wish for a truthful portrayal of life and a taste for scenes from the lower echelons of society. Both the German and English romantic movements were being introduced to the Paris literati through the salons. German romanticism brought an introspective mood and mysticism, English romanticism a sense of history. And the influence of Sir Walter Scott who had absorbed these romantic tenets was prevalent then.

Richardson adopted Scott's narrative technique; he presented the events up to a critical point through one set of characters, then returned to pick up the thread of another set of characters.

Scott's interest in chivalry was an interest of Richardson if only because his age was affected by medieval romanticism as in Cervantes' *Don Quixote*. The noble aspirations of the Knight of La Mancha, regardless how ridiculous they seemed, gave a sense of freedom of action which broke through social restraints and ridiculed ritual. This romanticism of action joined with another literary movement, naturalism, to form the basis of Richardson's art. George Brandes in describing naturalism provides a key to understand Richardson's writing:

> ...unconscious life is regarded as the basis and source of conscious life, and every earthly being is conceived of as having lain in nature's womb, an inseparable part of her until the moment when consciousness began.[34]

Naturalism laid the foundation for the romanticism of Jean-Jacques Rousseau, influences from which appear in Richardson's novels in varying degrees. Richardson used Rousseau's ideas but did not absorb them into his writing as completely as did the emotional romanticists such as Chateaubriand whom Richardson did not admire. While prizing imagination, he relied upon passages of introspection for a sobering effect. He wrote with powerful emotion yet he set up constraints within his novels to counterbalance it, as if he were opposing the freedom of romanticism with the restraining reason of classicism — for instance Delmaine's conscience is the restraining force upon his excesses.

Frascati's, the sequel to *Ecarté*, which he never acknowledged, does not fit into the underlying scheme of his novels, all of which work unconsciously toward an objective as if carried forward by the force of the author's energy. Its major characteristic is its purposelessness.

The protagonist, a middle-aged Irish bachelor, Rambleton Morris, travels to Paris with an Irish friend, Sir Brien O'Flaherty and his family. They encounter a number of rogues, among them an Irish dancing master and a gambler with a scientific method for winning at the card game of Rouge et Noir. The most engaging confidence trickster is Major Nimbleton

[34] Georg Brandes, *Naturalism in nineteenth century English literature* (New York: Russell and Russell, 1957), p. 39.

who subtly plays on the vanities of O'Flaherty and Morris to borrow heavily from them. This picaresque novel with its humourous satirical treatment of the major characters gives us an insight into Richardson's immeasurable sense of fun — even to the point where with tongue in cheek, he has the first person narrator, Rambleton Morris, unwittingly portray himself as a comical figure. In fact it is the portrayal of the weaknesses of the protagonists which eventually gives the novel its *raison d'être*, for it is these weaknesses upon which the swindlers prey. Major Nimbleton outdoes his competition in the effrontery of his swindling to become one of the most memorable confidence men in literature, and the prototype for later fictional characters such as Charles Dickens' Mr. Jingle. Nimbleton is last encountered in a chain gang on his way to the galleys, and cheerfully still borrowing whenever he can: "Old Cox managed to

hunt me out for that forgery... By the way, I have, still a little money left in his hands; could you oblige me with five Naps for a check on him?'"

The discursive and whimsical manner of the writing condemned it in the eyes of the reviewers who looked for moral messages and well-made plots. Richardson wrote the novel in 1829 with Justin Brenan, an Irishman, which may explain the predominance of Irish personages and the novel's whimsical charm. Since Richardson received twice as much payment as Brenan from Colburn and Bentley,[35] however, we assume he did most of the writing.[36] Yet one aspect of Brenan's contribution had a lasting influence on Richardson: Brenan was an exponent of Baconian inductive logic[37] which (in opposition to Aristotle's deductive reasoning) requires that the facts be known before a conclusion can be reached. In *Frascati's* many disparate events lead inductively to

[35] Richardson received 100 pounds and Brenan 50 pounds, according to the Bentley ledgers. (Bentley papers. B.M. Add. ms. 46, 674, p. 50). Of 750 copies printed 402 had to be sold off as remainders.

[36] A footnote in vol. III of *Ecarté* refers to an habitue of Frascati's gambling club: "More in relation to this individual may possibly appear in a second edition." Thus Richardson's penchant for sequels appears at the beginning of his novel-writing career.

Two clues to Richardson's authorship in the text of *Frascati's* are, first, the slipping of Manvers' coat from Morris's grasp as Manvers jumps a garden wall (II, 128) which reminds one of Richardson's escape from James in Kentucky, an event that left an indelible impression on Richardson: second, the quoting of Thomas Moore's line: "I know by the smoke that so gracefully curled" (I, 13). This line is from Moore's "Ballad Stanzas" written as he sailed from Niagara to Kingston in 1801, and continues:

Above the green elms, that a cottage was near,
And I said, "If there's peace to be found in the world,
A heart, that was humble might hope for it here!
Reputedly the smoke curled from the home of an ancestor

of the author (Richard Beasley) on Burlington Heights over-looking the head of Lake Ontario. Richardson's allusion to a Canadian scene made popular by an Irish poet would have been appreciated by Brenan, an Irishman.

Also, in *Frascati's* there are two allusions which connect Richardson rather tenuously to *The Confessions of Julia Johnstone:* (i) When Morris discovers his fiancee reading *Memoirs of Harriette Wilson*, he was surprised to find it "in the possession of a delicate female." (II, 107). (ii) Major Nimbleton "passes himself off for a major in the British army, though he never was any thing more than a needy adventurer in the Spanish South American service..." (II, 155). This description is similar to the charge made against J.J. Stockdale in *Confessions* (p. 330): "Let me ask the creature if he recollects a Cornet of his name, trying to raise some troops for the South American service, dubbing himself a Colonel much in the same manner Don Quixote was dubbed a Knight by the innkeeper!"

[37] Justin Brenan, *Old and New Logic* (Dublin: 1839). The Aristotelian system, Brenan explained, "looks for victory," whereas the Baconian system "searches truth...modesty is its leading feature."

resolution when the swindlers, through a long confession at the close of the story, are found to be working in collusion. Brenan and Richardson, therefore, seem to be experimenting with the inductive process as a framework for the novel. When the relatively innocent tourists discover that what they had considered chance had been planned by their relatively wicked acquaintances, the result is not a moral lesson but rather an impression of life as it is experienced. Richardson did not again trust to this discursive method, but he continued to use the confession to resolve the action in later novels. Published anonymously in August 1830, *Frascati's* marked the lowest point in Richardson's career as a novelist to be followed almost immediately by the highest.

Wacousta appeared in December 1832. Richardson began writing the novel in 1830 after he abandoned a plan to produce a major epic poem on London society. By his own admission James Fenimore Cooper's *The Last of the Mohicans* was the lightning bolt which turned him to the writing of *Wacousta*.[38] It suggested a romantic framework for Richardson's youthful impressions of savagery and sudden death.

In *Wacousta* Richardson employed historical details to give verisimilitude to the novel. For instance, he placed an incident in time with the statement "As far as our recollection of the Canadian tradition of this story serves us, it must have been the fourth night after the final discomfiture of the plan of Pontiac, and the tenth from the departure of the adventurers..."[39]

The action begins with the conversation of the British officers in Fort Detroit, which introduces personalities immediately. From the speculations of these officers about the strange events of the night, the story races forward, holding the reader's interest

to the end. Captain de Haldimar, the popular and athletic son of the fort commander, has left the fort during the night. The guard at the gate, Private Frank Halloway, is accused of treachery by Colonel de Haldimar, the stern and suspicious commander, when the slain corpse of Captain de Haldimar's servant is found outside the walls. Despite the frantic pleas of Halloway's wife, the Colonel condemns him to death. The Captain, however, is being guided by a squaw, Oucanasta, into the Indian encampment, where he learns of Indian plans to massacre the inhabitants of Forts Detroit and Michillimackinac, the events of which the remainder of the novel treats.

When Pontiac and his chiefs visit the fort, ostensibly to smoke the peace-pipe with the British officers in the council chamber, Indian wile is pitted against English caution.[40] Pontiac is revealed as a unique individual and a formidable leader. Colonel de Haldimar, who has learned of the Indian treachery from his son, shows himself as a commander of tact and cleverness. The scene of the council chamber where Indian and white minds spar to learn the intent of the other was drawn from the meetings between Indian nations on one side and the white settlers, fur traders, or army officers on the other, which Richardson witnessed, or which his father attended and described to him.

Robert Rogers, the backwoods hero was in Fort Detroit during the seige and kept a diary in which he told of the Indian attack on vessels coming to Detroit, and of how the Indians slaughtered the survivors on an island in the Detroit River in view of the fort. As for the massacre at Michillimackinac, Richardson had read Alexander Henry's *Travels* detailing that event. The remembrances of his foster grandmother

[38] *Wacousta*, 2nd ed., pref.
[39] *Wacousta*, 1st ed., III, 68.

[40] J.D. Logan, "Review of the Literary History of Canada, Essay II." *Canadian Magazine*, 48, No. 2 (Dec. 1916), 128, cites the scene as one of the best literary characterizations of Indians.

Cover of a late printing of Major Richardson's novel,
Wacousta, (New York: Dewitt 1875).

Askin, however, who had lived through the siege at
Detroit as a young girl, made the greatest impression
upon him. And his grandfather Askin, who helped
to bring supplies across Lake Erie in Schenectady
boats to the relief of the fort, could have added to his
knowledge at the same time.[41]

Some of the personages in the novel Richardson

patterned after fellow officers in the War of 1812.
Clara and Madeline de Haldimar were modelled upon
his aunt, Catharine Hamilton, and his own mother,
Madeleine Richardson. The model for the central
character in the novel, Reginald Morton otherwise
known as Wacousta, was his grandfather's friend,
John Norton or Chief Teyoninhokorawen.[42] Near
the end of the first volume the reader encounters
the protagonist, Wacousta, a white man dressed as
an Indian who is the confidante and chief advisor to
Pontiac.

His stature was considered beyond that of the
ordinary race of men, and his athletic and muscular limbs united the extremes of strength and
activity in a singular degree. His features, marked
and prominent, wore a cast of habitual thought,
strangely tinctured with ferocity; and the general
expression of his otherwise not unhandsome
countenance was repellent and disdainful...
His own eye was of a deep bluish-gray; his hair
short, dark and wavy; his hands large and muscular; and so far from exhibiting any of the self-
command of the Indian, the constant play of his
features betrayed each passing thought with the
same rapidity with which it was conceived.[43]

The novel turns on the mystery surrounding
this supernaturally strong man. He wishes to destroy
the English fort because of an all-consuming hate
for Colonel de Haldimar. His savagery is fascinating
and his cleverness is alarming. In the last part of the
novel Wacousta tells Clara de Haldimar, his captive,
that when he — Sir Reginald Morton — was a young
officer in Scotland he came across a beautiful girl
living in the hills with her recluse father. Falling in

[41] *Wacousta*, 2nd ed., pref.

[42] *Eight Years in Canada*, p. 231.
[43] *Wacousta*, 1st ed., I, 241.

60

love with her, he is tricked by a fellow officer — de Haldimar — his supposed best friend, who himself married the girl. De Haldimar connived to have Morton court-martialled under trumped-up charges and dismissed from the service. Morton took ship for Canada and joined with the French against the British army invading Quebec. Henceforth under the name of "Wacousta" he devoted his life to wreaking revenge on the de Haldimar family.

Richardson's inspiration for Wacousta is the most interesting facet in a study of the novel. As mentioned in Chapter One, above, the name Wacousta was derived from Wagousta, West Augusta, where John Norton had acted as a trading agent with the Cherokees and Miamis for Richardson's grandfather Askin. His personal history bears some of the marks which could have given rise to a feeling of resentment for white society. When he was a young private in a British regiment stationed in Canada in 1788, he was discharged by his commanding officer, Coffin, with whom, it has been said, young Norton quarrelled violently over his mother who was Coffin's housekeeper.[44] His father, John Norton Senior, a private in the same regiment, subsequently deserted and probably went to the land of his birth, the Cherokee country in present-day Tennessee and north Georgia.[45] From then on, he hated Coffin. He wandered to Kingston and ended up in Detroit working in the fur trade for John Askin. Joseph Brant, Chief of the Six

[44] Testimonial, Lt.-Gov. F. Gore, 1809, Public Archives of Canada, Q 312 pt. I, No. 38, 123.
[45] Carl F. Klinck and James J. Talman, eds. *The Journal of Major John Norton, 1809-1816* (Toronto: Champlain Society, 1970) Champlain Soc. Pub. 46. Prof. Klinck in his Introduction gives interesting details of Norton's life, including the fact that Norton's father was a Cherokee who at the age of 12 was rescued from his burning village by a British officer (possibly by the name of Norton) and schooled in Scotland. The ms. was given both titles, "A History..." and "Journey..." at different times.

Nations Indians in the land between Lakes Erie and Ontario, took an interest in him and found him work with the government as an Indian interpreter, but Norton resigned in 1800 because the pay was too poor. He took up Indian dress and ways and came under Brant's guidance. In 1804 Brant sent him to England to represent the Indian interests and before Brant died, he made Norton, or Teyoninhokorawen as he was now called, the Chief of the Six Nations Indians. In 1808 Norton went into the West Country to visit the Indian tribes for the British Government. He produced a book of his adventures "History of the Confederate Tribes, or Journey of 1,000 miles down the Ohio in 1809." It was published in 1970 from the manuscript in Alynwick Castle, where it was left when his friend, the Duke of Northumberland, failed to find a publisher for it.

Norton had children by an Onandaga woman. In 1808 he began living with an Indian girl, Catharine, whom he married officially in 1813. He took his wife and her young brother, whom he called his son, to England and Scotland in 1815. This is when he met Richardson in London. Leaving his wife and son to be educated in Scotland, Norton returned to Canada. He had attained distinction for leading the Indians in the War of 1812 and was made Brevet Major, though called "Colonel" by courtesy.

In 1821 his wife and foster son returned from Scotland. Norton had built a house, Hillhouse, on the Grand River, and occupied himself in encouraging agriculture and industry among the tribes. He studied masonic literature, translated the Gospel of St. John into the Mohawk language and corresponded with the American Board of Commissioners for Foreign Missions to enquire about work among the Cherokees. Then in 1823 he met with tragedy.

A young Indian, Onandaga Joe, was having a love affair with Catharine. Norton challenged him to a duel. The stories about the duel differ in detail, but

Onandaga died a few days afterwards. Norton was put on trial for murder at Niagara and fined one hundred dollars. He set out for Arkansas and never returned.[46]

The story of Norton's duel and disappearance was a sensational event in Upper Canada. The London *Times* carried a brief notice of the duel and referred to it approvingly as two savages adopting a civilized means of settling a quarrel.[47] To Richardson the news would have brought memories of the athletic white warrior in Indian garb whom he had known since he was five years old. Norton's hatred for the hypocrisy of government officials and their devious schemes for taking away Indian lands gave Richardson a basic ingredient for Wacousta's character.

The characterization of Wacousta, the demonic outlaw of superior strength who has been wronged by a hypocritical society, owes more to the literary influences of the early nineteenth century, however, than to the life of Chief Teyoninhokorawen.

The first popular representation in literature of the outlaw of great strength and fortitude who seeks revenge against the society which outlawed him is Karl Moor in Friedrich Schiller's *Die Räuber* (1781). Karl Moor has been called an angel-outlaw like Satan in Milton's *Paradise Lost,* who set the pattern for the untamed rebel in modern literature.[48]

There are interesting parallels between Satan of *Paradise Lost* and Wacousta. Satan and his tribe of fallen angels nursing their wounds after bloody war with the hosts of God are similar to Richardson's portrayals of the Indian warriors whom he accompanied in the War of 1812: "...they might have passed

for the spectres of those wilds, of those ruthless demons which War had unchained for the punishment and oppression of man."[49] These Indians were the basic inspiration for the creation of Pontiac's warriors in *Wacousta*. Like Satan, Wacousta is an outcast in whom revenge burns eternally. Like the fallen angels, the Indians have been expelled from their own territory. Milton strongly believed in heroic energy; Wacousta, who leaps and bounds through the forest and grapples with several of the enemy at one time, seems to be endowed with Satan's energy.

The Romantic writers of Richardson's day tended to agree with William Blake who said that Milton was of the devil's party without knowing it. Shelley wrote: "Milton's Devil as a moral being is as far superior to his God as one who perseveres in some purpose, which he has conceived to be excellent in spite of adversity and torture, is to one who in the cold security of undoubted triumph inflicts the most horrible revenge upon his enemy...with the alleged design of exasperating him to deserve new torments."[50] Despite the evil savagery which Richardson attributes to Wacousta, he appears to sympathize with the outlaw in spite of himself and to justify Wacousta's conduct by the enormity of the injustice shown him by Colonel de Haldimar.

If Milton inspired Schiller, certainly Schiller's *Die Räuber* laid the ground rules for a number of successors. Heinrich Zschokke's play *Aballino, der grosse Bandit* (1794) was translated into French and first played in Paris in 1801; it made the noble outlaw with a double personality a popular theme in romantic French literature. The play was translated into English and Monk Lewis adapted it to British taste as *Rugantino,* which was revived in 1820 at the Drury Lane Theatre when Richardson was in London.

The most popular exponent of the outlaw in this

[46] John Norton to John Harvey (n.d.). John Norton Papers, Ontario Archives. Years later a Toronto lawyer was prepared to prove that Norton died in 1831.

[47] *Times* (Oct. 1, 1823).

[48] Mario Praz, *The Romantic Agony* (Cleveland: World, 1951), p. 57.

[49] *War of 1812*, p. 34.

[50] Percy Shelley, "A Defence of Poetry," 1821.

impressionable period of Richardson's life was Lord Byron who not only was an outlaw from English society, but pursued the theme of the embittered outlaw in much of his poetry, particularly in "The Corsair," from which Richardson quoted a line in one of his works.[51] Similar in temperament to Byron — both were impetuous and quick to anger — Richardson could not fail to have been influenced by his poetry.

And yet aside from these contemporary influences, there was one great classic which Richardson admired, and which influenced him in writing *Wacousta:* Homer's *Iliad.* The siege of the fort by the Indian tribes, the council in the Indian encampments, the ruse to gain entrance to the fort, the great, seemingly invincible, warrior who counsels the supreme chief — all have obvious counterparts in the long siege of Troy by the Greek tribes. One of the causes of the war, in both stories, is the seduction of a fair and beautiful woman. Colonel de Haldimar, like Priam, fears for the lives of his children. Captain Frederick de Haldimar is a popular leader like Hector, and is personally defeated by the great warrior, though unlike Hector he survives; Lieutenant Charles de Haldimar, epicenely handsome and sensitive, is, like Paris, not made for battle. In both works there is a great unleashed energy; naked violence and frightening suddenness and unexpectedness carry the reader along in varying degrees of excitement.

Moreover, the naturalism in the novel is indeed akin to that of the Greeks. The forest is alive with the unknown. The human actors in the drama seem to belong to their surroundings — the whites to the fort, the Indians to the forest.

Wacousta, (New York: Dewitt & Davenport).

At times they fancied they beheld the dark and flitting forms of men gliding from tree to tree along the skirt of the wood; but when they gazed again, nothing of the kind was to be seen, and the illusion was at once ascribed to the heavy state of the atmosphere, and the action of their own precautionary instincts.[52]

[51] *Westbrook,* p. 40. "Link'd with one virtue and a thousand crimes".

[52] *Wacousta,* 1st ed., I, 267.

The skirmishing between the two camps is always sudden and unexpected, never a confrontation in battle as in European warfare. No doubt Richardson had taken note of Thomas Jefferson's remark about an Indian's education in which the point of honour consisted in the destruction of an enemy by stratagem, and in the preservation of his own person free from injury, "or," Jefferson added, "perhaps this is nature."[53]

This depiction of Indian strategy and cunning is probably what keeps Richardson's Indian from being romantic like Cooper's.[54] This is not to say that *Wacousta* is not imitative of Cooper. On the contrary, the romantic atmosphere of the forest and the romantic character of the ladies in *The Last of the Mohicans* are seen again in *Wacousta*. Wacousta, in pursuit of his ideal — woman — personifies the romanticism of action. Yet in contra-distinction to Cooper's men of action, he is an embittered seeker after revenge. His romantic illusion having been broken by the betrayal of his love, he has experienced the reality of life but will not accept it. He must have his revenge because it is a motivating emotion that shields him from the even more painful acceptance of reality. In so doing he himself becomes a harsh reality for the whites in the fort. One of them, a young officer, is passionately in love with Clara de Haldimar whom he has never seen, but whose beauty has been described to him by her brother. His dream becomes real after he rescues Clara from the slaughter at Fort Michillimackinac. But Wacousta captures them and tying the officer to a tree, he makes love to Clara in front of him. The Rousseauist's dream, love engendered in the mind,

is confronted with the reality of the present.

Wacousta, therefore, personifies reality at the same time as the romanticism of action. When Wacousta has the terrified Clara in his power, he tells her the story of his love for her mother with romantic nostalgia. His story humanizes him, and wins him the reader's sympathy for the moment. But rather than bearing an attachment for Clara, at least out of sentiment, Wacousta plunges a knife into her heart and throws her body into a ravine.

Such action, of course, shows Richardson's indebtedness to the Gothic novel — the long confession by Wacousta and the violent action — but it also marks the weakness in the novel. Having involved the protagonists in the action for most of the story he then has to explain their motivations and their relationships to give meaning to the story. This allows the reader to understand the up till then inexplicable actions of Colonel de Haldimar who, it appears, knew Wacousta's real identity all the time.

In these two persons lies the core of the novel: de Haldimar, "all coldness, prudence, obsequiousness and forethought," and Wacousta "all enthusiasm, carelessness, impetuosity and independence" represent the extremes of classicism on one hand and of romanticism on the other. De Haldimar as the fort Commander remains the hope for salvation of the band of Europeans in peril of being destroyed by seemingly irrational savages. His stern control over his troops is in sharp contrast to Wacousta's incitement of Pontiac and his Indians. Whereas de Haldimar speaks and moves only through his troops as it were, Wacousta acts as if apotheosizing the individual. In the end de Haldimar dies from grief at the murder of his children, and Wacousta is killed by an Indian warrior — thus exemplifying the internalizing of emotion in contrast to the uninhibited expression of emotion. In the quiet manner of his death de Haldimar rises above the charges of hypocrisy and insensitivity leveled against

[53] Thomas Jefferson, *Notes on the State of Virginia* (Boston: 1801), p. 89. Richardson refers to Jefferson's *Notes* in his "Notes" to *Tecumseh* which implies that he had read the book.
[54] J.D. Logan in his "Reviews of the Literary History of Canada", *op. cit.*, discusses what makes Richardson's Indians more credible than Cooper's.

him by Wacousta. Through decorum or strict discipline Colonel de Haldimar attains a greater sense of freedom for the inhabitants of the fort by convincing the Indians of the fort's invincibility. On the other hand, Wacousta as impetuous as a child of nature, brings tragedy to himself and others and defeat to the Indians. Restraint, therefore, is the saving grace of civilization.

It is Wacousta's imagination, or in other words his sensitivity, which caused him to twist his unrequited love into a desire for murderous revenge. Ostensibly then, his revenge like that in the *Iliad* is for the seduction and abduction of a beautiful woman. But there is a far more consuming urgency for revenge which underlies the fabric of the novel: racial revenge. The Indian side of Wacousta's personality expresses the deep restless hatred of the Indian tribes for the militant white usurping their lands. The ceaseless wars between Indians and Americans which followed the American War for Independence had united the Indians in 1812 when Richardson witnessed the violent expression of their revenge. Richardson had seen the enduring power of revenge in the example of Tecumseh who had been fighting American armies for years before 1812. Perhaps, too, Richardson could the more readily empathize with the Indian owing to his blood relationship to the Ottawa nation.

As if to emphasize the racial aspect of Wacousta's revenge, Richardson cited lines from Edward Young's play *The Revenge* (1721) on the title-page of the novel. The lines merely describe the evil fascination that the idea of revenge has for the protagonist, a noble Moor, enslaved in battle to a Spaniard. But when the Moor has wreaked revenge upon his master, his exultation reveals its racial nature:

Let Europe and her pallid sons go weep,
Let Afric and her hundred thrones rejoice.[55]

And again,

If cold white mortals censure this great deed
Warn them they judge not of superior beings,
Souls made of fire, and children of the sun
With whom revenge is virtue.[56]

Richardson's "children of the sun" were the warriors under Pontiac.

The reviews praised *Wacousta* for "originality," "truth and force," "the higher merits of historical truth," "consistency of truth." Barnard Gregory, the pungent wit of the day, wrote in his newspaper, *The Satirist:*

Wacousta afforded us more satisfaction than anything of the kind which has fallen within the range of our reading for many a long day... united simplicity with eloquence of style...the author...bred to a military life...is a man of very superior acquirements and possessed of intellect and taste that must render him an ornament in the tented field, as well as the field of literature.[57]

No reviewer attempted to examine the novel closely;[58] recognition of its "truth" seemed sufficient. By "truth" the reviewers meant "reality." Richardson, however, was apparently not satisfied because he began work on a sequel which attempted to draw closer to real life.

The Canadian Brothers; or, the Prophecy Fulfilled (1840) tells the story of the descendants of Captain

---

[55] Edward Young, *The Revenge* (Edinburgh: J. Robertson, 1774), Act. V, p. 61.

[56] *Ibid.*, p.62.

[57] See "Extracts from Notices of Wacousta, by the London Press" in the back pages of *The Canadian Brothers* (1840).

[58] In that day novels were not considered worthy of close examination. Richardson, who insisted on having his writing regarded seriously, *vide* pref. to *Ecarté*, was of the new breed of novelists.

Frederick and Madeline de Haldimar who are living under the curse uttered by the mad Ellen Halloway in *Wacousta*. Like *Wacousta*, this novel is again concerned with the nature of revenge — the revenge of woman's pride. And in this novel as in *Wacousta*, revenge is discovered to be the motivation of its principal character only near the end of the story.

To catch the elusive moments of reality Richardson used an autobiographical-historical approach. In the opening scene at Fort Malden in Upper Canada just prior to the British and Indian attack on Detroit in 1812, he introduced Tecumseh, Captain Barclay, and General Brock, as if to establish the authenticity of the story.

Detroit falls to the British and Indians. There follows a chapter of conversation between an American Major (fashioned after General Hull) and a Canadian Colonel (after Charles Askin) about the employment of Indians in warfare. The Colonel makes the point that the Spanish inflicted worse tortures on their prisoners than did the Indians. Richardson sent this chapter to King William IV while he was writing the novel, and on the strength of its realistic treatment of the subject, William consented to have the novel dedicated to him.[59]

The remainder of the story centers upon Matilda

Montgomerie although it is told from the point of view of the Grantham brothers. Gerald Grantham cannot see Matilda as "the child of the devil" as others, including Henry Grantham, see her. Captured in the battle of Fort Sandusky by a chivalrous American Colonel Forrester, Gerald is sent as a prisoner to Frankfort, Kentucky. In the wilds he barely escapes death at the hands of a personal enemy, Desborough. At Frankfort Matilda asks him to murder a man to whom she was affianced but who, on leaving her, accused her of "vile intercourse with a slave." Gerald driven by his love for her to an act repugnant to his nature is about to stab his victim when he discovers him to be Colonel Forrester. Matilda wrenches the dagger from Gerald's faltering hand and stabs Forrester. She poisons herself. Forrester recovers and forgives Gerald who returning to Canada, crosses the Niagara River where the American forces are attacking Queenston Heights. Henry Grantham fires at a figure approaching him from the American side, and discovers to his horror that he has killed Gerald. Moments later, he wrestles with the wounded Desborough who manages to drag them both over the cliffside to their deaths. In the meantime it has been revealed that Desborough is the son of Wacousta and Ellen Halloway and that Matilda is really Desborough's daughter. Consequently Ellen Halloway's curse on the de Haldimars has been enacted by the offspring of Wacousta upon the offspring of de Haldimar.

Matilda's revenge, however, was not directed against the Granthams, but against her false lover, Forrester. Nevertheless, Gerald Grantham believes that Matilda was chosen by "Destiny" to fulfill Ellen Halloway's curse on the Granthams. This conflict in motivations weakens the novel.

The story was inspired by the famous Beauchamp murder in Frankfort in 1825, the facts of which were carried in newspapers throughout the English- speak-

[59] Letter H. Taylor to J. Richardson, Windsor Castle, Aug. 12, 1833 in pref. to *The Canadian Brothers*. William's interest in the North American Indians was well known. A point should be made here about Richardson's experimentation with forms of realism. Diderot, who began the search for literary realism, used dialogue for this purpose. Richardson was using the Diderot form in this instance, and followed, as well, Diderot's advice generally in this novel: "Only that description which makes the reader see lifelike expressions, actual gestures caught in suspension and convincing character should be the concern of the realistic author." J.R. Loy *Diderot's Determined Fatalist* (New York: King's Crown Press, 1950). p. 112.

ing world. Ann Cook from a prominent but impoverished family was jilted by Solomon Sharp, a rising young lawyer who became Attorney-General of Kentucky. Sharp was accused during an election of being the father of her stillborn child. Jereboam Beauchamp, an idealistic lawyer of twenty-one years of age, fell in love with the thirty-eight year old Ann Cook, knew of her desire for revenge upon Sharp, and, after marrying her, challenged Sharp to a duel. Sharp refused. Beauchamp, incensed by a political handbill referring to Ann Cook's child as mulatto, rode to Frankfort and killed Sharp. The Beauchamps were to be hanged on July 7 1826. Both took laudanum but lived. Ann killed herself with a knife. Beauchamp, nearly dead from knife wounds, was saved to be hanged.

The evil side of Matilda's character would seem to owe nothing to Ann Cook. Matilda becomes vicious at Gerald's failure to murder Forrester; "To see you writhe thus, under the wound inflicted upon your vanity is some small atonement for the base violation of your oath."[60] She seems to delight in torturing Gerald and he appears powerless to escape from his fascination for her. Throughout the novel he is like a moth attracted to the light of her flame. Indeed, there was a taste of algolagnia in the air of the Romantic period, even to the point where some men yearned to be whipped by a domineering mate. A critic of the period writes:

The following point must be emphasized: the function of the flame which attracts and burns is exercised, in the first half of the century, by the Fatal Man (the Byronic hero) in the second half by the Fatal Woman; the moth destined for sacrifice is in the first case the woman, in the second the man.[61]

---

[60] *The Canadian Brothers*, II, 182.
[61] Mario Praz, *The Romantic Agony, op. cit.*, p. 206.

MATILDA MONTGOMERIE
OR, THE
PROPHECY FULFILLED.
BY MAJOR RICHARDSON,
AUTHOR OF "WACOUSTA," "ECARTE," "HARDSCRABBLE" "WESTBROOK," **Etc.**

Complete in one Octavo Volume.

Richardson's sequel to *Wacousta*,
Matilda Montgomerie, or, the Prophecy Fulfilled,
(New York: Dewitt & Davenport).

Matilda Montgomerie would seem to be, therefore, an example of the Fatal Woman in literature. When the novel was republished in 1851 in New York it was retitled *Matilda Montgomerie*, which properly emphasized her significance.

Gerald Grantham is the quixotic character in search of an ideal who, when he becomes disillusioned, dies. Yet the novel is not born from romantic action as much as from Rousseau-like nostalgia and reliance on the truth as found in Nature.

> Here is to be heard, neither the impertinent coxcombry, of the European self styled exclusive nor the unmeaning twaddle of the daughter of false fashion, spoiled by the example of the said exclusive, and almost become a dowager in silliness, before she has attained the first years of womanhood...The sneer of contempt — the laugh of derision — is nowhere to be heard... (rather here) fashion has not superseded the kindlier emotions of nature.[62]

Richardson returned to the question of morality which plagued Delmaine in *Ecarté*; the moral dilemma of Gerald Grantham, urged to commit murder out of love, implies that there are limits to trusting to one's natural emotions. Opposed to reason is the powerful desire of Matilda. Thus Matilda's emotion overcomes Gerald's conscience; romanticism overcomes the restraints of reason and brings misfortune to all.

Richardson wrote in *Ecarté* that Delmaine at the age of twenty-four became convinced that he had "too rosy a picture of society." That novel unveiled social-climbers and hypocrites. In *Kensington Gardens in 1830*, a poem, Richardson satirized the mannerism and foibles of London society. His disillusionment with society was complete, but it was accompanied by a cynical humour which seemed to unburden him of the effects of his disillusion, and helped him regard the social life as a game of play separate from the reality of living.

Being an active man (he called the long period required to write a novel "vegetating") he had applied repeatedly to Frederick, the Duke of York, Army Chief of Staff at the Horse Guards, after he returned from Paris, to be taken on active service,[63] which would take him to distant lands far from West End Society.

His poem, then, was written before the publication of *Wacousta*, when he was stymied in his aborted career as a soldier, and frustrated by his lack of success as a poet and novelist. He intended to publish *Kensington Gardens* canto by canto in the manner of Lord Byron, but only the first canto came out.

His father's impoverished family needed the money which a fashionable poem would bring him. Surgeon Richardson of the Indian Department died in Amherstburg on May 1, 1829, leaving a widow and many children, four of whom were infants. His widow "in straightened circumstances" petitioned the Commander of the Forces for some provision in recognition of Dr. Richardson's life-time military service, but the Lords of the Treasury rejected her plea, though she received a kind letter from Downing Street.[64]

At the close of the Canto, Richardson announced that his next would review the female beauties "whose various charms in song should be preserved" — a certain sale in any age.

Richardson's targets were not only the dandies at whom he laughed because of their long dark look "making love in the Turkish manner, forcing the sex to range beneath their banner;" he also made fun of the phalanxes of women:

> Here mothers group to get their daughters mated,
> (A goodly brood from thirty to sixteen)
> While wives of twenty, with their husbands sated,

[63] Return of Service, Dec. 2, 1828, *op. cit.*

[64] Sir James Kempt to Sir John Colborne, Aug. 20, 1829 (enclosing a letter from Downing Street, Aug. 20, 1829) Public Archives of Canada, RG10, Vol. 5, 259.

[62] *The Canadian Brothers*, I, 207.

Seek out wherewith to lay their rising spleen:

These dames of fashion communicate with the Guardsmen over a background of marches and waltzes: their "softened souls pass through their burning eyes, and wake the fulness of responsive sighs." He scored British merchants who cared little whether Greek or Turk won the War for Greek Independence as long as they profited from their barter. But his greatest disgust was reserved for the men of society:

Thus certain apes — comparisons are odious —
Besides these men have their respective merit:
Some have the thrilling tone — the lisp
    mellodious,
Others the loud coarse laugh which proves their
    Spirit,
And so on to the end; the sly Asmodeus,
Who stole through house-tops like a thief or
    feret,
Could scarce have shown so much to Don Cleofas
As they recount of easy dames and sofas.

Richardson stands aloof from this crowd; he gives the impression that he is an altruist and, like Quixote, a defender of the ideal woman.

The "ideal woman" in this poem was Elizabeth Green, the beautiful daughter of a West Indian planter, who married the wealthy Leicester Stanhope shortly after the Canto came out.[65] Her marriage may have brought death to the poem. Richardson admitted that the theme had worn thin — "sameness to verse is deleterious;" apparently his contemporaries agreed with him.

The publisher of the poem, William Marsh, listed Richardson in *The Literary Blue Book* of 1830 as a novelist. Richardson preferred to keep his authorship a secret because the military attached a stigma to any form of learning or literary expression.[66] Some military men, however, were intellectual. Richardson's future father-in-law, William Drayson, was of this kind. He was a student of chivalry and kept a notebook in which he traced the lineage of his family back to the Norman invasion under William the Conqueror.[67] As a young engineer in 1807 William Drayson was sent to the Royal Gunpowder Factory at Waltham Abbey and soon became Clerk of the Works. He had a home on its grounds and raised a large family. Because the works were under the Ordnance Department he was made an honourary Colonel and required to report periodically to the Chiefs of Staff at the Horse Guards. His second daughter, Maria Caroline, was twenty-four years of age in 1830; she proved to be the attraction which drew Richardson on visits to Colonel Drayson in Waltham Abbey.

In 1831 Richardson was writing *Wacousta* in the picturesque village of Waltham Abbey, thirteen miles north-east of London Bridge; he lodged on the opposite side of the village from the Gunpowder Works, that is, by Epping Forest. The mills of the Gunpowder

---

[65] Married on April 23, 1831. Richardson remembered the beauty of Miss Green's eye years later (*Lola Montes*, p. 6). Ned Willis encountered her beauty when on a visit to London (*vide* his *Literary London in 1835*).

[66] Francis Place, a tailor, told a parliamentary inquiry how he lost the business of a military man when he was discovered to be a reader of philosophy. Richardson refers to the problem in *Frascati's* (I, 72): "The name of author is not reputable now-a-days, and especially for a military man. It is too much after the vulgar taste of that old Roman Cincinatus. Moreover, among persons of family and fortune, an author is considered a mere drudge, — a sort of literary mountebank at so much per sheet...."

[67] Rear Admiral Edwin Drayson to D. Beasley, Lustleigh, S. Devon, Oct. 15, 1967. The family lineage was traced to D'Arlanzan or Dalencon who came to England with William the Conqueror. The name was converted by stages to Drainer, Draison and finally Drayson.

Works were turned by the River Lea which for centuries had powered the Abbey Mills for grinding corn. The dominant feature was the ruins of the Abbey Church founded by King Harold before the Norman invasion. Public houses lined the main street for the painters and poets attracted to the place. Richardson, who was courting Maria, visited frequently with the Draysons.

He had a terrifying experience after one visit in mid-August.[68] Two other guests, an officer and his bride of two weeks, offered to give him a lift in their phaeton. As he sat in the back seat he had an inexplicable presentiment of danger. When they had almost reached his lodgings, an itinerant organ-grinder suddenly began to play and startled the pair of horses into a frantic run. The officer and Richardson together were unable to stop the animals. The officer dropped the reins and jumped, but Richardson remained for the sake of the young lady. At last Richardson managed to direct the horses toward the sodden ground beside the road, plunged them into the mud, and brought the phaeton to a stop. Richardson and the lady learned that the officer had hit his head in the fall and was dying.

The young bride suffered for weeks from the shock. When there was a doubt that she would receive a pension because she had been married only a short time, Richardson used his influence at the Horse Guards to secure it for her. In gratitude she gave him an antique ring set with a beautiful Indian stone which had belonged to her husband. This gesture became symbolic to him; he saw it as representing a tri-union of hearts, and he employed it as a romantic device in his novels. He first used it in *Wacousta* which he completed early in the following year; Madeline de Haldimar gave Oucanasta a beautiful ring for preserving her life and the life of Captain de Haldimar whom

she knew Oucanasta secretly loved. In a later novel, *Hardscabble*, Richardson used the gift of a ring to unite the heroine, her Lieutenant fiance, and an Indian brave who was romantically attached to the heroine. The symbolism in *Hardscrabble* was carried much farther, however, by the fact that the heroine, Maria Heywood, seems to have been fashioned after Maria Drayson, and the Lieutenant and the Indian brave represented the different natures of the two races from which Richardson sprang. Richardson in describing this heroine was probably giving a picture of the girl he married on April 2, 1832: above middle height, oval face of a delicate olive tint, hazel eyes, raven black hair, small mouth, full lips... "a forehead, high for her sex, combined with a nose, somewhat more aquiline than Grecian, to give dignity to a countenance that might, otherwise, have exhibited a character of voluptuous beauty."[69]

After his marriage Richardson rented the squire's house called Langton's Cottage in the tiny village of Farnham Royal, Buckinghamshire, and farmed the flat fertile land. Nearby were the Burnham Beaches where he and Maria could ride and picnic. It was here that Richardson began to write the sequel to *Wacousta*, which he intended to call "The Brothers; or the Prophecy Fulfilled." As Richard Barham, another writer of the day, said about sequels, they simply extended the denouement: he called them

---

[68] *Eight Years in Canada*, pp. 125-128.

[69] *Hardscrabble*, p. 69. Their marriage is recorded in *Burke's* genealogical and heraldic history of the landed gentry (ed. L.G. Pine) 17th ed. (1952), p. 692 (Drayson of Kilnsey). In the Hardinge Papers at the McGill Univ. Library are letters from Richardson which were sealed with red wax stamped with his ring leaving this impression: a cross set within a shield over which is a horseshoe with a spur atop it and the phrase *"nonquam non paramus"* encircling the shield. This phrase was the family motto of Johnstone (incidentally a family name connected with the Richardsons) in *Wacousta*, 1st ed., I, 208.

"literary monsters, stories with two tails."[70] This opinion may have been the reason for the novel's rejection by English publishers.

Meanwhile, the publication of *Wacousta* brought Richardson wide recognition. Alaric Watts, a poet and enterprising journalist, who thought it deserved to sell better than it did,[71] enlisted Richardson as a contributor to a newspaper on military affairs, *The United Service Gazette,* which he began in February 1833. King William IV and his court relished *Wacousta,* according to the King's secretary, Sir Herbert Taylor. Possibly Maria Richardson had prompted Richardson to send a copy to the King. Maria was closely related through her mother to Mrs. Maria Fitzherbert, the secret wife of the late George IV.[72] William had great respect and compassion for Mrs. Fitzherbert, and being made aware of Richardson's connection, he was indulgent to Richardson's soliciting his aid in selling a secret remedy for dry rot to the Royal Navy in July 1833.

Since the Admiralty was continuously besieged by men who had a secret cure for dry rot, the Lords were not prepared to pay Richardson for it until it could be tested — character references from the King and Admiral Hardy notwithstanding. Richardson mistrusted them, and after negotiating all summer, sometimes from his officer's club on Bond Street where he lodged in London, he gave up.

Sir Herbert Taylor, who remembered Richardson from the days when Taylor was secretary to the Duke of York at the Horse Guards, tried to comfort him: "I am perfectly convinced that you would not have brought forward any thing that you had not proved to be useful and important."[73] Taylor also may have remembered Richardson's efforts to be brought on to full pay and he would have recalled Richardson's admiration for the late Duke whose first name, Frederick, Richardson preferred to be called, rather than John.[74] Therefore, when the Spanish began recruiting British troops in the summer of 1835 to fight in the Carlist War in Spain, Taylor, on the authority of the King, recommended Richardson for a Captaincy.

Spain

THE BRITISH AUXILIARY LEGION was initially formed along lines which doomed it to fail. The English Tories objected to sending a British force to aid Queen Christina of Spain in her fight to subdue the uprising of the Conservatives, who were predominantly northern Basques, led by her brother-in-law, Don Carlos. On the other hand, the Whigs, the governing party in England, were concerned with the plight of liberalism on the continent. When the Spanish ambassador to England suggested that a mercenary force of English soldiers be raised and paid by the Spanish government to fight for liberalism, the Whigs agreed. George de Lacy Evans, a Whig who represented the constituency of Westminster in the House of Commons, was chosen to lead the force. The Spanish remembered the valiant

[70] R.H. Dalton Barham, *The Life and Remains of Theodore Hook* (London: Bentley, 1853), p. 202.

[71] "Editor's Note," *United Service Gazette* (Jan. 21, 1837).

[72] Rear Admiral Edwin Drayson to D. Beasley, June 4, 1972. Mrs. Drayson's father (William Hodges) was first cousin to Mrs. Fitzherbert whose marriage to George IV was secret because she was Roman Catholic.

[73] "Correspondence" (Between H. Taylor and J. Richardson *et al.*) "respecting a secret for keeping the Dry Rot out of Timber," Public Archives of Canada, RG5, C1, Vol. 169, p. 11.

[74] A.H.U. Colquhoun (ed.) *Tecumseh and Richardson. The Story of a Trip to Walpole Island and Port Sarnia* (Toronto: Ontario Book Co., 1924), p. 14n. writes that Richardson preferred to be called by his second name, Frederick. In the List of Passengers entering New York Harbour in March 1838 on the SS *Ontario* he listed himself as Frederick Richardson (Passenger Lists on Microfilm, National Archives, Washington, D.C.).

fighting of the British under Wellington, whose troops had once freed them from Napoleon, but Evans was no Iron Duke.

Son of a small landholder, Evans had risen in the army to the rank of Lieutenant Colonel. He had his horse shot from under him in three different battles, and he had been the leader of the small force which captured the American Houses of Congress in 1812.[1] When Evans was made Lieutenant-General in the Legion, he appointed his brother, R. de Lacy Evans, who had seen service in India, as Brigadier-General. He made another applicant, Gaspard LeMarchant, a Colonel. LeMarchant was the son of a famous Brigadier-General and the brother of an influential Whig who was to become Minister of the Board of Trade the following year.[2]

Not all the officers were adventurers and political appointees; some were excellent military men with distinguished records who had had no opportunity to follow their profession for some years. Some English mercenaries who had been sent to aid the Portuguese throne against rebellious elements in 1834 were also a part of this new venture. One of them was Charles Shaw, an idiosyncratic figure, whose cunning was underrated by everyone, including Evans. Both Shaw and LeMarchant became Richardson's enemies.

The trouble with the Legion lay with its officers. They were more concerned with being promoted in rank — which would mean prestige when they returned to social life in England — than in fighting for a cause.[3] Unfortunately the more unscrupulous the officer, the more likely he was to be promoted. Richardson, of course, wanted promotion as badly as any of them.

The rank and file joined the Legion, not for glory and certainly not for promotion, but for money, which, ironically, most of them did not receive. Recruited through a Central Office in London, they comprised Irish, poor rural folk, and Scots, unemployed handloom weavers, most of whom had never handled a gun. Throughout the summer of 1835, they left in ships from Glasgow, Gravesend, the Thames, and Portsmouth, all bound for San Sebastian on the northern coast of Spain.

Richardson, accompanied by Maria, left Portsmouth with the Right Wing of the 2nd Regiment on July 23.[4] Near the end of the trip, when they were just off the coast of Spain, a storm threatened to blow their steamer upon some rocks. Everyone gathered on the deck and prepared to leap into the sea, but fortunately the engines kicked them out of danger. The incident appealed to Richardson's sense of drama, which was further tantalized the next day when the steamer entered the San Sebastian harbour under a blue sky, in the heat of mid-day. He saw the precipitous headland, the succession of lofty green hills "studded with an infinitude of antique looking houses, harmonizing admirably with the romantic character of the whole,"[5] and the Spaniards waving their hats and cheering from the hillsides. With a telescope he picked out the mountain posts of the Carlists and showed Maria where the enemy lay.

Maria stayed in a posada in town while Richardson marched with his regiment to the Convent of San Francisco. Already the streets were swarming with redcoats and the officers held banquets frequently. The townspeople were jubilant at their presence:

---

[1] D.N.B., 6.

[2] D.N.B., 39.

[3] Long lists of honours awarded to officers many of whom were not on the battlefield attest to this. Evans stated that his officers "are peculiarly desirous of their distinctions." A.L.S., Evans to Villiers, Vitoria, Jan. 2, 1836, Villiers Papers, c460.

[4] Journal of the Movements of the British Legion, p.1.

[5] Ibid., p.3.

as mercantilists they supported the Queen and her liberal policies.

At lax times, such as the weeks after their arrival, drinking, gambling, and duelling were the soldiers' main interests. Richardson's first duty was to lead about a hundred men, as a military police brigade, about the streets of San Sebastian to pick up drunken soldiers and prevent others from spending their bounty money on drink. It was sometimes a delicate task when officers were involved in the drinking, and many duels were fought as a result.

The Legion soon had its first defeat. Evans led the storming of the Carlist outpost at Hernani, but his advance line misunderstood an order. They fell back on the rearguard, sending two-hundred of them to their deaths in a ravine. For his next confrontation with the enemy, Evans sent for reinforcements, which included Richardson's regiment. By the time Richardson's men reached the place, the battle had been won. Evans then ordered the men to march to Bilbao, a town which had been under siege by the Carlists for two years. By winning a few skirmishes and dealing with snipers along the roadways, the Legion succeeded in raising the siege. Richardson received orders to countermarch to a village nearby. As the troops had not been permitted to train in England, Evans intended to drill them on long marches. Richardson's men, hungry and exhausted, sank to the ground and yet made no murmur of complaint. Richardson felt they had performed well.[6]

Richardson was thoroughly enjoying military life and the prospect of seeing combat. In a journal in which he put down his impressions of the Legion's activities, he created a valuable historical record as well as a readable book. Many officers saw the Legion as good material for journalism, but none had Richardson's talent. The "correspondents" who sent letters to English newspapers were often officers of the

⁶ *Ibid.*, p.29.

Legion. Since much of the English press attacked the Legion, Evans suspected his officers of betraying him.

Evans next received orders from Christino generals to join forces with the two armies under the Queen at Vitoria, a town on the far side of the Cantabrica mountain ranges. He led the Legion upon a long semi-circular trek skirting the mountains. Richardson recorded the march in his journal. Not only did the men travel over rough country, but they also had to contend with Carlist ambushes along the route, which reminded Richardson of the tactics of the North American Indians.[7] Along one stretch, outlaw bands who had previously worked the iron mines in the hills, attacked the women and children travelling with the troops and subjected them to horrible acts of sadism. These all-day marches themselves exacted a terrible death toll. Evans later defended himself against charges of inhumanity by stating that over two-thousand of the seven-thousand men on the march were sick and crippled to begin with and would have died anyway.[8] Richardson, as an officer, was on horseback, but he sympathised with the marchers:

...some unfortunate soldier's wife, from whom pain and fatigue amounting almost to exhaustion had drawn tears of bitterness, as her swollen feet carefully met the ground, and her anxious gaze bent itself on the far distance, as if to discover the haven of rest which was to terminate her sufferings for the day...one woman — young and of interesting appearance, walked the whole way, shoeless and with shrinking feet; and yet, to the close, there was a cheerfulness of manner about her that touched one more, efforced as I saw it was, to encourage her husband, than all

⁷ *Ibid.*, p.24.

⁸ Great Britain, Parliament, *Debates and Proceedings*, 41 (March 13, 1838) 829ff.

the tears that were shed by her less uncomplaining copartners in suffering.[9]

When they reached Bilbao, Richardson was promoted to the Quartermaster-General's staff. This suited him, for it enabled him to travel at will in pursuit of his duties and observe at the same time. He was fascinated and puzzled by the contrasts of Spanish culture which he encountered in the towns the Legion passed through. The dire poverty of a string of villages suddenly would give way to a huge and richly adorned monastery in which the whole Legion could have been quartered. In Bilbao the women spat on the streets, breast-fed their babies in public, and enjoyed lewd pantomime at the theatre. Yet the townspeople showed a cultural sophistication and a joie-de-vivre: in spite of the siege they attended the opera twice a week and held dances every night.

He was sent ahead by sea, thus avoiding the arduous march over the larger mountains:

From the sea — as the small boat in which I was embarked moved slowly on — I could distinctly command a view of the whole ascent, and imposing in truth was the sight. The eye embraced the continuous line of troops, followed and preceded by their baggage mules, winding up an extent of little less than a league, until they finally and successively reached the highest point of elevation, where their forms and glittering arms, thrown into bold relief against a cloudless sky, formed a picture in itself as instinct with interest as with life. At length the scene faded like a closing panorama from my view, and I beheld no more than a confused mass of moving atoms, resembling rather the serpentine march of an army of ants, than one of human beings.[10]

But his new tasks gave him little time for musing on scenes of romantic grandeur. He had to find provisions for this army in one of the poorest regions of Spain, in cold and rainy autumn weather, from a peasant class which sided with the Carlists and which would sooner fire upon a Britisher than give him sustenance. Hampered by the peasants, Richardson advocated burning their houses in order to lure them back from the Carlist bands in the hills to protect their families.[11] His proposal provoked an acid response from *Blackwood's Magazine*. Reviewing his *Journal* in 1837, *Blackwood's* gave the Tory point of view:

But what might the Carlist peasant say upon the subject? Would he not be entitled to ask, what had brought the Legion here? There was no war between England and Spain: the Legion could have no personal interest in the quarrels of the country; they were simply strangers who sold the use of their bayonets for Spanish coin, and earned their hire in Spanish battle! What difference was there between them and the highwayman, except that they wore red coats and the highwayman brown or blue; that they were twelve-thousand instead of one; that they were commanded by a chief missionary, who called himself a general; and that they did, in one month, twelve-thousand times more mischief than had been done by all the highwaymen of Spain in the last one-hundred years? And for resisting the slayers of the red coats was the Spaniard to be put to death rather then for resisting the robber in the brown?[12]

The Legion halted on the plains at the town of

[9] *Journal of the Movements*, p.61.
[10] *Ibid.*, pp.66-67.

[11] *Ibid.*, p.112.
[12] *Blackwood's Magazine*, 42, (Aug. 1837) 173.

Brivieska — a muddy, cold, and inhospitable spot — while the officers counted the survivors from the exposure in the mountain snows, the starvation, the ambushes, and the exhausting pace. The officers had additional problems. Several were court-martialled for incompetence, others quit, still others turned upon their men. One young officer had twenty-one of his men flogged for selling pieces of their kits for food to keep from starving. Eleven of them died as a result of the flogging.[13]

To help him in his many duties Richardson employed a servant, Paul Carçanada, a Frenchman who spoke fluent Spanish. Because Carçanada was fat, Richardson humourously likened the two of them to Sancho Panza and Don Quixote. He purchased a mule for Paul to ride, but there the resemblance ended, for Paul was a proud man and resented riding behind Richardson on a lesser animal.

Richardson sometimes mixed pleasure with business. On a visit to the Governor of Burgos he toured the Cathedral and marvelled at Murillo's alto-relievos of the trial, death, and ascension of Christ. The picture of Christ and the thieves dying on the crosses particularly attracted him; he may have seen in it the theme of his own art; a hero betrayed by hypocrisy and portrayed publicly as no better than the thieves — the irony of the terrible injustice of life.

On this visit to the Governor, Richardson and an officer accompanying him, waited for some time in the hallway. The Governor knew the British were there for accommodations for the troops and treated them like any petitioner. Richardson, angered, reported his conduct to his superiors, and the Governor was relieved of his post. The Queen's politicians were eager to find ways to ingratiate themselves with the British, for since the politicians had lost the confidence of the Madrid bankers, the Spanish Government was unable to pay the British troops.

Richardson drew a picture of himself at this time:

After finishing a sad apology for a dinner, I am now warming my toes and my nose over a braziero, which I have managed to procure, yet in which there are infinitely more ashes than coals. The window of my room is hermetically closed, to keep out as much of the cold air as possible, and a horse-cloth is placed under my chair to receive my heels — the toes resting upon the braziero: — my servant's regimental great coat is on my back, and yet despite all this luxury, all this comfort, I can scarcely hold the pencil that traces my note. We are allowed wood, it is true: but alas! where are the chimnies in which to consume it? And yet these Spaniards talk of liberty. Ye Gods! Who would accord liberty to men so far besotted — so far behind all the rest of mankind, as not to know the comfort of a cheerful fire?[14]

It was December when the Legion reached Vitoria, a picturesque and colorful town surrounded in the distance by snow-capped hills. The two Spanish armies, under Generals Cordova and Espartero, met the British with bands and parades. Richardson's duties took him to the villages around Vitoria where he foraged for food for his troops. These villages, although open to attack by the Carlists, became infinitely preferable to Vitoria which was turning into a foul pen of disease and starvation for the Legionnaires. Near the end of December typhus struck. About eight to ten men died each day. The British, unpaid by the Spanish, could not afford hospital care; their living quarters were crude — the men lacked even beds.

Richardson wrote a strong letter of complaint to his superior officer, LeMarchant, who had been promoted to Adjutant-General. LeMarchant ignored his

[13] Alexander Somerville, *The History of the British Legion and War in Spain* (London: James Pattie, 1839), *passim*.

[14] *Journal of the Movements*, p.99.

The Plains of Vitoria, by Henry Wilkinson.

ments.

Accomodation for the rank and file was generally the cold and wet floor of a convent or church. The officers were billeted in private houses, but if they caught typhus, their landlords promptly turned them into the street. Some men, unable to move or left uncared for, were attacked by rats, starved to death, or were neglected by the so-called surgeons, who preferred not to risk their own lives in the course of their duty. Richardson also observed the irresponsible behaviour of officers who did nothing to correct the abuses. Evans himself refused to demand payment for his men because he thought it impolitic to embarass the Spanish government.[15] Rations were low because no one bothered to stock food. The cavalry was forced to go out daily to seek it in the face of the enemy. Richardson wrote strong passages in his journal describing the incompetence of LeMarchant, and the useless skirmishing in which Evans and the Spaniards were involved. Richardson felt that the indifference of Evans was largely to blame. He was a man without principle. He forbade flogging the military because public opinion was against it, yet he overlooked the fact that a dozen men were flogged every day at Vitoria for the smallest

letter. When Richardson found that these sick men lying in unheated rooms four and five to a mattress or blanket, had not been issued rations until late at night because the commissariat could not be bothered with them earlier, he wrote a letter critical of the whole procedure. Apparently LeMarchant, who did nothing to improve conditions, considered the criticism a reflection upon himself.

The typhus was raging out of control in mid-January when the French Foreign Legion, consisting of strong and healthy Scandinavians and Germans, marched in from North Africa. Both Legions and the two Armies of the Queen skirmished with the Carlists without decisive gain. This type of guerilla warfare favoured the Carlists. With short legs and sturdy physique, the nimble Basques easily moved through the mountain terrain in front of the exhausted Legionnaires. Only the Chapelgorries, those Basques who fought for the Queen and who usually led the British Legion in the attack, could meet the Carlists effectively on their own ground. Also the cold and the ice which was two inches thick hampered the Legion's move-

76

15 Evans could not deal effectively with his superior, the Spanish General Cordova, upon whom the Legion depended to secure its funding. When the Legion was in Vitoria "Cordova received ample means from Madrid with instructions to pay the Legion; but instead of doing so he paid the Contractors, because he was allowed twenty per cent discount, which sum he pocketed." (Alexander Ball, *A Personal Narrative of Seven Years in Spain* (London: J. Chappell, 1846), p.39). To begin with, the amount due the Legion in mid-June 1836 was 37,532 pounds minus 800 pounds which was in the military chest. On July 1 the government owed the Legion 4,310 pounds for the field allowance for three months (Villiers Papers c460). In 1838 it was estimated that the Spanish government owed the Legion from 200,000 to 250,000 pounds (T. D'Eyncourt in Gt Brit., Parliament, *Debates...* Mar. 13, 1838, *op. cit.*).

offences.[16] He professed to lead a highly disciplined force, yet he would not punish drunken officers who behaved dissolutely in the cafes in the evening. Richardson sarcastically ascribed Evans' reluctance to the fact that these officers were influential in his Westminster constituency.[17] An historian of the Legion who served with it said of Evans:

If he had any dread of infection in going into the hospitals he ought not to have had such fear, for he who could expose himself so coolly, often unnecessarily, to the enemy's balls should have exposed himself to the dangers of disease among his men. But it was not the dread of the mortal diseases; it was a dread to see men so overwhelmed with wretchedness that kept him from inspecting the quarters; and therefore, I conclude he never knew our real state of suffering which he ought to have known.[18]

How close he was to the truth may be seen by a letter from Evans to George Villiers, Envoy-Extraordinary to Madrid, in which he suggests that he be replaced:

The pain and annoyance and distress of feeling to which I am subjected from the situation in which my force has been left — and especially the Hospitals — would be in such case comparatively removed from me. And also with regard to shoes — we have five Battalions at Vitoria which are

almost barefooted and incapable of marching.[19]

Evans' staff officers formed a clique around Evans whom they flattered for their own ends. There are indications that the group was closely knit and homosexual, and depended on Evans' brother, the Brigadier, to exert his influence over Evans. LeMarchant was intimate with the Assistant-Military Secretary, Major Herman, whom Richardson characterized as a "yesman", and who was said to have been so supercilious and haughty that he was repeatedly challenged to duels. General Reid, nicknamed "Peggy Reid", conducted the parade from a manual in his hand; he formed an attachment for his aide-de-camp MacIntosh, who was promoted from private to captain within a few months. Colonel Charles Shaw seems to have fitted well into the group too. He had shown his cruel side to his men in the Portugese campaign: he withheld their payment, relied heavily on the whip to keep order, and constantly boasted of his bravery and military prowess. Evans promoted him to Brigadier General.

With the Commandant of Vitoria dying of typhus, Richardson was appointed to that position. In addition, he still served in the Quarter-Master-General's department. As Commandant, he visited the sick in the hospitals, kept the ill officers from being thrown out of their billets, and did whatever he could to relieve the suffering of the men. The strain on him was tremendous. His aides fell ill and died. He asked Evans, through LeMarchant, for a promotion, but LeMarchant blocked it or so Richardson believed, and Evans appointed Charles Shaw to the post of Commandant on January 20th. Shaw wrote home: "I knew they would give me a disagreeable post, out of my turn of duty."[20]

On February 2, while writing in his journal describing the Spanish citizens' plundering of the sick,

[16] "Whenever a man came on parade with his coat dirty or not properly folded, he received two dozen lashes." (Statement by Col. Dickson quoted by Hardinge in parliamentary debate, Mar. 13, 1838).

[17] *Personal Memoirs*, p.111.

[18] Alexander Somerville, *The History of the British Legion and War in Spain, op. cit., passim.*

[19] ALS, Evans to Villiers, Feb. 20, 1836, Villiers Papers c460.

[20] Charles Shaw, *Personal Memoirs* (London: H. Colburn, 1837), letter, Vitoria, Feb. 2, 1836.

Richardson was struck down by typhoid. He did not know that he had been replaced as Commandant; and while he was sick, Evans put one of his brother's favourites in Richardson's post on the Quarter-Master-General's staff.

Richardson was unconscious for nine days. He would have died had not a surgeon been particularly attentive to him. During this time his servant, Paul, went through his papers, possibly on orders from LeMarchant, and took certain passages from his journal to the Adjutant-General. Evans, worried by reports that a high-ranking officer had been writing strong attacks on the Legion for the Liberal newspaper the *Morning Chronicle*, informed Shaw and others whom he trusted. Richardson's abilities as a journalist were known to a few, so that suspicion was readily focused upon him. The journal gave no proof of guilt, but LeMarchant was angered by entries critical of him.[21]

For six weeks Richardson lay in his enfeebled state, sometimes crawling to the window to watch his successor muster the scantily-clad sick, who could barely stand, and order them off to their regiments. Both LeMarchant and Shaw sent out the convalescents before they were well, and flogged them if they did not obey. They marched men in the cold so unmercifully that some fell down on their beds and died without removing their packs.

Shaw had a particular manner of approach, Richardson observed. He seemed to suspect that every soldier was trying to pretend sickness in order to avoid being sent to the front.

Shaw was proud of his efforts. He wrote home in mid-February:

The hospitals at this time were choke full, four or five in a bed: discharging none except to their graves (about fifteen or twenty daily) and having exclusive of those in hospital (twelve hundred),

a depot of convalescents of nearly eight hundred. To this depot I bent my steps, seeing numbers of officers in the streets. I fell in all the men who could stand, taking a Portuguese surgeon with me, and in less than one hour had turned out upwards of 300 stout fellows, by means of words and the flat side of my sabre. I ordered them to march next morning to join their regiments.[22]

The typhus abated at the close of January, and by the end of February death statistics could be drawn up: seven-hundred men and forty officers. At the close of March Richardson was able to hire a coach with other officers and set out for Santander on the coast. Although seven mules pulled the coach, it was a slow journey over the mountain passes. His disillusionment with Evans increased when he reached Santander. Determined to uphold the honour of the Legion against its many critics, Richardson requested leave to return to England to find a publisher for his journal. The leave had been granted, yet when he tried to board the ships leaving for England, he was abruptly informed that only field officers could be taken. Brigadier Evans, carrying dispatches, arrived in Santander and sailed immediately. To Richardson, it was a deliberate insult. The regiments from Vitoria arrived daily as preparations were made for their transfer to San Sebastian. Evans and his staff also arrived. They held a banquet and a marchpast. Ship after ship transported the soldiers up the coast, but Richardson remained behind. He called on Evans at his posada, ostensibly to inquire about his promotion, though he wanted to learn if there was some reason for denying him passage.

The Lieutenant-General had an easy charm. He told Richardson that he had been wanting to promote

[21] *Personal Memoirs*, pp.88-9.

78

[22] Charles Shaw, *Personal Memoirs, op. cit.*, letter, Vitoria, Feb. 18, 1836.

him for some time and would do so as soon as the first post became vacant. Then he turned to the subject of politics and the difficulties he had in informing the British public of the true nature of the war. For instance, the battle of Hernani, which the newspapers called a defeat, was in reality a reconnaissance. Then there was this long march which had been criticized; the Legion had drawn a semi-circle about the Carlists which cut off their supplies from the rest of Spain and the sea; the troops had only to tighten the semi-encirclement to achieve a complete victory. Richardson could have argued that the Carlists would have received all the supplies they needed through the north from France. Finally, Evans expressed a wish to read the journal. Richardson obligingly fetched it from his own posada. This, then, was the unspoken reason for his detainment.

Although Richardson had erased all the passages critical of LeMarchant, treated events without bias, indeed, lauded the courage of the Legionnaires and defended Evans's military decisions, he did not win his approval. Evans wanted a passage on the whipping of a soldier cut. Richardson was willing to omit remarks on individuals, but he was not going to cut out a dramatic scene which, far from representing an isolated case, was typical of what took place among the Legionnaires.

At last a ship did find room for him as far as San Sebastian, where, sensing the preparations for battle, he offered his services. Evans replied that Richardson was not required. Still very weak, Richardson had thought that he could be of more use on the staff where he would be able to ride, but now he turned to the infantry. On the disbandment of the 2nd Regiment he was appointed Captain with the 6th Scotch Regiment. Since the command of a Major was badly needed in the Regiment, he was asked by its young Colonel to become Acting-Major.

Richardson could not check his enthusiasm. First, he was thrilled at discovering that one of his Lieutenants was the son of the Major under whom he had stormed the battery at Fort Meigs on May 5th, twenty-three years before. Second, he remarked that the Carlists were occupying the Convent of San Francisco where he had stayed with his Regiment after arriving from England. He drew up a plan of attack in which he illustrated its vulnerable points and offered to lead a small group to storm it. He sent his plan to the staff officers. But, unwilling to adopt his ideas, they replied, disingenuously, that no Carlists occupied the Convent.

Nothing could dampen Richardson's spirit. At last, after twenty-three years, he was to experience the glory of battle.

The Battle

JUST AFTER MIDNIGHT on May 5, 1836, the Legionnaires were mustered on the road leading to the enemy. Wet fog hung thickly about them in the dark as they marched quietly. Before dawn they arrived at the Convent of San Bartolomew, and, at the first streaks of light, dashed into the valley and up the heights at the stone wall of the Carlists' first line of defence. The 6th Scotch were with the regiments on the Right Wing under the command of General Reid; the Centre was commanded by Charles Shaw; and the Left by General Chichester. General Evans watched from a vantage point.

Richardson, as second Major, was expected to wait at the Convent until the regimental rear had come up, but he noticed with surprise that his superior, Major Ross, who was supposed to lead the attack, also remained behind. Richardson immediately ran over to fill in Ross's place and head the Right Wing. He was one of the first to ascend the height and cross the open ground to the first parapet from which the Carlists were firing with everything they had. The break was made by the Centre. Shaw surprised his men as he stood out bravely waving his sword and bellowing encouragement. His reddish-yellow whiskers made a bright target in the drizzle. The Carlists retreated to their second line while the cannonading

from their third and final line fell on the British who were regrouping behind the first wall. Richardson and the Right Wing took shelter in some stone houses and waited for Reid to give the next order. The Carlist shells were not greatly effective, although they wounded several men. Richardson watched the engineers level the stone parapet and expected Reid to order the troops over it and charge the second line. Instead, Reid commanded the brigade to form a line behind the Chapelgorries on the high road and march into the face of a heavy crossfire. Richardson was astonished, because as the column holding its fire advanced, the men fell like lead.

"I was in the centre of the regiment," Richardson wrote,

and we were all close under the formidable barrier, which appeared already won, when I observed a large body of the Carlists in full retreat. In the excitement of the moment, I called out to the men, 'Now, my lads, hurrah! for the honour of old Scotland! See! They run! They run!' and I pointed with my sword. Suddenly to my astonishment, I saw the head of the column waver. They were the Chapelgorries, who, unable to surmount the barrier, had turned back upon the leading company of the 6th... The 6th in their turn finding the impossibility of effecting an entrance without scaling ladders, gave way also, and all became confusion and dismay. I tried to stop the fugitives, but in vain — a sudden panic had seized them, and they knew not the voices of their officers. In their haste to pass me, on their way to their recent cover, they threw me down — my face falling into the mud. As fast as I attempted to rise, a rude foot was placed upon my back and down again I fell. The men neither cared nor thought about the matter. They must have now supposed me wounded, and could not but know that, if left behind there was no chance of my escape from the ground. I could not help reflecting, even as I lay, on the extreme selfishness of man, while labouring under the influence of panic.[1]

Owing to descriptions such as the above, which he wrote with some bitterness against the Legion and especially the 6th Regiment, Richardson was accused of exaggerating the situation to win sympathy for himself. Some critics readily surmised that he suffered from a persecution complex.

On retreating to his line, Richardson found the officers trying to sort out the regiments amidst great confusion. As Reid was grazed in the neck by a musket ball and retired to San Sebastian, Adjutant-General LeMarchant had to assume command. Standing in the shelter of the houses, LeMarchant ordered the Colonel of the 6th to lead another charge, but the Colonel replied that his men had done all that was humanly possible. LeMarchant turned to the colonel of another regiment, but received a similar reply. "He then turned to me, who had been standing near him at the time," Richardson wrote,

and said, 'Captain Richardson, lead on your company and carry that battery,' I simply said, 'I am now not in command of a company, but of a wing, sir,' — 'Wing or company — all the same', but I knew my duty too well to disobey. I answered, 'Very well. Colonel LeMarchant, have the goodness to assist me over the parapet?' The Adjutant-General gave me his hand, and I ascended the wall. Most of the 3rd, and 6th, were at the time sheltered by a row of houses, which extended about twenty yards beyond the parapet. I ordered the officers of the left wing of the 6th. to bring up their men for another

advance. Most of those in command of companies had already fallen, so that the task devolved on some of the juniors, who but indifferently understood their duty. Not more than two companies could be got together, and with these I again attempted an advance upon the high road. No sooner, however, had the men uncovered themselves, than a heavy fire of musketry was immediately poured into them from various points, and the young soldiers, perceiving the impracticability of effecting that which a whole brigade had vainly attempted to accomplish, a short time previously, again retired to their cover, whence it was impossible to withdraw them. I was a good deal annoyed at the time, for the Lieutenant-General was looking on: yet it was absurd in the extreme to suppose so small a force could have effected any thing against the obstacles they were sent to destroy.

He was struck in the chest and lower arm by shot from the enemy, then . . .

Finding all my endeavors vain to urge the men from their cover, I told them that, since they were afraid to move forward, I would not remain to share their disgrace. Forcing my way through the crowd, I gained the parapet, which was greatly exposed to the fire of the enemy, and where several officers had already been picked off by the Carlist sharpshooters, while in the attempt to cross it. I had not stood more than five minutes on this parapet before I received a blow on my left arm which knocked me off the wall. So acute was the agony, I thought the limb was fractured, and I hastened to the ambulance, which had been established about a hundred yards in the rear.[2]

[1] *Personal Memoirs*, p.10-11.

[2] *Ibid.*, p.13.

San Sebastian, 1836, by Henry Wilkinson.

The surgeons advised him to retire from the field. He was caked with mud and so exhausted that he fainted as his arm was being looked at. His stamina, debilitated by typhus, was failing. But swallowing some brandy he insisted that he was all right and returned to the parapet.

It appears that he exposed himself foolishly to the enemy's fire not so much to embarrass his men as to impress Evans. He should have spared himself. Evans blamed his commissary officers for the suffering at Vitoria, and bore resentment towards them for as long as they remained in the Legion. Unfortunately the typhus epidemic reached its peak when Richardson was Commandant, hence Evans gave him a large share of the blame.

Major Ross who, at last, found his way to the front lines, looked down at Richardson's swollen arm and suggested he have it examined.[3] Richardson declined as he could see no external mark, though he felt faint with the pain. At half past nine o'clock in the morning the surgeon from the ambulance came to him to return his pistols which he had forgotten. About an hour later, when Richardson could bear it no longer, he finally decided to let the surgeon examine his arm. The same surgeon, who had already told him that he looked too exhausted to carry on, met him on the way, sat him on a rock, and cut the sleeve about the wound. The arm from socket to elbow was inky black. Richardson took one look at it and fainted. With his arm in a sling, and leaning on the arm of a fellow officer, he began the long walk back to San Sebastian. Other wounded men fell along the wayside, but some were revived by the women of San Sebastian who came up from the town and offered them fruit and wine. By late morning he dropped into bed in San Sebastian. At about the same time the battle was won.

If the British battleships had not landed reinforcements from Santander, and then proceeded to lob shells from off shore onto the second line, the battle might have raged on inconclusively, because the Carlists were firmly entrenched. But with the aid of the shelling, a breach was made. The Carlists fled to the third line, hotly pursued by the Left Wing under General Chichester which stormed and took it. Evans and his staff jubilantly called the encounter "a great victory." At the most, though, they had won some ground from which they could attack the Carlist outposts on the heights around San Sebastian, and drive the enemy further into the mountains. No prisoners were taken. The Legion lost ninety-seven officers and five-hundred men out of a force of five thousand.

To a journalist such as Richardson, the battle was a scoop he could not resist. He left his sick-bed on the evening after the battle to look for transportation by ship either to England or France. Refused passage, he returned in frustration to his lodgings.

[3] *Ibid.*, p.84; B.M. copy has written in margin "True": by hand of an eyewitness one wonders.

Not wasting a moment, Richardson wrote an account of the fighting which he intended to submit to *Galignani's Messenger* in Paris. He thought that this time, to ensure his passage, he should see Evans. The Lieutenant-General, vain about his victory, was haughtier and regarded him superciliously. The interview was short; they spoke about the battle, then Richardson casually mentioned his article. Evans immediately asked to see it, read through the account and angrily handed it back. "Why, *my good man,* this will never do. The Chapelgorries, the Chapelgorries, it is always the Chapelgorries first, as if we could do nothing without the Chapelgorries. The people in England will seize hold of this immediately."[4] Richardson had attributed the failure of the Legion's assault on the second line to the Chapelgorries, and he upheld that no shred of blame should be attached to the Legion. Evans, however, was adamant, until he agreed to expunge the passage. Richardson suspected that Evans envied his ability to write.[5] He secured Evans's permission to board a ship the next day to Socoa; from there he could travel through France

[4] *Ibid.*, p.18.
[5] This was Richardson's explanation to his readers, but he was less than candid. Richardson's problems began in Vitoria, about the time he believes that his servant took passages from his journal to Le Marchant. Shaw wrote in his *Personal Memoirs* that on the march from Vitoria, Evans wrote to him that he had learned "that an officer of rank in the Legion had been furnishing the *Courier* newspaper with some very ill-natured remarks about it." Evans was looking for the culprit; Richardson, known to some officers as a writer, was a likely suspect. Elsewhere Richardson states that Evans turned against his Quarter-Master-General, Col. Boyd, and those officers who worked under Boyd such as W.A. Clarke (not to be confused with Fred Clark, Richardson's rival) and Richardson himself. Indeed there was much general criticism of this dept. at Vitoria. George de Lacy Evans, *Memoranda of the Contest in Spain* (London: J. Ridgway, 1840) was written in a wooden style.

and stay a day or two in Paris.

Before leaving San Sebastian Richardson lunched with Ross. He wanted Ross, who was now a Colonel, to support him for promotion to Major for which he was first in line. Ross's promotion to Colonel had come as a result of the death of the Colonel of the 6th Scotch in the battle. Before he died, however, the Colonel, a cousin of LeMarchant, reportedly expressed a desire to see Captain Clark promoted. Clark was junior to Richardson but a great friend of LeMarchant. Richardson did not believe LeMarchant's report of the Colonel's death-wish. He felt it was another ruse to keep him from being promoted.

On the 11th of May, Richardson was at last free from Spain. He had originally been given two months leave, April and May, but during his last interview with Evans he obtained permission to extend his leave through June.

Just before he reached England an interesting duel took place. Brigadier Evans, the brother of the General, had intrigued against a young Captain in Spain to make the Captain appear dishonourable, but the Captain followed Evans to England and appealed to the United Service Club in London which exonerated him. Evans, obliged to accept the Captain's challenge, was wounded and recuperating in a London hotel. Learning that awards were to be given to those who had distinguished themselves on May 5th, Richardson wrote a letter detailing his services to the Military Secretary in Spain, and took a copy to Brigadier Evans at his London hotel. If there were honours to be dispensed, Richardson did not want to be overlooked. He read the newspapers with anticipation.

On May 25th the lists of officers honoured and promoted appeared. Richardson read through them with alarm, dismay, and then fury, as he searched vainly for his own name. Everyone but Richardson seemed to have been promoted. Fred Clark, his junior officer, was appointed Major over his head. All Evans' friends and favourites were honoured and promoted, men who were returning from India to rejoin the Legion, men who were not even in the battle. Richardson, deeply hurt, wrote to the Military Secretary that he suspected an officer on the staff was his secret enemy, and that he would "strip" some officer of "borrowed plumes" some day. He marked this letter "private" and followed it with an official letter stating that he was returning to San Sebastian immediately. He sent a copy of the official letter to LeMarchant. Five days later, on May 30, his bitterness having built up to an overwhelming urge for expression, he dashed off a preface to his journal which was now set for the presses. Revealing his anger and disappointment, it spoke of the injustice done him, and promised that at a future date he might relate the true circumstances of the battle. He explained later to Evans that ". . . goaded by the very natural astonishment expressed by my friends and acquaintance, I felt it to be a duty which I owed myself, and to my character as a British officer, to promise public explanation of a wrong which had been publicly done to me."[6] He had a few copies printed and sent one to Brigadier Evans at his hotel with the warning that he would publish this preface if justice were not done him. He did not send a copy to Spain, but the Brigadier forwarded his with comments to his brother.

With Maria he caught a ship for Falmouth, Cornwall, where steam packets left regularly for Spain and Portugal. The long trip down the Thames and round the southern coast was passed in a tumble of ugly dreams and impatience. While he waited for a ship at this sea town, his temper cooled and he began to be tormented by second thoughts. How foolish a personal grievance would read, when it was attached as a preface to an unbiased account of the Legion! He scrapped

it and wrote another on a different theme which he sent to his printer.[7] As far as his relations with Evans were concerned, however, the damage was done.

Herman, acting for the Military Secretary still recovering from wounds, replied to Richardson's official letter that he had tried to get Richardson a promotion but was unsuccessful. The idea of Herman who was hand-in-glove with LeMarchant, supporting him for promotion was insulting and gave him a feeling of misgiving that Herman had opened his confidential letter. Brimming with impatience, he finally secured passage for Spain in the second week of June.

Although Richardson had been returned "severely wounded," Ross and LeMarchant reported him as "slightly wounded." Inevitably, another rumour went around that Richardson had behaved with cowardice in leaving the battle early. This rumour was to cause lasting damage to Richardson's reputation. In spite of public evidence to the contrary, the author of the *History of the British Legion* wrote in 1839: "He (Richardson) left the service shortly after the action of the 5th. of May, that engagement having been, as was supposed, too hot to warrant his waiting for a repetition of it."[8]

Ross was very successful in turning the charge of cowardice from himself to Richardson. But then he had a lot of help. As Richardson had suspected, Herman did open the "private" letter and ran with it to LeMarchant, who showed it to Evans. The rumours about the letter were rife, and exaggerated. It was said that Richardson belittled the late Colonel of the 6th, and that he slandered the Regiment. So when Ross went to recommend Richardson for a vacant Majority about this time, Evans called out to him in the hearing of other officers, "Beware how you recommend Captain

[7] He took his frustration out on Capt. Henningsen, who had just published a book favoring the Carlists, in his pref.

[8] Alexander Somerville, *History of the British Legion....op. cit.*, p.707.

[6] *Personal Memoirs*, p.25.

Richardson. He has threatened to publish us all in England, and I am not to be intimidated by threats."[9] Thus Ross himself was intimidated from proposing Richardson.

Richardson joined his regiment on the Heights of Alza, which had been won from the Carlists during his absence, and took up a post with his companies on the front line. The following day, June 18, he received a letter from a Captain of the 6th Regiment. The officers of the 6th charged him with slandering them and their late Colonel. Richardson refuted the charge and asked on whose authority it was based. The Captain merely reaffirmed the charge, adding: "There is only one course for the officers of the 6th Regiment to pursue, and it becomes my painful duty, as the senior Captain present, and in the name of the officers, to announce to you, that with Captain Richardson we can no longer associate as an officer and a gentleman."[10]

Instead of challenging the Captain to a duel as was expected, Richardson sent copies of the correspondence to Ross, the Regimental Colonel, and requested that the Captain be put under arrest for presuming to address a senior officer in such a manner. Ross was obliged to imprison the Captain.

Richardson took copies of the correspondence to Evans with a covering note asking that the Captain be court-martialled. The Chief of the Legion was in the hallway when Richardson arrived. This was the first time they had met since Richardson's return, although Richardson had spent a whole day waiting to see him immediately on arrival.

Evans, with mocking affability, refused to see him privately and would not accept the correspondence because he said the affair was private.[11] Richardson insisted the affair was public and handed the papers to Herman who was standing among the staff officers,

looking on with amused condescension.

Evans, believing that the correspondence Richardson had given Herman was the original, told Herman to destroy it and write a letter to Richardson stating that it was being returned separately through his commanding officer, which was the proper channel of communication. (When Richardson complained to Herman that he had not received the correspondence, he was told it had been mailed by mistake to England.) Evans then ordered Shaw, the commanding officer of the 6th, to release the Captain and notify Richardson.

Richardson, ever resourceful, was not dismayed by Evans' high-handedness. He sent Evans another set of copies of the correspondence directly, since he doubted it would reach him through the normal chain of command. He then sent copies to Shaw, accompanied by a note which charged Shaw with helping instigate the officers of the 6th against him and which demanded that a court of inquiry deliberate his case, since Shaw by releasing the Captain, implied that he, Richardson, was guilty of the Captain's charge. It was a clever move, but he was playing from an inferior position. Shaw had the power to ignore the letter.

On rejoining his troops on the Heights of Alza, Richardson noticed that the Legion's morale had dropped. Many experienced officers either had been killed or had quit the Legion which left gaps in the staffing, and overworked the young, inexperienced, and often indifferent officers remaining. Since the San Sebastian victory and the winning of the Heights of Alza and Ametza which followed on its heels, Evans had become even less concerned with the state of his troops. His attitude of superiority and his unconcern filtered down to the lowest ranks. Drinking, fighting, and all kinds of laxities went unchecked. Richardson, the optimist, believed it could be rectified,[12] but then he also had his own problems to contend with.

[9] *Personal Memoirs*, p.28.
[10] *Ibid.*, p.30.
[11] *Ibid.*, p.31.

[12] *Ibid.*, p.93.

The harassment began in deadly earnest. Richardson's fellow officers of the 6th avoided and annoyed him at every opportunity. Led by Colonel Ross and Major Clark, they resorted to such tricks as informing him at the last moment that he was to take the morning watch. They held a dinner for General Shaw to which all the officers of the regiment except Richardson were invited.

Fortunately Richardson had friends in the Legion from the early days of London escapades. Colonel Fitzgerald, "Ould Charlie" as his Irish soldiers affectionately called him, had been keeping Richardson posted as to what was being said and secretly planned against him. Learning of this attempt to disgrace Richardson, the generous Fitzgerald invited him to have dinner at Ametza that evening. Richardson accepted with relief. He relaxed in Fitzgerald's company. Both men were raconteurs and had adventures and acquaintances in common which made for an entertaining few hours. For once he did not have to measure the effect of his words before he spoke them, or of his actions before he acted. As for Fitzgerald, he loathed Shaw.

Since it was late and Alza was some miles distant by road, Fitzgerald asked his aide to notify Shaw on his authority that Captain Richardson was staying the night at Ametza. Richardson, although exhausted, was not meant to have a peaceful sleep. He was awakened by a messenger from Major Clark who brought word that Shaw had authorized Clark to declare him absent without leave. At last Shaw and company had caught Richardson on a legitimate charge which would ruin him. Richardson turned to Fitzgerald with an idea. If he could get back to Alza before morning roll call, he could not be considered absent. This meant cutting through enemy territory, as the route by road between the positions, would take too long. The night was black. Richardson was prepared to chance it. Fitzgerald informed him of the countersign which would allow him to pass his own sentries.

86

Shortly after midnight Richardson disappeared into the darkness. His regiment was mustered between one and two in the morning, so that he had to travel swiftly with great stealth to make it in time. Both Carlist and British lines were manned tightly over that mountainous area; their greatest fear was that a breakthrough would be made in the night which could surround one section of the army and cut it off from the remainder. Richardson made his way with difficulty past the Spaniards, and reached his regiment just as roll was being called.

Ross, at a loss as to what to do next, put Richardson under arrest and notified Shaw. Standing Richardson at attention on the parade ground, he accused him of treating him with no respect.

Richardson commented:

I have often since wondered at my self-possession on this and several other occasions, for I am not naturally of the most forbearing temperament; and three and twenty years in the King's Army had not exactly fitted me for the endurance of anything like undue severity in so limited a service as that of the British Legion, particularly from an officer who must have been learning his alphabet at the time I was studying the practical rudiments of war, in many a hard fought battle field . . . But the fact is, I had traced out a line of conduct I intended undeviatingly to pursue. I knew that a powerful conspiracy was in agitation, at the head of which was the Lieutenant-General, and I felt that his satellites from Brigadier Shaw to the very meanest in rank of the clique, would omit no opportunity of making any unguarded expression of mine, a matter of the most serious accusation against me.[13]

13 *Ibid.*, p.43.

Ross had to release Richardson from arrest, but he issued an order forbidding any officer to leave the line for any reason. Colonel Fitzgerald fired off a strong protest to Shaw for overlooking his message concerning Richardson. Shaw apologized and claimed he had no knowledge of Fitzgerald's request. But the issue had been forced into the open, and the clique now had the task of justifying its actions. Shaw was compelled to answer Richardson's letter demanding a court of inquiry. He asked Richardson to visit him at his posada in San Sebastian.

The meeting was between a brown-skinned, steel-eyed officer of martial bearing with a Byronic air of destiny, and his red-haired blustering commanding officer whose egotism was revealed in his mannerism and speech. Richardson was only five years older than Shaw, but those five years bridged two radically different periods in the history of the British Army. Richardson was trained in the correct behaviour of an officer as practiced during the Napoleonic wars; Shaw in the lax period of relative peace after Waterloo, when England assumed an air of superiority, and concentrated all her efforts on collecting territorial possessions. The army, no longer fighting to save the nation, was a political tool to maintain the commercial prospects of British investors.

Shaw was prepared to admit that Richardson had not slandered the officers of the 6th Regiment, but he asked Richardson to retract his letter demanding an inquiry. Richardson agreed to withdraw his letter and was dismissed. If Shaw congratulated himself on his tactful handling of Richardson, he must have been shocked shortly afterwards to receive another letter from Richardson withdrawing his previous letter but substituting another with the same demands in stronger terms. Richardson pressed Shaw once more for his Majority.

Richardson realized with cautious optimism that the clique was now on the defensive. Evans had tried to placate Richardson's anger by including him on the list of those to receive the Order of the Knight of Saint Ferdinand, Spain's highest military honour, but he under-rated Richardson's determination to get a formal inquiry into his supposed cowardice.

Anticipating a court martial, Richardson wrote to some of his friends who had been connected with him in the Legion. His senior officer in the Quarter-Master-General's Department, who at one time had served as aide to the late Duke of Gloucester, replied: "Those friends who have known you in the British Service, and in the closer ties of private society, will join with me in pronouncing you incapable of acting derogatory to the highest principles of honour you have always professed and advocated."[14]

On the 28th, having received no word from Evans, he sent in his resignation to Headquarters effective on the 29th, terminal date for his contracted one year of service. Evans was caught by surprise; he was occupied with plans for another campaign, and was also ill with fever. Richardson had to be taken care of somehow, and the only way possible now was to find him guilty in a court-martial. When Evans promoted to brevet rank three Captains of the 6th Regiment, whose disdainful attitude to Richardson had been obvious, Richardson interpreted it as an example to those officers who were to sit in judgment on him on June 30th at Alza.

[14] *Ibid.*, p.48.

Tribulation

SEVEN OFFICERS sat in judgement on Richardson. General Chichester, the mainstay of the Legion,[1] was president of the court. LeMarchant represented Evans at the trial.

Richardson was charged with dishonouring the Legion. Noting this, he made it clear that as of the preceding day he was not a member of the Legion but, strictly speaking, a Lieutenant in the British Army, and therefore under no circumstances could he be considered on trial. Indeed, he asserted, he was staying for the inquiry only because he asked for it. This statement sent the courtroom into confusion. Le Marchant called for a temporary halt until he could get directions as to how to continue.

Since a Court of Legionnaires passing sentence on an officer of the Regular Army for dishonouring them,

would have been unprecedented, Richardson' enemies had to think up another charge. Soon, a Lancer arrived from San Sebastian with a letter for Chichester. Evans had changed the charge to "cowardice in battle." The court resumed.

Richardson relished the unimaginativeness of this new charge. The certificate making him a Knight of the Order of Saint Ferdinand for his bravery had been delivered to him just before the trial. Evans was correct in assuming that Richardson would be very pleased by the award, but wrong in conjecturing that his anger would be mollified. He was not to be bought off.

Richardson addressed the court with an eloquence that must have indicated it was to be an unusual trial:

> I find myself in a position, at once novel, painful, and triumphant — novel, inasmuch as I, who have ever been the most zealous advocate of this Legion, am accused of being its principal detractor — painful, in so far as I am called upon to justify myself from an infamous imputation — and finally triumphant, because in my review of the past, and anticipation of the future, I foresee but the warm approval of every generous and manly mind.
>
> Gentlemen, I fear I shall have to trespass much on your patience by the production of matter necessary to my defence, but when it is considered, that the honour of a soldier is concerned,

---

[1] Chichester was a clever military tactician (*vide* D.N.B.). He kept a diary at this time and in after-years in Canada in which he referred to his British Legion experience as the happiest months of his life. He was not a cruel disciplinarian; when Evans left some privates with him to be given one hundred lashes immediately, he preferred to ignore the order until the men could be turned over to their proper regiment at which time he passed on Evans' order (Diary, Nov. 7, 1836). Surprisingly he made no mention of Richardson; the diary for the period of Richardson's trial is missing, possibly purposely destroyed. His diaries reveal his willingness to accomodate to the wishes of Evans and his high-ranked colleagues out of a desire for personal advancement. Richardson could not have assessed his motives better than he did in *Personal Memoirs* (p.123): "(He) had all along evinced but too much readiness to fall into the views of the Lieutenant-General, and therefore there was more of indignation than regret in the feeling I entertained towards him." The Chichester Papers are in the County Archives, Beverley, Yorkshire.

and that soldier one, who in return for his anxiety to maintain unsullied the reputation of this Legion, has been met by a tissue of injustice, as varied in detail, as persevering in object, I am sure prolixity will be forgiven, and your patience not unwillingly accorded.[2]

The court voted to consider his letters to the Military Secretary strictly private. But his correspondence with the Captain of the 6th Regiment and the controversial preface were read aloud. The Captain was called to the stand. Richardson cross-examined with the adroitness of an experienced court-lawyer. The Captain admitted that Major Clark gave Richardson's private letter to the officers of the 6th and that Colonel Ross told the officers of the 6th that Richardson had made imputations against them.

Ross was next called to the stand. He denied that he had refused Richardson's promotion because he left the field without sufficient reason ' "I saw him do his duty in it" — but did it because Richardson had not had enough experience with the regiment and was returning to England in any case. Evans, he said, was the one to hint at Richardson's "cowardice."

Richardson then reviewed his service with the Legion. Since Chichester had visited him when he was recuperating from typhus in Vitoria, and knew how hard he had worked, he had no fear of being misunderstood. He analyzed the preface and showed that there was no attempt in it to slander the Legion or any officer. Then he produced the officers he had met in Paris and London after the action, and the surgeons who had treated him. To a man they told of his praise for the Legion and of the seriousness of his arm wound.

Already confident that he had disproven the charge of cowardice, Richardson planned to clinch the matter with Major Clark's testimony. He hoped to

[2] *Personal Memoirs*, pp.59-60.

show that Clark had listed him as "severely" wounded but that Ross and LeMarchant changed it to "slightly." When asked whether he had returned Richardson as slightly or severely wounded, Clark unhesitantly said "slightly," although he had told Richardson the reverse just prior to the trial. But Richardson was prepared for this. He asked Clark to answer the question again, but honestly this time, or else Richardson would be forced to say something he would rather leave unsaid. The unsuspecting Clark repeated "slightly." Richardson asked him if it was true that he had been dismissed from the 12th Regiment of the British Infantry for making a false report. The court, aghast, interrupted. It was decided after a short recess that Clark did not have to answer. When Clark refused to answer, he was dismissed.[3]

Richardson then turned to the subject of his wounds. Officers who had seen him return to San Sebastian testified to the seriousness of his condition. Richardson took off his coat to reveal the gash on his chest and the large lump of flesh on his left arm. The court considered wounds that would leave such marks to be serious. As Richardson let them be inspected, he thought wryly of Frank Halloway, the private soldier he had created in *Wacousta*, who had to undergo the

[3] Clark and Ross worked their way together to high commands in the Second Legion which was formed in 1837 from remnants of the First Legion. Alexander Ball in his *A Personal Narrative... (op. cit.)*, p.93, referred to them: "Military men, I am convinced, must startle at the Staff-officers named by General O'Connell in his farewell order (which for a number and rank might have satisfied Napoleon) when they are informed that the force never mustered 1100 effectives. The first mentioned is Colonel Ross, to whom the General felt deeply indebted for his "unwearied exertions," had he added *at playing billiards* he would have been perfectly right." The General's address was written by "Assistant Quartermaster General Colonel Clerk at Colonel Ross's dictation." Ball, of course, was punning on the name Clark.

same inspection.[4]

Meanwhile LeMarchant having to leave for England on Legion business, gave written answers which were produced to the court. LeMarchant admitted the truth of Richardson's description of the battle. Because Chichester intimated to Richardson that he should not indulge in recrimination, Richardson did not pursue the matter of Ross' cowardice with LeMarchant, but determined to make one point clear, he recalled Ross to the stand. He was asked exactly when Evans had implied that Richardson lacked courage. The answer was: after Richardson returned to Spain on July 12.

In his summation (which was deleted from the transcript as recriminatory) Richardson pointed up the injustice of the charge against him. The court voted unanimously in his favour. It was July 5. Richardson anxiously awaited Evans' reaction to the verdict.

Many officers, whose one-year term had expired, were shipping back to England on July 10. Richardson was anxious that they should learn the outcome of the trial before they carried a wrong impression to England, but Evans did not publish the results in the Orders until after their departure. His comments clearly indicated his displeasure with the findings.[5]

Before the notice appeared in the Orders, Evans sent an officer to Richardson with the message that if he withdrew his resignation from the Legion in writing, Evans would promote him to Major as the verdict of the trial indicated he should. Richardson did withdraw his resignation in writing but only under the condition that he appear in Orders as Major with the 6th Scotch from May 5, and that he be allowed to retire at his own discretion. On reading Richardson's letter Evans returned it and instructed the officer to tell Richardson that he would promote him if he made no mention of any conditions. Richardson rewrote his

[4] *Personal Memoirs*, p.69n.
[5] *Ibid.*, pp.75-6.

letter without stating his conditions but he mentioned the conversation with the officer. That very day he saw the pejorative manner in which Evans published the verdict of his trial, and bitterly regretted writing the letter. Luckily Evans returned it by the same officer because he wanted no mention made of the conversation. Richardson tore the letter to pieces and sent the officer back to Evans with a curse. He at last saw through Evans' strategy. Evans who had planned an attack on Fuentarabia for the following day, would conveniently have forgotten his promise to promote Richardson, if Richardson had withdrawn his resignation and re-entered the service without a written promise of promotion. Then Richardson, who would not have consented to act as a Captain, would have had to refuse to join the expedition to Fuentarabia. Evans would then have published in Orders Richardson's refusal to fight at Fuentarabia and made it appear that he was indeed a coward. Richardson had to do some quick thinking, but he was tiring of the pettiness of the whole affair.

The "affair" of Fuentarabia worsened Evans' reputation back in England. The Legion marched miles over the mountains to descend on this Carlist town by the French border. As the battle raged, the French climbed every available tree and roof to watch it, and the French army stood by. Evans claimed that his design was to draw the Carlists from the interior to defend the town and thus give the Spanish armies an opportunity to attack in the south, but the attack was badly conducted. An inferior Carlist force fought off the British — who made excellent targets on the hillsides. Colonel Ross was dangerously wounded. The Captain of the 6th, who had challenged Richardson, was shot, became ill with fever and died. Evans' fever had not been helped by spending the night on the cold and wet mountain side. Sick with a raging temperature, he had to be transported by ship back to San Sebastian. When his men straggled back, Evans notified the press that he had conducted merely a reconnaissance.

Richardson returned to the subject of his promotion after the battle. In a letter to Evans phrased with a subtle sarcasm, he referred to his disappointment at not being able to accompany the expedition: "However, as I understand since, it was only a reconnaissance, I do not so much regret the circumstances of my absence."[6]

Finally Evans, faced with a series of misfortunes, including the newspaper accounts of his defeat, a wracking fever, and badly officered troops in a state of rebellion, had Herman *write* that he would promote Richardson if he withdrew his resignation. Only then did Richardson withdraw his resignation. He read the announcement in Orders that he had been made a Major with the 6th Regiment, vice Ross, and was transferred to active service with the 4th Regiment stationed on the Heights of Passages.

Another reason for Evans' reinstatement of Richardson may have been the shocking revelation that Brigadier General Shaw wrote scurrilous accounts of the Legion for the London *Chronicle*. Shaw had been betrayed by his chief weakness: in his published account of the attack on Fuentarabia Shaw overshadowed Evans.

Although the officers were allowed to observe the end of their service under the contract terms, the rank and file were not given the same treatment. Evans would allow none of them to terminate. The soldiers of Scotch regiments refused to obey orders unless paid. The 8th Scotch protested successfully and was paid, but when the 6th Scotch insisted that Evans recognise the terms of its contract, the men were marched instead to the glacis at San Sebastian and addressed by General Shaw. Scotland at this time was the only European country with a general public system of edu-

George de Lacy Evans.

cation. Richardson said of these soldiers: "I have heard them express themselves in terms which few of their officers could hope to attain."[7] Through threats and promises, Shaw persuaded half the regiment to return to duty, but the other half remaining obstinate, was forced at bayonet point by the 10th Irish Regiment to

---

[6] *Ibid.*, p.79.

[7] *Movements of the British Legion...*, p.273.

board ships. They were taken to Santander and imprisoned. A few weeks later when the rebellious 8th Scotch wanted to return to England, it received the same treatment. The morale of the men was so low that they sold their clothes for drink. They were imprisoned, suffered filth, deprivation, starvation, death, and even slavery. Some of them, half-naked, cleaned the streets or cut wood for a bare sustenance. Many Legionnaires deserted and, trying somehow to reach home, they wandered emaciated and ragged across France. Evans manufactured letters for the home Government to obscure the circumstances of the soldiers.[8] The chronicler of *The History of the British Legion in Spain,* who served as a Private and Sergeant, bitterly commented: "But we must be fair with him; — he did what other Commanders would have done — he hires subterfuges for defence. And be they who they may, that have become famous in war, they rose by setting at defiance every tie and right, and every affection and law of humanity."[9]

In the last week of July Richardson joined the 4th Queen's Own Fusiliers on the Heights of Passages which was a strategic pass through the mountains, particularly since Ametza, which overlooked it, had been retaken by the Carlists.

The 4th Regiment was in decay. Its present Colonel, Harley, who had been one of the judges at Richardson's trial, was ill in town where he retained the Regimental Surgeon to attend him. The Senior Major was ill in town also. There was neither Adjutant, Sergeant-Major, nor Medical Officer, and the few officers remaining knew little about their duties. The troops were in a mutinous mood.

While riding along his lines Richardson heard gunfire and galloped to the area where a skirmish was

taking place. A Captain of the 4th had ordered sappers and miners to blow up some Carlist fortifications. Richardson arrived in time to see the officer arrange for a covering fire to bring off their retreat. He commended the young man's military skill, and gave a full report of the incident to Colonel Harley. But unknown to him his Legion enemies were at work again.

Reid had sent his special aide, Captain MacIntosh, to help Colonel La Saussaye, another member of the Evans clique, to keep an eye on Richardson. During the skirmish MacIntosh crept into the field behind the sappers and miners of the 4th and told them to drop their tools and retreat. The soldiers ignored the invitation and later reported the incident to their officers. La Saussaye made out a long, abusive report about the 4th Regiment, accusing the men of retreating from the batteries, lacking discipline, having rusty firearms, and so on. He sent the document to Evans, who fired off an angry letter to Harley demanding an explanation and remarking that the Commanding Officer should be court-martialled. Richardson as Commanding Officer had to take full responsibility. Since Harley knew the facts and should have refuted Evans' charge, Richardson suspected him of complicity with Evans.[10] He demanded to know which officers were being alluded to, and the identity of the parties making the report. He sent his request through his Brigade Commander to Evans and, of course, received no response.

Sickening of the whole affair he asked for a leave of absence, was refused, then sent in his resignation. Fresh officers were arriving from England so that he felt no compunction about leaving. "I saw it was resolved I should have no release from perpetual espionage, and wilful misconstruction of my motives for

---

[8] Alexander Somerville, *The History of the British Legion..., op. cit., passim.*

[9] *Ibid.*

[10] *Personal Memoirs,* p.92ff. Harley was indicted for peculation in concert with the Paymaster of the 4th Reg. and dismissed from the Legion.

[11] *Ibid.,* p.96.

action."[11] He stayed in Spain to observe military manoeuvres, because, he explained, he felt it incumbent upon himself to report the state of the war for the British public.[12]

Although it was customary for officers to retain their quarters until they had passage for England, Evans sent La Saussaye to inform Richardson to get out of his billet in town. Richardson had been waiting some time to even things with La Saussaye whom he suspected of spying on him at Passages, and this incident of the billet whetted his temper. That very day the officers of the 4th were giving a dinner for the Commandant. Richardson had not been successful in eliciting from Harley the names of those officers who had given the false report on the behaviour of the 4th. After the dinner and the departure of the guests, Richardson chatting with his fellow officers, turned suddenly to Harley and demanded to know the author of the slanders upon them. Harley tried to evade the question, but Richardson held him to the subject until he admitted it was La Saussaye. The next day Richardson sent a note to La Saussaye accusing him of the slander and naming MacIntosh as an accomplice. He wanted La Saussaye to admit his guilt, or he would lay the whole charge before the Lieutenant-General. But Evans, claiming that Richardson had called La Saussaye a coward during the regimental dinner, sent the Chief of the Quarter-Master-General's Department to challenge Richardson on La Saussaye's behalf.

When he arrived on the sands of San Sebastian with his second, he found La Saussaye surrounded by members of the clique who, Richardson insisted, had to leave the immediate area before he dueled. A number of townspeople had also gathered to watch from the glacis in the distance. He and La Saussaye stepped forward with the count to wheel and fire, but the soft sand, ankle deep, caused them to slip as they shot. After

several attempts and a change of pistols, it was obvious that no harm would be done by this method — prearranged by the seconds. Richardson volunteered that La Saussaye was not a coward since he was duelling at that very moment, but La Saussaye who at first demanded an unconditional withdrawal of all Richardson's assertions finally accepted Richardson's apology. As they walked from the sands, the clique ran toward them — "they threw away the ends of their cigars — bit their lips through mortified spleen, and surrounding and questioning their champion, rode sullenly back into the town. 'Sic transit gloria duellae'," wrote Richardson.[13]

One hour later, as he was resting in his posada, Richardson received a challenge from MacIntosh, co-author of the slanders. The clique was still trying to make the affair private to escape public inspection. When Richardson demanded that Harley immediately make an investigation, MacIntosh confessed to Harley that his accusation of cowardice had been intended for an officer other than Richardson. This officer requested a Court of Inquiry, at which the officer was acquitted and MacIntosh reprimanded.

When no official notice was taken of MacIntosh's guilt (in the eyes of an officer defamation was a crime of the lowest sort), Richardson wrote to Chichester asking if the transcript of the trial had been sent through to Evans. Chichester replied that it had, but also implied that nothing was likely to be done. A few

[12] *Movements...*, p.268.

[13] *Personal Memoirs*, p.105. Evans seemed to use his officers as surrogates against Richardson. Another source, unconnected with the Legion of Spain, commented about Evans: "...he seems to have a *penchant* for dueling. I have often seen him ... go out of his way, when personal altercations were going on in the House of Commons, in order that he might stand a chance of receiving a challenge." (James Grant, *Random Recollections of the House of Commons...*, Philadelphia; Cary and Hart, 1836, pp.134-5). The aggressiveness, then, was not all on Richardson's part.

days later Captain MacIntosh was appointed Deputy-Quarter-Master-General and soon afterward obtained his Majority.

Richardson continued to keep his journal to reflect the change in his views about Evans and the Legion. Maria was with him: "...he is to be seen walking about every day with his wife, supposed to be picking up materials for his second volume," wrote one of his detractors.[14]

Aside from articles of pungent satire about the Legion which he wrote anonymously for London periodicals,[15] Richardson was easily recognized as the author of a letter signed "Quiz" to the *United Service Gazette*:[16]

> Gents — Nothing of moment has taken place . . . You know, of course, that General Shaw has left in high dudgeon. Some verses of a ludicrous kind have been circulated here among the officers, in which the quarrel is described as a "grand fracas betwixt Tweedle-dum and Tweedle-dee." . . .
> Some one facetiously asked if it was in conse-

quence of its being the General's birthday that his long brevet had appeared, as he seemed anxious to assume to himself a king's prerogative. The fact is, it was done with a view to bring over General Shaw's friends to his own side . . .
> The circumstances of Herman's introduction to the Legion was owing to his being a *so-much-a-line writer* for the *Courier* newspaper, to which publication he has contributed all the eulogistic papers you have seen in that journal, as connected with the Lieut-General . . .
> . . . the whole of the riband for May 5th has been monopolized by the Adjutant-General, who swears that no officer shall wear it until he has admonished the natives with it himself for a short time. He intends leaving it off when it becomes more common . . .

It led to the "affair of the Spanish Club." Some Legion officers on forming a club insisted that Richardson join it. It was not to his taste:

> Certainly nothing less resembled a place appropriated to gentlemen. The coarse card tables were without cloths, and the players had even their hats on — la cigarre en bouche — and a glass of brandy at their elbow, while to crown it all, the waiters were permitted to remain in the room, and in the most familiar manner to overlook the players.[17]

But since the evenings were long and lonely, and he enjoyed a good game of cards, he went again to the Club on November 4. As he stood with some officers near the fire, the head-waiter addressed him rudely. Richardson threatened to throw him out the window. In his account of the episode Richardson did not say

---

[14] "Letter to the Editor...Veritas (viz: Le Marchant)" *United Service Gazette* (Oct. 29, 1836). It is not likely that Richardson was preparing the second edition of his *Journal* in the three and one-half months he remained in Spain; it would have taken him less than a week to do. Rather he was surveying the terrain in order to describe the battles of Wellington's troops for his *Peninsular War* (London: 1837). A copy of this book has yet to be found; Morley thinks it a mistake for the *Journal*. Palau, *Manual del librero hispano-americano*, 16 (Barcelona: 1964) 492; Jaime del Burgo, *Bibliographia de las guerras carlistas y de las luchas politicas del siglo XIX...*3 (Pamplona: 1955) 437.

[15] "Letter to the Editor...'A Friend to Truth'" *United Service Journal*, 21 (Aug. 1836) 554-6.

[16] *United Service Gazette* (Oct. 1, 1836). "Quiz" also wrote "Maxims for Officers Joining the British Legion," *Personal Memoirs*, pp.i-iv.

[17] *Personal Memoirs*, p.117.

what started the argument: his enemies claimed that he refused to pay for a pack of cards. Colonel Sloane, President of the Club Committee, took the waiter's side, much to the astonishment of Richardson and his friends, and demanded that Richardson leave.

The stage was set for another battle. Richardson went to his lodgings, dashed of a note of resignation from the Club and returning, set it on the reading-room table. That very evening placards were put in the streets calling all club members to a general meeting the next day.

About fifty officers mostly Portugese, who, Richardson claimed, had never served in the military prior to joining the Legion, rejected Richardson's notice of resignation, then proceeded to try him in absentia so that they could kick him out. Two friends objected on grounds that Richardson was not present to defend himself. But every other vote passed a resolution stating:

> that his conduct last night was such as to outrage the feeling of the members, being a breach of the regulations of the Club—that his subscription be returned to him, and his name erased from the list of members of the Club.

The officers of the 6th Regiment threatened to horse-whip him. Their anger was fuelled by Richardson's rejection of Colonel Ross, their Commanding Officer, as unworthy to be received when he came to Richardson's lodgings with a challenge note from Sloane because Richardson had called Sloane "no gentleman." Fortunately, a friend of Richardson's won apologies from both sides. But the clique had achieved what it wanted, namely, the humiliation of Richardson and this it intended to have printed in the London papers.

The weather was stormy. No ships were leaving port. Richardson stayed in his posada until, fed up with the threats, he put on his pistols and went into the streets. Some officers jeered at him, but they did not attack him. Richardson believed that if they had, Evans would have supported them.

As the days dragged on and he could not find passage out of the country, he suspected that Evans was holding him again. On November 12 he addressed a bitterly sarcastic letter to Evans, thanking him for "all the goodness and loving kindness," and enclosing an account of the heavy sums which Evans had been pocketing monthly. According to Richardson the account had been given him for publication in England by an officer close to Evans.

This staff officer's willingness to expose Evans is an indication of deep dissatisfaction with Evans' administration of the Legion. Evans had sent Gaspard Le-Marchant to England the day after the Spanish Club affair "to state plainly to the British Government that unless we (the Legion) have their guarantee for pay, arrears, gratuity, and above all for the pension to the wounded men, it would be necessary to withdraw the Legion."[18] LeMarchant did not return to Spain; and some months later Evans wrote to Villiers: "I am told Brigadier-General LeMarchant (of whose riddance from this force I am very glad) has been passing his high censures on my conduct as a Commander — but I hope his good judgement, experience and capability to do so will be duly appreciated."[19]

In response to Richardson's letter, Evans allowed the Richardsons to embark for France on November 16.

Richardson invited the four Clubmen, who had signed the resolution to expel him, to Bayonne where they could duel without interruption, but when after three days none of them arrived and the wind changed,

[18] Diary, Nov. 6, 1836, Chichester Papers, *op.cit.*
[19] ALS, Evans to Villiers, April 10, 1837, Villiers Papers c461.

hindering ships from sailing, Richardson left word that they would find him in Bordeaux.

Unfinished Business

BORDEAUX was a grand showcase of architecture with beautiful churches and remnants of Roman sculpture. Its women colourfully dressed, carried baskets and amphoras on their heads which displayed their elegant forms.

A book about the Basques, *Essai historique sur les provinces basques (Alava, Guipuzcoa, Biscaye et Navarre) et sur la guerre dont elles sont le theatre,* was published anonymously in Bordeaux two or three months earlier.[1] Recognizing its timeliness for the English, Richardson began to translate it. The Basques, as presented in the book, seemed ideal; they had a strong sense of individuality and a concept of justice and fairness unknown in other parts of the world; England was even then legislating on some freedoms which the Basques had always enjoyed. The new mercantile society in Spain, however, threatened to end these traditions and the prosperity of their lands.

The author was the Comte de Boislecomte, brilliant French Ambassador to the Ottoman Empire, who was in temporary retirement in Bordeaux. Had Richardson the good fortune to meet him he would have found this scholar most interesting upon another subject: the Middle Ages and the knights who journeyed from Spain through the castled regions of Périgord and the Dordogne, north to Clermont and Orléans. These regions, among the most beautiful in Europe, still harboured many chateaux from the Middle Ages standing on rocky precipices overlooking twisting rivers and valleys. Either Boislecomte or some knowledgeable resident told Richardson the story of the Castle of Cordes in that mountainous country which was once called Ricordane.[2]

Richardson wanted to see the chateau. Maria went on to Amiens and Richardson set out along the banks of the Dordogne River in mid-December with, as he described it, "a gun on my shoulder, and a bottle of the best cognac of the Hotel de Lille in the side pockets of my shooting jacket."[3] Freed from the interminable quarrels of the Legionnaires, he hunted for his food and relaxed in the comforting silence of nature.

The Romans had called Orcival, the village in the valley below Cordes, the valley of hell for some obscure religious reason, but the Virgin had ruled there since the early Middle Ages. The giant wooden carving of Mary, which still stands in the ancient church, dominated the life of the region. Richardson climbed the road to the chateau and stepped into its great cobble-stoned lane under soaring trees. The magnificent turreted structure bordered on a forest that swept semicircularly round its wings. Two large gardens, with a cascading fountain in the centre of each, lay on either side of the lane. A coat of arms on the wooden door spoke of its chivalric past. But no one answered his knock. He wandered about the grounds until he chan-

---

[1] Charles Joseph Edmund, Comte de Boislecomte, *Essai historique sur les provinces basques* (Alava, Guipuzcou, Biscaye et Navarre) et sur la guerre dont elles sont le theatre (Bordeaux: R. Teycheney, E. Lalouberse, C. Dulac, 1836), 361p.

[2] Boislecomte was made French Ambassador to Spain that autumn, but he did not take up his post in Madrid until the beginning of the new year.

[3] *The Monk Knight of St. John,* p.3.

ced upon the gameskeeper, a friendly old fellow, who, charmed by his interest, told him that the owner lived in Paris but that he was welcome to remain as a guest. The gameskeeper produced a parchment relating the history of the chateau. Richardson read it late into the night. In this manner, he introduced his historical novel about the crusades, *The Monk Knight of St. John*, which he wrote more than a decade later. That there really was such a parchment is doubtful, but that Richardson stayed overnight in the Castle and was deeply impressed by its ancient character should not be doubted.[4]

The following day he took a coach to meet Maria in Amiens. Together they reached their home on Bloomsbury Square in time to celebrate the New Year of 1837.

Not until they went to Chatham, to stay at her father's home where the family had moved on Drayson's retirement in 1835, did he learn that a letter had been printed in the *United Service Gazette* which told of his expulsion from the Spanish Club. The letter identified him as "Major Richardson of écarté notoriety."[5]

Richardson replied deftly turning the meaning away from his notoriety at cards: "If by this your correspondent means that I am the author of a book so called, unwilling as I have hitherto been to identify myself publicly with any work, I cannot deny 'the sweet

Cordes, 1965.

implication'." He promised to publish "an *exposé* of General Evans' tyranny, oppression and injustice, as will with difficulty be credited by his favouring 'independent electors of Westminster' to whom it is intended to be inscribed."[6]

The *Gazette* editors who were under the impres-

---

[4] The author of this biography and his wife searched for the chateau in the summer of 1965. Richardson had not recorded its name. The only facts available to the author were that the chateau was eleventh or twelfth century, it was three leagues from Clermont and it bordered on a forest that swept semi-circularly round its wings towards the front. A league may be interpreted as three or four miles. There are many chateaux in and around Clermont, but the period of the architecture and the semicircular forest clearly distinguished this particular chateau which the author discovered after a good deal of driving along back country roads near Clermont. It was bolted and deserted but the carved crest of arms still

emblazoned the weather-beaten door. The fountains still cascaded in the gardens overgrown with weeds, and a shed beyond the coach-house harbored piles of empty wine bottles. There was no groundsman to welcome the author and his wife, only a faded sign on a small wooden booth at the gate which listed the price and hours of tours, a memento from a previous occupant in a vain attempt to attract sightseers. Somehow the author was grateful to have found it uninhabited as Richardson had a century ago, rather than as a spectacle at five francs per person.

[5] *United Service Gazette* (Dec. 3, 1836).

[6] *United Service Gazette* (Jan. 21, 1837).

sion that Richardson had "thrown the first stone" in this Legion "squabble" were quickly persuaded by Richardson that he was "more sinned against than sinning." They warned: "From what we know of his talents, his assailants will find that they have caught a Tartar."[7]

Richardson discovered that Kirby, the officer who had proposed the motion to expel him from the Spanish Club, was in London. He sent accusatory letters about Kirby to the *Gazette* but its editors refused to print them: "We have something better to occupy our columns than . . . the personal squabbles and acrimonious recriminations of the disputants of the Anglo-Spanish Legion."[8] Kirby agreed to meet him with pistols at Chalk Farm. Richardson's friend in the affair wisely persuaded Kirby to write that he was merely following General Chichester's lead and did not understand the serious nature of expelling a member from a Club. The *Gazette* reported on the settlement, but still refused to take sides.[9]

At Chatham the genial Drayson and his houseful of young daughters restored Richardson's good temper. Unfortunately Mrs. Drayson was seriously ill and Maria had to care for her large brood of young brothers and sisters until Mrs. Drayson died in April, when the family broke up.

Richardson arranged for the printing of the second edition of the *Journal* to be called, *Movements of the British Legion, with strictures on the course of conduct pursued by Lieutenant-General Evans*.[10] It marked the first time he put his name to a published work. Appearing in April 1837, *Movements* was reviewed in magazines and newspapers throughout the country. The Tories

referred to it in the Commons to attack the Whig Government which defended Evans.

Hardinge, a leading Tory, referred to *Movements* in the Commons debate on Spain in April. The Whigs replied to the charges of mutiny and low morale cited by Richardson by attacking Richardson's character. A letter from Charles Shaw was read stating that Richardson's fellow officers declined to serve with him.[11] Captain Henry George Boldero, a friend of twenty-two years standing, vouched for Richardson's character and defended him against the charge of cowardice by reading the verdict of the Court of Inquiry clearing him.[12] Daniel O'Connell, the Irish firebrand, said that owing to Richardson's behaviour at an Officer's Club, no officer would sit at the same table with him. Boldero cried that O'Connell had "grossly, outrageously and wickedly calumniated" Richardson. General Hardinge rose to say that he had enquired into the character and background of Richardson and found them such that he could believe Richardson's assertions. This statement, coming from one of the first gentlemen in the country, could not be doubted. Boldero closed the dispute by emphasizing that Richardson, in praising the bravery of the Legion, regretted the system of taking no prisoners, and by quoting Richardson: " 'But,' said the gallant officer with great energy, 'if I saw a man before me who would stick me through and show me no mercy, by George I'd do the same myself' (Cheers and laughter)."[13] Enthusiastically Richardson wrote the *Times* on April 22: "I beg to take

---

[7] *United Service Gazette* (Jan. 28, 1837).

[8] *United Service Gazette* (Feb. 11, 1837).

[9] *United Service Gazette* (March 4, 1837).

[10] *Literary Gazette*, No.1015 (July 2, 1836), p.420, noted Richardson as author of the *Journal*.

[11] Great Britain, Parliament, *Debates and Proceedings*, 37 (April 19, 1837) 1329ff. Shaw was referring to the letter written by the Captain (Calder) of the 6th Reg. stating that the officers did not regard Richardson as one of them because of what he had written about the regiment. Shaw, of course, blamed the whole dispute on Richardson, whose "irregular service" seemed to make him inferior in judgement and forgetful of proper army decorum.

[12] *Ibid.* (April 19, 1837).

this public opportunity of expressing to Sir Henry Hardinge and Captain Boldero, the deep and heartfelt gratitude I must ever owe them for the truly noble and gallant manner in which they have rescued my fair name from the abyss in which it has been sought to engulf it."[14]

At this point the *Gazette* admitted: "It is clear that Major Richardson has suffered considerable persecution at the hands of General Evans and his friends, for having written an account of the Legion not sufficiently *couleur de rose* to satisfy those gentlemen. . ."[15]

The excitement was too much. Richardson suffered a relapse of typhoid fever and was unable to answer Hardinge's letter asking for details of the inhuman treatment shown to prisoners. Hardinge was not concerned about the injustices in the Legion. He explained his position to one of his colleagues: "My object was to shew the ferocity with which the War was carried on by both parties and thus to compel the Government to abandon so vicious a system of making war."[16] On May 17 Richardson wrote to Hardinge explaining that he had been sick for three weeks and was too feeble to write more.[17] On the same day the *Times* carried an article by "Major Richardson, K.S.F." entitled "History of the Manners, Customs and Privileges of the Basque Provinces from the earliest ages (Compiled from Authentic Documents with Notes on the Causes of the Present War)."[18] It was a direct translation of the first fifty-five pages of Boislecomte's book. The following day a friend of Shaw's, who had recently been in Bordeaux, wrote to the editor that

Richardson was passing off a translation as his original work.[19] Richardson, denying it, wrote that the facts were taken from many sources.[20] This barefaced lie was not apparent to people in England who had little opportunity of purchasing the book. Hardinge clipped the article and the ensuing correspondence from the *Times* and kept it with his papers. On May 20, Richardson wrote him a fifteen page letter answering his questions.[21]

Richardson, although supported by the Tories in Parliament, had already requested the Whig government for help in starting a newspaper in Upper Canada to support the political interests of the mother country,[22] and for a position "under the Crown." When he wrote his public thanks to Hardinge and Boldero, he may have felt uncomfortable, for he added: "Sir Henry Hardinge has inferred from the book I have written that I am a Liberal. I feel that I am too humble an individual to be of any political party."[23]

His younger brother, Charles, was encouraging him to establish a conservative newspaper in Canada to fight the vociferous Radicals. Charles, as a member of the House of Assembly in Toronto, saw the efforts of

---

[13] *Ibid.* Britain, Parliament, *Debates and Proceedings, op.cit.*

[14] *Times* (April 22, 1837).

[15] *United Service Gazette* (April 29, 1837).

[16] ALS, Hardinge to Lord Ebington, Whitehall Place, May 2, 1837, Hardinge Papers.

[17] ALS, Richardson to Hardinge, London, May 17, 1837, Hardinge Papers.

[18] *Times* (May 17, 1837).

[19] *Times* (May 18, 1837).

[20] *Times* (May 19, 1837). Richardson admitted a debt to the *Essai Historique* as one of his sources. At this moment when his character was being questioned in the House of Commons, even the smallest admission of deceit could take on unnatural proportions for political reasons. I have surmised that Richardson met the Baron de Boislecomte, and now surmise that he respected the Baron's need for anonymity, particularly important when in the diplomatic service. In this connection it is interesting to note that Richardson named a protagonist in *The Monk Knight* the Baron de Boiscourt, which is close to Boislecomte.

[21] ALS, Richardson to Hardinge, May 20, 1837, Hardinge Papers.

[22] ALS, Richardson to Lord Glenelg, March 22, 1837, Public Archives of Canada Q ser. MG11, Vol. 401, p.2.

[23] *Times* (April 22, 1837).

Canadian Radicals to effect reforms as an attempt to unite Canada with the United States. He had articled in the conservative atmosphere of Chief Justice Beverley Robinson's law office. In 1826, then 21 years old, he broke into William Lyon Mackenzie's home in Toronto with a handful of prominent citizens, smashed Mackenzie's printing press and dumped his type into Lake Ontario.[24] Mackenzie, made of stubborn stuff, got a new press, entered politics and won a fair-sized following. It was not surprising therefore that the Conservatives needed someone like Richardson who could reply to the fiery journalism of Mackenzie and his radical followers.

Richardson, absent from Canada for over twenty years, had not seen the poverty of the Canadians who were badly neglected by the British Government and the abuses of Church and officialdom upon the land. He had to rely solely on occasional letters from his brother and English newspaper accounts, which inevitably represented the Radicals as disturbers of law and order and advocates of American republican principles.

"I am myself a Canadian by birth," he wrote to Lord Palmerston "and as such deeply interested in the welfare of the Provinces which I esteem to be dependent on their continued union with the mother country. . ."[25]

With hopes for an appointment in Upper Canada, Richardson settled down with Maria to enjoy the fashionable life in London. An adaptation of Theodore Hook's recent comic novel, *Jack Brag*, opened at the St. James Theatre on May 23. It was merely an incident from Hook's novel which told of the social climbing of a young chandler into the ranks of high London society, who finally became disillusioned, fell deeply in debt, and enlisted in the British Auxiliary Legion as Acting-Assistant-Deputy-Assistant-Commissary-General. Richardson was inspired to write a sequel, *Jack Brag in Spain*. Its characters were easily recognizable as officers in the British Legion. Jack Brag was LeMarchant. Don Lasho, the Commander of the Legion, was unmistakably Evans. Reid was caricatured as Brigadier Stick, who was continually consulting his drill manual. Shaw was Brigadier Wash, whose face was barely visible behind his bristling red beard. The amusing incidents were drawn to show the disorganization and jealous innuendos throughout the force. A sample paragraph illustrates its humour:

Meanwhile Don Lasho had worked himself into what Jack called a fit of the dumps, occasioned partly through the conduct of Cordova (who he now felt persuaded, instead of advancing his interests with the Queen Mother, was rather inclined to "sell" him to the enemy) partly through his inability to prosecute his customary reconnaissances, to which hobby he was quite as much devoted as Brigadier Stick was to any in his way — and also in some degree from the apprehension he began to entertain that he might be cut off by fever, before he could accomplish any of those stupendous movements by which he hoped to immortalize himself. True, there was the glorious affair of Arlaban, but what was one victory, even sweet and romantic sounding as that last named, to one of his ardent temperament? Psha, a mere flea bite, giving him a greater taste for blood than ever. Be that as it may however, Don Lasho did most hermetically shut himself up in his private apartments, surrounded with pen, ink, and paper, and scarcely deigning to hold communion even with his Aides — his favourite Brag not excepted.[26]

---

[24] *Elgin-Grey Papers*, III, 1054.

[25] ALS, Richardson to Lord Glenelg, *op.cit.*

[26] *The New Era* (Jan. 26, 1842).

While Richardson wrote, the Legion was disbanded in Spain. Evans returned to England in June and prepared to defend himself in the Commons. The soldiers were supposedly paid, though stories were told in the Commons of hundreds of destitute men, barely clad, deserted in the towns of Spain without transportation home. Many officers also went without pay or gratuity and insisted that Evans represent their cause in Parliament, which Evans just as insistently refused to do. The many accounts of the indiscriminate floggings, the barbarism shown prisoners, all the charges brought against Evans by those who had left the Legion were said in sum to his face in Parliamentary debate and published in the newspapers. He belittled them all, and with the backing of the Government, survived the criticism.

Some officers stayed in Spain and formed a second Legion by recruiting soldiers from England as well as those who did not return. La Saussaye became its Commander. MacIntosh, who still intrigued with La Saussaye, this time to drive a popular young officer of the Artillery out of the new Legion,[27] was made a Colonel and appointed Artillery Commander. Colonel Ross became a staff officer, and Fred Clark, promoted to Colonel, took the post of Assistant Quarter-Master-General. This Legion was massacred at Andoain in the fall.

Its sad fate darkened the mood of the English public. Some may have regarded a humourous book about the Legionnaires in bad taste, though this was probably not the reason why Richardson could not find a publisher. He sent the completed manuscript to Theodore Hook who wrote to Bentley, his publisher:

I send you herewith a novel of a novel character, which I think would make a hit if done directly...

the characters introduced are portraits and blended with the humourous parts would no doubt be very attractive. Its correctness geographically is unquestionable, its being from the pen of an officer of the Legion itself; I believe you are acquainted with the author's name through other works — Major Richardson — I wish you would look over it and the sooner you come to a decision the better, as Major Richardson leaves England on the 20th.[28]

Richardson was expecting to leave for Canada as special correspondent to the *Times* on Canadian affairs.

Bentley said that the characters were too easy to identify in real life. Hook tried to get the price of copyright for the book from Colburn as well, but received the same reply. Obviously the characters were thinly disguised, but in 1837 this was no matter for libel charges. Most likely Richard Barham had been the publisher's reader and rejected the manuscript; he hinted at this in his biography of Hook: "... the vicissitudes of the Spanish Legion would, in the hands of the gallant eyewitness, supply ample materials for a very entertaining work, we have no doubt; but our protest has already been entered against [sequels]."[29]

The winter of 1837/38 was particularly severe in London. The Thames was frozen solid when the Richardsons were scheduled to embark. Their ship, the *SS Ontario*, could not push downstream through the ice. Departure was expected momentarily, as a slight thaw would be sufficient to get the ship far enough downstream into the stronger current. Isaac D'Israeli, the author, and father of Benjamin, came in from the country to say good-bye; it was his old home on Bloomsbury Square which the Richardsons were renting.[30] At the end of the year, the Richardsons moved into the man-

---

[27] Alexander Ball, *A personal narrative of seven years in Spain* (London: J. Chappell, 1846), p.212.

[28] R.H.D. Barham, *The Life and Remains of Theodore Edward Hook*. rev.ed. (London: Bentley, 1853), p.202.
[29] *Ibid*.

101

sion of Lady Shrewsbury.

The atmosphere of the Regency had lingered on through the reigns of George III's sons, but now a commercial, bourgeois element of restraint seemed to have taken over society. A new group of merchants, enriched in the aftermath of the Napoleonic Wars, guardedly moved into prominence. Richardson sensed that the world of the gentleman was adopting new values which he could not accept; he felt it encouraged hypocrisy by allowing the individual to place legal contracts before his honour.[31] Moreover, all the action was in the colonies. His intention to set up a newspaper press in Canada indicates that he had chosen to settle there, but not forever. Maria, when she left her family, expected to see it again in a few years.[32]

Richardson, in preparation for his assignment, made himself thoroughly familiar with Canadian affairs. Alarmed about the poor state of the military he wrote a long letter under the pseudonym of "Nemo" to the *Morning Post*[33] in which he berated Parliament for adjourning for three weeks when it appeared that Canada was in imminent danger of invasion from the United States: "What Sir, are the members of the Houses of Lords and Commons schoolboys, that they must enjoy their terms of holiday, merely because it is their privilege?" He called for the immediate sending of troops from England on a large scale to reinforce the regiments in Canada, "principally rifles, to suit the nature of Canadian warfare." He warned that if the revolutionists were joined by the American backwoodsmen "whom I know from experience to be the very best guerillas in the world," Canada would be lost without the support of the Indians. Identifying himself as a Canadian, he opposed independence for Canada. "In the breast of no man on God's earth glows the spirit of independence more fervently than in my own, and yet were the whole of Canada — my own native land — ungratefully to spurn from her the parent that has nurtured her into life and prosperity, I should be one of the first to repudiate her."

In spite of his alarming cry for troop reinforcements, Richardson was appalled by the members of ex-British Legion officers who were being sent to Canada. A week later he commented to the *Morning Post*[34] on a meeting of Legion officers at Peel's Coffee House for organizing a militia in Canada: ". . . such a step would rather injure than benefit the cause, as independently of the fact of the Canadian Loyalists having no desire to see other than the regular troops of the mother country quartered upon them, very many of these "ever-ready" applicants would be more fitted to create disturbances than to quell them." The *Morning Post* published another letter from "Nemo" and the enclosed first chapter of *Wacousta* under the column title "Geographical Sketch of Canada"[35] communicating Richardson's anxiety that the English realize what a magnificent territory they possessed.

In the early morning of February 18, after they

---

[30] David Lester Richardson, *Literary Chit-Chat* (London: J. Madden, 1848), pp.147-8. Letter from Isaac D'Israeli to D.L. Richardson, Feb. 4, 1839: "...rec'd a year passed, your very acceptable *Literary Leaves*... I am very rarely in London, — but I remember calling on Mr. John Richardson to acknowledge the receipt of your volume, and, as he was in communication with you, to send, through him, the letter I intended to write." A plaque marks D'Israeli's residence at 6 Bloomsbury Square.

[31] Richardson gives his views on this question in his *The Guards in Canada*.

[32] The Richardsons had every reason to expect that the *Times* would pay for their return passage after Richardson's assignment was concluded. But in this they were to be disappointed.

[33] *Morning Post* (Dec. 28, 1837).

[34] Letter to the Editor from "A British Half-Pay Officer," *Morning Post* (Jan. 2, 1838).

[35] *Morning Post* (Jan. 3, 1838).

had returned from a fancy dress ball and fallen asleep, Maria awoke with a start and shook Richardson. She had a psychic premonition of their ship leaving the port.[36] Unable to dissuade her, Richardson dressed, and yawning, braved the cold night air with the determined Maria. At the dock where their luggage was stored, they learned that the ship's Captain had no intention of embarking. Richardson had just begun to poke fun at Maria's clairvoyance when they received orders to load their luggage immediately, as the SS Ontario was taking advantage of a thaw to get downriver.

Richardson was seasick for most of the 35 day voyage. The entrance into the New York harbour surprised him by its openness and cleanness which he contrasted to London's raucous docks crawling with the poor.

The Richardsons stayed at the best hotel, the Carleton on Broadway, the fashionable section where everyone of distinction lodged. New York with its cobbled main streets, flagged sidewalks, wells at every alternate corner and beautiful natural surroundings was one of the prettiest cities of the world. The clean sweep of the shores of Bay Ridge leading to distant Brooklyn and the lower shores of New Jersey gradually rising to the Heights, and the Orange mountains with the villages of Communipaw and Jersey City above it, acted as a background to the bright grass and trees of the Battery. The range of houses and tree-lined avenues stretched through twentieth street and past the farms and isolated homes which lay beyond.

Since the Times was one of two giant newspapers which molded British opinion, Richardson had a great opportunity to serve the cause of justice for Canada with fair reporting. He signed his despatches "Inquisitor" which indicated his intention to inquire into and report on the facts. But until he arrived in Canada he fed his readers' prejudices.

Mackenzie is here, seeking to extricate himself from the almost utter ruin in which his mad and impotent career of treason has involved him, by having recourse to his old weapon — the pen. The ex-speaker Bidwell and Dr. Rolfe are also here; and yet, with all these colossi of mind within their city, the people of New York absolutely eat and drink and perform their customary avocations as though insensible of a more than ordinary visitation.[37]

Since the roads were muddy, Maria stayed behind until travel was easier in the warmer weather. Taking a steamer up the Hudson River to Albany, and the railroad to Utica, Richardson passed the first part of his journey comfortably. At this point he transferred to stagecoach and encountered the system of American free enterprise.

The Yankee coachman insisted that only a certain amount of baggage could be carried in proportion to the amount of seating space purchased. In order to accomodate all his luggage, Richardson had to buy all the seats in the coach. The idea of a coach to himself was appealing, so he paid the Yankee and sat inside. Presently a troop of heavy men clambered into the coach and sat in all the remaining places which Richardson had purchased. The driver would not listen to Richardson's arguments, but collected fares from each of the gentlemen. Richardson began to understand what it was to be at the mercy of the money-wise Yankees, so well described by that humourous Nova Scotian, Haliburton, whose Sam Slick stories had travelled the English-speaking world.

On the road to Syracuse, the mud was so deep that the driver asked the passengers to get out and walk for short distances, which Richardson, still sulking, refused to do. He was damned if he was going to walk

---

[36] Eight Years in Canada, p.6-7.

[37] Times (April 30, 1838).

beside the coach he had paid to carry him. Finally when it was late in the night and they seemed to be making no progress in the darkness, he got out with the others and immediately lost his boot in the mud. He searched about for it, feeling along his track, but the darkness was so opaque and the mud so thick that he had to give up all thought of finding it. He trudged on alone for hours until he came to an inn where the other passengers were waiting. He was a sorry sight, covered with mud, minus a boot and exhausted. It was dawn. Turning to look down the road, he saw the stage-coach about a quarter of a mile away. He realized with a stiff upper lip that he had walked in circles with one boot off for most of the night. But the coach was truly unworthy; it had gone fifty miles in twenty-five hours. Hereafter the roads were better and travel swifter.

Along the way he gauged the views of the people upon the Canadian rebellions and found that sympathy was confined almost completely to the lower classes, who formed meetings in towns along the frontier: "among whom, as in all other countries, there were to be found plenty of needy adventurers, both ready and eager to embark in any contest, however unjust, which promised a change in their social condition."[38] In Rochester, he learned that the English-hating Mayor, and his corporation, supported by a violent press, had fanned the citizens to a state of excitement. The citizens of Buffalo marched in a show of enmity and called upon the Rochester folk to join them in an invasion of Canada. They had not forgiven the Canadians for burning their village in the 1812 War. The canals were frozen, therefore many were unemployed and ready to war under the patriotic banner. The Canadian forts were in ruins without a workable gun. Invasion appeared easy, except for one thing: "the Rochester heroes could not muster more than a dozen rusty old muskets, and without arms

an expedition of the kind might be attended by some risk and inconvenience."[39] To add to the difficulties, General Winfield Scott was sent by the U.S. Government to quell their enthusiasm.

The utter desolation of the Canadian forts gave Richardson his first shock. When he looked across the Niagara from Lewiston he saw signs of the ragged living which Canadians endured. He took a ferry across the river where Charles welcomed him into his home in Niagara. He admired his younger brother, brown-skinned like himself, dark-eyed, and clever, who at age 32 had accomplished a great deal.

Charles Richardson fulfilled predictions that he would make a good lawyer. He had a reputation for excellence as a public officer, for gentlemanliness, for strong intellect, noble feelings and quick perception. He was a good public speaker. He also had faults, the major one being his intolerance of anyone who did not agree with his political views. This particular failing earned him many unnecessary enemies and provided his older brother with ready-made opponents whom he could well have done without. During his tenure at the Legislature in Toronto, Charles mailed his shirts home for laundering, a habit he could not overcome from his parsimonious days. The Radical papers used it to make him the butt of public ridicule. His first wife having died in childbirth, he married again and had children, who now doubtless were awed by the visit of their famous uncle.

There was plenty to talk about. Charles was nine when Richardson last saw him. The family, scattered in the western end of the province, had suffered tragedies and disappointments not least of which was the death of their brother, Robert, from tuberculosis in 1819.

Forming a party Charles took him to see Niagara Falls, which did not impress him, for he had always

---

[38] *Ibid.* (May 17, 1838).

[39] *Ibid.*

imagined it was grander. His disappointment was sharpened when he witnessed the idleness of many of the citizens and the large number of taverns which kept them in long periods of stupefaction. It was very well to speak of the wonders of nature, but what wonders had the people created? — none! The British Government was largely to blame. Pitt had surrendered the island of Montreal to the Lower Canadians, thereby depriving Upper Canada of a port of entry. English immigration was discouraged by the French, and surprisingly by the British Government as well. The clergy reserves, politically supported by the Family Compact rulers, broke up the land so as to isolate settlers from one another. All large landholders whose greatest wish was to open the country to settlement were doomed to become "land poor" waiting for government policy to change. Indeed the country was in need of reform.

Richardson despatched an article to the *Times* in which he said he was going right away to Toronto to see the hangings of Matthews and Lount, who had just been convicted of treason. It seemed that many respectable people were implicated in the rebellion and had fled the city. But his next published account reported the anger of the citizenry that an American called Theller was not given the death sentence. Theller had led a band of patriots across the Detroit River to Amherstburg. When he was cannonading the town, the wind blew his ship almost into the arms of angry Canadians on shore, among whom was Richardson's young half-brother, Henry Wellington Richardson, who, Richardson proudly reported, personally captured Theller.[40]

While in Toronto Richardson sent a letter of introduction to the Lieutenant-Governor of Upper Canada, Sir George Arthur. Arthur was trying to get the economy running. No politician, but a practical man of

Charles Richardson, ca. 1830, by Grove Gilbert (painting in the possession of Miss Elida Clench, St. Catharines, Ont.)

experience with a fine sense of humanity (he had fought against slavery and oppression when Governor in Honduras), he had been promised complete control, but he was soon to learn that the forthcoming Governor-General, Lord Durham, had extraordinary powers which impinged on his own. Arthur invited Richardson to dine with his family and would have offered him a government post, if Richardson had not wished to remain with the *Times*.[41]

[40] *Ibid.* (May 24, 1838).

[41] *Eight Years in Canada*, p.27.

View of the harbour, Montreal c.1850.

Returning to Niagara, Richardson met Maria arriving from New York. Then immediately he was off to Montreal by steamer and coach. He left Maria behind with instructions to wait until he sent for her.

Canada's first city was more to his liking. When he arrived in Montreal at the beginning of May the weather was beautiful. The heat of the sun was making itself felt after a cold winter, and the streets became dry. Unfortunately the citizens were tormented every summer by clouds of dust stirred up in the streets. The Macadamized method failed because the stones used for the paving were ground to powder bringing dust to the face and eyes and into the apartments of the town and causing the citizens to complain of bad lungs. An old friend of Richardson's, John Jones, proprietor and editor of a French-language newspaper in

Montreal, *L'Ami du Peuple, de l'Ordre et des Lois*, editorialized angrily about Notre Dame street, where on some days there were lakes of mud in which a regiment of cavalry could be lost, he said, and on dry days there were holes big enough to bury a horse and monstrous stones thrown here and there as if to inconvenience passers-by.

Ever since Jones' newspaper carried a report of the disembarkation of the Richardsons in New York,[42] the nascent literary community in Montreal had been waiting expectantly for the nation's most successful writer. As if announcing his return Richardson had advertised in the Canadian newspapers from Niagara a forthcoming Canadian edition of *Wacousta* and stressed its historical importance to the country.[43] He seemed to be promoting the idea of a national literature which had an immediate effect on a Montreal publisher, John Lovell. In late June, Lovell began to advertise a monthly magazine, *The Literary Garland*, which he hoped would start a native Canadian literature. After the magazine appeared in December it developed into the best of its kind on the continent. To the fourth number Richardson contributed a chapter from his unpublished novel "The Brothers" called "Jeremiah Desborough or the Kentuckian."[44] *L'Ami du Peuple* reviewed the chapter: *"On y trouve tout le faire de Walter Scott, et la maniere de mettre les acteurs en scene est bien superieure à celle de Fenimore Cooper."*[45] In the following number of the *Garland* appeared the chapter entitled, "The Settler."[46] Its editors hoped that his new novel would be published "from a native press setting an ex-

[42] *L'Ami du Peuple*, (Avril 4, 1838).

[43] The prospectus, dated May 15, 1838 at Niagara, offered a "revised Canadian edition" in eight monthly parts at 25 cents each.

[44] *Literary Garland* (March 1839), pp. 181-7.

[45] *L'Ami du Peuple* (Mars 6, 1839).

[46] *Literary Garland* (April 1839), pp.225-31.

[47] *Literary Garland* (March 1839).

ample for other authors,"[47] and expressed concern over the delay in the publication of the Canadian edition of *Wacousta* which they expected would soon be found "in every boudoir from the Atlantic to Lake Erie."[48]

While busy stirring up a new literature with one hand, Richardson occupied the other in politics. He established contacts and set up a network of news runners who brought him the latest developments. One of his contacts would have been Pierre-Edouard Leclère who had founded *L'Ami du Peuple* with Jones and now was the Superintendent of the secret police which kept a close check on seditious activities. The alert Leclère was one of the key reasons for the failure of the uprisings.[49]

Richardson's contacts probably helped him prepare for an important confrontation, although he reported it as accidental.[50] One evening near the end of May while chatting in the lobby of his hotel, he caught sight of a familiar figure — it was Charles Chichester, now a Colonel in the regular army, and passing through Montreal. Richardson had unfinished business with him.

Murdoch Morison, a Montreal lawyer, acted for Richardson in this affair. Chichester refused to apologize for seconding the motion to expel Richardson from the Spanish Club and referred Morison to Colonel Weatherall, Commanding Officer of the British Regiments in Montreal. Although the reports Weatherall received about Richardson brought him to the point of scarcely controlled hostility, he was prepared to negotiate. A statement was prepared admitting that Chichester did not understand why Richardson was expelled from the Club, and that he bore no animosity to Richardson who in his opinion was innocent of the

charges brought against him. Richardson wrote:

> If the energies of the principal player should seem to have been occasionally put forth with a vehemence disproportioned to his subject, let it be recollected, that on the wide stage of action, on which he had been forced, often without study or preparation, he has stood almost alone and unsupported. One false emphasis in his acting, and he must have failed, not only through the glaring disinclination to perform their parts as they ought, of those with whom he had been brought in contact upon the scene, but by the unanimous voice of that most imposing and severe of all audiences — the world.[51]

In retrospect Chichester's attitude to Richardson seemed ambivalent. He visited Richardson when he was ill in Vitoria, and presided at the court-martial which exonerated Richardson, but nowhere in his diaries, which he kept rather conscientiously, did he mention Richardson: as if he were unwilling to leave any record of his association with him.[52]

The Personal Memoirs of Major Richardson, which included Chichester's letter, though advertised in July for publication on September 1, did not appear until September 19. *L'Ami du Peuple* saw it as an object lesson:

> La manière dont l'auteur s'est tiré des positions vraiment difficiles où il s'est trouvé plusieurs fois placé par la malice de ses ennemis et l'injustice

[48] *Literary Garland* (Feb. 1839), p.144.
[49] Richardson mentions his activeness in *Eight Years*, p.58.
[50] *Personal Memoirs*, p.143.
[51] *Ibid.*, p.144.
[52] Chichester Diary, Nov. 6, 1836, Chichester Papers. In the entry for this day Chichester stated that he joined the Legion solely for experience and reputation. Later, while stationed at Lake St. Clair in the backwoods of Ontario, he bewailed that his services were overlooked while Evans, Shaw and Le Marchant were knighted.

de ses supérieures, peut servir d'example et de lécon dans bien des circonstances de la vie surtout de la vie militaire, et montre ce que peut la force d'âme et la fermété.[53]

The *United Service Gazette* commented that it was a mistake: ". . . we assure him that we consider that he has shown very little wisdom in thus endeavouring to perpetuate the recollection of the petty squabbles, and still more despicable intrigues, which appear to have been of such frequent occurrence in the British Legion."[54] Wheatherall wrote to Chichester: "It is impossible to say what lies that man Richardson may have circulated . . . he has made many efforts to get into military society here but has naturally been repulsed... he aims at notoriety, and to answer his book would, I imagine, gratify him much — the fellow is a vulgar charlatan. . ."[55]

For the moment, Richardson took passage for Quebec to report on the arrival of the new Governor-General, the much heralded Lord Durham, with whom rested the hopes of the Canadian people for a united and strong nation.

[53] *L'Ami du Peuple* (Sept. 26, 1838).
[54] *United Service Gazette* (Nov. 24, 1838).
[55] ALS, G.T. Weatherall to Lt.-Col. Chichester, Montreal, Nov. 12, 1838, Chichester Papers. Weatherall's brother was the Paymaster for the British Legion under Evans, a circumstance which may have influenced his judgement of Richardson.

Times Correspondent

AS THE TIMES CORRESPONDENT, Richardson had ready access to Lord Durham who was anxious to use the Tory organ to convey his radical views. Richardson left his card, was invited to a lavish dinner the following Sunday and made the centre of attention while the Governor-General explained his hopes for responsible government in the Canadas. Flattered, Richardson found Durham's frankness stimulating. He soon became a staunch supporter and reported favourably to the *Times* on Durham's assuming temporary control of the Legislative Council in Lower Canada, his banning of rebel leaders to Bermuda, and his arrangements with the United States to prevent invasions of sympathisers over the border.[1]

The *Times*, finding that its editorials criticizing Durham were at odds with the "Inquisitor's" reports, planted a report critical of Durham as if it were by the "Inquisitor,"[2] which upset Durham and embarrassed Richardson. Finally unable to persuade Richardson to desist from eulogizing Durham, the *Times* footnoted one of his despatches: "The writer of these letters is an occasional correspondent; it will be seen that he is a sort

[1] *Times* (June 30, 1838).
[2] *Ibid.* (Aug. 7, 1838).
[3] *Ibid.* (Sept. 18, 1838).

of partisan of Lord Durham."[3] Shortly thereafter, at about the same time that Durham lost all support in the English Parliament, the *Times* notified him that his contract would not be renewed.

An example of how closely Richardson fashioned his articles after Durham's suggestions is seen when a letter to Richardson from Charles Buller, Durham's secretary, dated August 14, 1838, is compared with Richardson's despatch of August 22. "Whatever you say in favour of Lord Durham," wrote Buller, "I think you may satisfy the Toryism of the Editor of the *Times*, by commenting on the weakness and perfidy of the Ministry who understood so little of the policy of their own Governor, in supporting it so weakly and insincerely."[4] Subsequently Richardson's despatch carried the comment:

> . . . exception should be taken (not of Lord Durham's measures) but to the unexampled ignorance of a Ministry, who seem neither to understand what is necessary to the good government of the country, nor even to know what are the extent and nature of the power they have vested in him whom they have sent to govern it. . . A Tory Government would at least have the courage to defend an absent servant, no matter by whom and in what manner assailed. . . .[5]

Was Richardson so convinced of the rightness of Durham's plans for Canada that he prepared to risk losing an employment which he prized highly and which he expected would eventually take him to other parts of the world? Or did Durham's handsome personality overwhelm him? He wrote to Durham: ". . . the highly flattering manner in which your Lordship's confidence has been reposed in me has ensured my utter

Lord Durham.

devotion to your Lordship's person and interests. . ."[6] and later "Oh! My Lord if it be presumption on my part to offer counsel on this occasion, let it be ascribed to its true cause the deep deep interest — I am sure I know not how conceived — I entertain in all that relates to Your Lordship's public acts."[7] Their correspondence reflects an open friendship. Early in July, Durham offered him a government appointment on a mission to

[4] *Eight Years in Canada*, p.228.
[5] *Times* (Sept. 18, 1838).

[6] ALS, J. Richardson to Lord Durham, Montreal, July 31, 1838, Public Archives of Canada MG24, A27, Vol.26, 972.
[7] ALS, J. Richardson to Lord Durham, Montreal, Sept. 22, 1838, Public Archives of Canada MG24, A27, Vol.27, 205-6.

the Indians which Richardson declined because he could better serve Durham, he said, as a correspondent. Richardson lent him his only copy of *Wacousta* and later in his book, *Eight Years in Canada*, he pictured his meetings with Durham during the summer of 1838: talking privately in Durham's study, chatting by the betting stand at the Montreal race course, discussing politics on board Durham's steamer the *John Bull*, and finally a sad parting at Quebec as Durham embarked for England: "We had been standing all this time near a window of the study which overlooked the beautiful harbour of Quebec, Point Levis, and the country beyond; and as I cast my eyes on the stately frigate which was to convey his Lordship to the noble land for which I myself sighed, I was reminded of the lapse of time and motioned to withdraw."[8] And yet underlying their correspondence is the understanding that Durham would repay Richardson for his support. Possibly Richardson had hoped to receive a high post in the new responsible government. He found, however, that by backing Durham he lost all prospects when Durham was recalled. He tried to persuade him to remain as Governor-General, but Durham replied: "All real power is taken from my authority — all civil power is annihilated. Nothing remains but military force which I cannot wield as well as an officer, and would not if I could."[9] But Durham, saddened by Richardson's dismissal from the *Times*, promised to find him a post in England.[10] Richardson, as if to keep his services to Durham in mind, wrote to Charles Buller:

. . . By the way, you might possibly contrive on your return to England to procure me another Master, one who may prove rather less *exigeant* than *those* I now serve. . . I should think the Chronicle a likely paper to require a correspondent, only as I have little money in the Whig Ministry of the present day, *that* may prove an objection. But if not the Chronicle, some other journal may be found.[11]

In three letters to the Montreal *Courier* Richardson defended Durham's position and attacked the English Parliament, in particular Lord Brougham, who had betrayed Durham and undermined his policies.[12] Certainly Richardson's loyalty to Durham cannot be questioned; he defended that nobleman editorially in Montreal months after Durham had left the country, although Richardson was fully aware of the enemies his stand would bring him and of his defencelessness now that his champion had been defeated.

Meanwhile he was busy at other projects. Maria joined him in Montreal in late June. They bought a large Newfoundland dog, Hector, to guard Maria in their cottage on the city's outskirts while he was away. During the winter of 1838-39, he busied himself with journalism, contributing anonymous political articles to newspapers, planning a book on Durham's administration in Canada, and possibly editing from Montreal the Prescott *Sentinel*, a weekly which ran from Septem-

---

[8] *Eight Years in Canada*, pp.51-2. Durham's offer to send him on a mission to the Indians is declined in ALS, J. Richardson to Lord Durham, July 3, 1838, Lambton Papers, Box 22(29).

[9] *Ibid.*, p.229.

[10] *Ibid.*, p.52. Richardson had written to Durham: "They certainly greatly mistook my character when they imagined I could condescend to become a hireling scribe — or a paltry caterer for more news — next year they may possibly find some more willing and pliable instrument." ALS, J. Richardson to Lord Durham, Montreal Oct. 16, 1838, Public Archives of Canada MG24, A27, Vol.27, 361.

[11] ALS, J. Richardson to Charles Buller, Montreal, Oct. 16, 1838, Public Archives of Canada MG24, A27, Vol. 27, 357.

[12] "The Late Bill in Parliament. . . "Anglo-Canadian"." *Morning Courier* (Sept. 20, 21, 22 1838). Richardson lifted the main parts of these letters, slightly edited, and inserted them in *Eight Years in Canada*, bottom p.53 to top p.57.

ber 1838 to the spring of 1839.[13]

On November 17 the *Sentinel* carried an account of the Battle of the Windmill. Prescott had been invaded on the 12th by a makeshift army of "Patriots" including Canadian rebels and their American sympathizers. One of the leaders of this raid was Nils Von Schoultz, a Scandinavian by birth who had been a freedom fighter in Poland, and on emigrating to America passed himself off as a Pole.[14] A brilliant tactician, he and his men captured a windmill near the town and though aband-

oned by the intended support troops, fought on tenaciously until overwhelmed by superior odds. Richardson visited the scene of the battle shortly afterwards and discussed the engagement with officer friends who had taken part in it. Although proof is lacking, he may well have written the *Sentinel* account, later re-issued in Montreal (January, 1839) as a pamphlet under the title *Sketch of the Late Battle at the Wind Mill.*[15] On a copy in the McGill University Library is a pencilled annotation attributing the authorship to Major

---

[13] *Brockville Recorder* (Sept. 6, 1838). The *Sentinel* actually may have begun in August as the *Recorder* refers to an issue of Aug. 30. The editor of the *Sentinel* strongly supported the Tory address to Lt.-Governor Arthur. Another faint clue to Richardson's editorship is provided by a letter to the *Morning Courier* (April 5, 1839) from Murdoch Morison who, citing de Bleury as his source, refers to Richardson as "being the author of the "Little Peddlington Gazette"." The title may have been in satirical reference to the mythical English town of Little Pedlington created by the popular comic novelist, Poole. No doubt Prescott was regarded as a Little Pedlington by Montrealers of that day.

[14] R.A. Pierce, "Nils von Schoultz — the man they had to hang," *Historic Kingston*, No.19 (Feb. 1971), pp.56-65. He was born 7 Oct., 1807 at Kuopio, Finland, of Swedish parents.

[15] *Eight Years in Canada*, p.66. Richardson was taking copies of his *Personal Memoirs* to booksellers in Upper Canada. It is likely that when he first heard the news of the invasion, he set out immediately on the trip he had been contemplating for almost two months (the book was published on Sept. 19). Strangely, the "Introduction" to the *Sketch* refers to its appearance in the *Sentinel* of Nov. 16, when it was actually in the issue of Nov. 17. This slip of memory seems to indicate that the account was written on Nov. 16, perhaps significant to the writer because it was the day of his arrival in Prescott. In Richardson's case news of the invasion of the 12th would have reached Montreal on the 13th. If Richardson had set out late on the 14th he could have travelled the 125 miles by public transportation, allowing for stop-overs, in a night and a day, arriving early on the 16th. The "Introduction" continues with an apology for errors "as

invariably will be the case among the different conflicting statements made by persons who were actually in the battle, and upon whom we must rely for much of our information," thus indicating the writer was not present during the battle. (This, also, rules out the assumption that the author was Duncan Clark who took part in the battle: *vide* W.F.E. Morley, *Bibliographical Study of Richardson*, p.59. Major Jessup, Richardson's friend from Waltham Abbey, as a participant in the battle probably was one of Richardson's sources.) It adds that the account is "hastily drawn," perhaps in one day. The question arises, who wrote the "Inquisitor" dispatches from Montreal for Nov. 16, 17, 18, if Richardson was in Prescott? The dispatches to the *Times*, dated Nov. 7, 8, 12, 16, 17, 18, (*Times* Dec. 10, 1838) cover almost three full columns devoted strictly to detailing military movements. Those of Nov. 16, 17, 18, which cover only three-quarters of a column seem to have been written by someone other than Richardson, probably by Maria. Expressions such as "what is to become of the unfortunate wives and children of these misguided men during the inclement season which is approaching, Heaven only knows" (Nov. 16) and "these guilty, selfish men, deserve no mercy" (Nov.17) are not from Richardson. The Drayson family produced talented writers: one of Maria's sisters, Caroline Agnes Drayson, was a novelist, and her youngest brother, Maj-Gen. Alfred Wilkes Drayson wrote popular adventure novels, books on games, treatises on astronomy, and articles on Spiritualism. As for Maria: "All, however, agree in saying that she was accomplished, talented, and possessed of some literary ability. . . ." (A.C. Casselman, "Biography of Richardson," *War of 1812*, p.xxv.).

John Richardson "Who edited the few numbers of the Prescott Ontario Sentinel which were printed."

Leaving Prescott, Richardson went on to Kingston where he placed copies of his *Personal Memoirs* with the booksellers and also visited Von Schoultz imprisoned in Fort Henry. He took an instant liking to this soldier of fortune who frankly admitted that he had been misled and misinformed. Although defended at his court martial by John A. Macdonald, then a rising young Kingston Lawyer, he was sentenced to be hanged. Richardson, when he reached Toronto, tried to persuade Lieutenant Governor Arthur to mitigate the sentence but was informed that only Sir John Colborne could exercise clemency on Von Schoultz's behalf. As Richardson was returning to Montreal, Arthur entrusted him with despatches for the Governor General concerning an invasion by patriots at Windsor. He left in all due haste but was delayed in Kingston by having to wait for the ordinary mail coach, with the result that a military messenger got to Colborne half an hour before he did. Apologizing for the delay, he blamed the Post Office, but Colborne assured him that "after all, the despatch happened not to be of much importance."[16] Richardson stayed to dine with the Governor, but his pleas for clemency to Von Schoultz were of no avail. Although he admired Colborne as a soldier, his relationship was on a less friendly and personal basis than it had been with Lord Durham.

There was also the matter of his *Personal Memoirs*. Since its publication, Richardson gradually became convinced that orders had gone down from the highest

officers to the lowest in rank to ignore him. He continued to be hospitably received by the Highland Regiments, especially his own 92nd or Gordon Highlanders, though on two occasions he showed his anger in public at two young subalterns, whom, he thought, were insulting him. The military which had had to put down insurrections immediately after Durham's departure, was in a position to indulge its humours under Colborne's military administration. By Richardson's account it planned a strategem intended to put him through a series of humiliations.

In mid-March while driving a light carriage on Rue Sanguinette, he was rammed by a large wagon loaded with firewood. Convinced that it was a contrived accident and angered at the names he was being called, he leapt from his carriage and horse-whipped the driver, who promptly charged him with unprovoked assault. Richardson had to post 20 pounds bail and report at the Court House on April 22, and every day thereafter until he answered the charge and the case was dismissed.[17] He was accompanied by two friends, one of whom, Murdoch Morison, soon turned against him.

The next incident, in which Morison played the leading role, was bizarre and left a lasting mark on Richardson's reputation in Canada. The figures behind Morison were two prominent French-Canadians, who, as *vendus*, had strong ties with the British military. They strongly opposed Durham's policy of uniting the Upper and Lower Canadas because they wanted French Canada to be governed as a separate state by England. In the background was Charles-Clément de Sabrevois, fourth seigneur de Bleury, elegant man-of-the-world, member of the Legislative Council, and proprietor of *Le Populaire*, a Montreal newspaper which the government shut down in the fall of 1838. Out in front was de Bleury's journalistic defender and editor

---

[16] *Eight Years in Canada*, p.72. As a result of his being delayed by post-masters, Richardson contributed an article of constructive criticism to "Report of the Commissioners appointed to inquire into the affairs of the Post Office in British North America," Canada, Legislative Assembly, *Journals*, 9 (1846) App. F, (M) No.63, (o) No.17. He advocated the giving over of control of the Post Office in Canada from the GPO in London to the Canadian Government.

[17] The Queen vs John Richardson, Assault and Battery, March 19, 1839, Office of the Peace, Montreal.

of *Le Populaire*, Hyacinthe Leblanc de Marconnay.[18] Both men detested Richardson for his eloquent and unequivocal support of Durham. Leblanc had written articles critical of Durham in *L'Ami du Peuple*,[19] but Richardson destroyed his argument in reply. "I had effectually silenced (him) by a leading article in the Herald,"[20] he wrote to Durham.

While the Loyalist French-Canadian faction and the Tory-minded military (the latter represented in Montreal at the time by its top regiment, the Grenadier Guards) while these elements might well have joined

forces to silence a vociferous supporter of Durham's views, it is difficult to see their connection with the lawyer, Murdoch Morison. Critics of Richardson regard the affair of honour which followed as confirmation that Richardson was his own worst enemy — he turned his best friend against him and unnecessarily alienated powerful social and military forces in Montreal; indeed, he must have been a troublesome, quarrelsome liar as his enemies claimed. But Morison's choice of Leblanc for his friend in the affair lends some credence to Richardson's claim that it was a stratagem. In what followed, Morison seemed to have chosen Leblanc for his journalistic talents.

According to Richardson, Morison came into Richardson's cottage when Richardson was away, and, in front of Maria, he went through Richardson's papers to find evidence of Richardson having written an article critical of the Grenadier Guards. He found none, but his action infuriated Richardson, who said that he was no gentleman. Morison responded by sending Leblanc with a challenge to duel. But Richardson refused the challenge from Leblanc whom he considered no gentleman. When Richardson drove into the city he found placards on the lamposts calling him a coward. And as he stood chatting with two Guards officers who were to dine at his cottage that evening, Morison rode by, called him a coward and whipped him to the ground when Richardson tried to drag him from the saddle. Richardson shouted that he would duel him in half an hour. His officer friends stood back and he knew suddenly that he could expect no help from the military. His civilian friends also turned him down, possibly from fear of the penalty for duelling which was a real risk with Richardson since the police had been alerted and were after him. He turned up at the appointed place alone and asked that one of Morison's men second him. Morison refused. Richardson offered to stand alone, but was refused, and left, asking for more time. Finally he found an acquaintance, the As-

[18] Le Blanc wrote *La Petite Clique Dévoilée où quelques explications sur les manoeuvres dirigées contre la minorité patriote* . . . Rome (N.Y.) 1836 in support of de Bleury's political position, and later ghosted de Bleury's book which blasted Papineau (*Refutation de l'écrit de Louis Joseph Papineau.* . . Montreal, John Lovell, Octobre 1839) for which de Bleury was given a sinecure in the Dept. of Public Works (*vide* Jacques Monet, *The Last Cannon Shot; a study of French-Canadian Nationalism* 1837-50, Toronto, Univ. of Toronto Press, 1969, p.43). Since the Dept. of Public Works was to show Richardson some injustice throughout the following ten years, one might reasonably question de Bleury's role in Richardson's misfortunes. (Richardson hinted at as much in *The Guards* (1848)).

[19] *L'Ami du Peuple* (Nov. 10, 14 1838).

[20] ALS, J. Richardson to Lord Durham, Montreal, April 26, 1839, Lambton Papers, Box 19, No.1. When *Le Populaire*, a newspaper that advocated for reform but condemned violence, was shut down by the government in the fall of 1838, its editor, LeBlanc, who was imprisoned, issued a statement that the paper shut down only owing to financial loss (a statement that was disbelieved by the editor of *L'Ami du Peuple*). Consequently LeBlanc was released from jail after only two days, and a short time afterwards he began attacking Durham from the conservative point of view in letters to *L'Ami du Peuple*, an organ for the Lower Canadian Tories and the only French language newspaper allowed to continue publishing. After the fracas with Richardson, *L'Ami du Peuple* changed proprietors and LeBlanc became its editor.

sistant Commissary, who, shocked by Richardson's state of nervous exhaustion prevailed upon Leblanc to postpone the duel to the next day. But when they arrived at the appointed hour, Morison's second said that the affair was terminated as Richardson should have fought the day before. Again he was placarded as a coward, but this time he had a witness who could belie the charge, and he in turn put up posters charging Morison with cowardice. Morison and Leblanc repeated the charge in the newspapers and a man was hired to call "coward" after Richardson in the streets.[21]

Morison knew that Richardson, as a result of his fracas with the wagon driver in March, faced a prison term should he break the peace. When Richardson was angry enough to accept the risk, however, Morison was unwilling to meet him. It appears then, that Morison may have been an opportunist forwarding his interests with those in power.[22]

The final humiliation came within the week when the Commanding Officer of the Guards formally notified the Richardsons that their invitation to the regimental ball and dance, the most important social event of the year, had been withdrawn. Richardson asked Colborne to hold an enquiry to clear his name; Colborne replied that he could not for half-pay officers. Yet Richardson did win an admission from the Commanding Officer that no insult was intended, and that he would not have sent the letter had he not been prevailed upon by others. The newspapers published this admission but the hurt had been done.[23] Ostracized, Maria and Richardson could not remain in Montreal.

Before leaving for the west, Richardson received from Durham his *Report on the Affairs of British North America*. He wrote to Durham that it "commanded the unfeigned admiration of all parties here — those alone excepted whose false political views and selfish personal interests promise fair to be frustrated thereby..."[24]

---

[21] Months later LeBlanc claimed that he never wrote that Richardson lacked courage, but simply that he was precipitate and indiscrete. He wrote as if his conscience bothered him: "Il doit être entendu, une fois pour tout, que nous ne consentirons jamais à accepter un role qui pourrait tendre à nous élever aux dépens de qui que ce soit, et surtout à trahir la vérité." *L'Ami du Peuple* (Oct. 5, 1839).

[22] Morison neglected to pay his share of Richardson's bail money at the time of Richardson's altercation with the carter: perhaps he foresaw that the money might have to be forfeited. De Bleury and Morison were fellow members of the bar and both, therefore, had a stake in the ruling merchant class which had carefully built its power upon French-Canadian institutions for some decades. Richardson hinted at Sir John Colborne's role in the affair by giving the names of the officers with whom he was speaking when Morison provoked him, but who refused to act as his seconds: both aides-de-camp, one being Col. Barnard, special aide to Colborne for carrying dispatches. Richardson's description of the affair has the ring of truth, but at that time he seemed singularly blind to the passionate hatred of the military for him, and, therefore, unable to appreciate its motivation. Col. Weatherall's outburst against him in his letters to Chichester (op.cit.) must have typified what the officers said about him in private. How could Richardson expect that after attacking the sacred cow in his *Personal Memoirs* that the high priests could feel any friendship for him behind their cordial facade? He wanted it all on his terms, a trait which was exemplified by Byron whose defiant life style seems to have served as a model for Richardson.

[23] Montreal *Herald* (May 3, 1839).

[24] ALS, Richardson to Lord Durham, Montreal, April 26, 1839, *op.cit.*. In this letter Richardson revealed that he had begun to write "a brief history of events in this country"; this was the genesis of *Eight Years in Canada*.

the axe to be laid at the root of trees which had existed for ages, and in removing the dark curtain which the sun invariably goldened with his rays, before dipping finally from view, destroyed a beauty which no human hand — no human ingenuity can renew.

The town was changed, the council house was gone as were the Indian wigwams and watchfires.

. . . if a solitary Indian exhibited himself, he was so changed in character and in appearance from the warriors of those days, and presented so uninteresting an exterior in his unbecoming garb of civilization, that his presence only added to the melancholy.

Townspeople met them as they landed, including his stepmother, Ann, and her youngest children.

Some familiar faces there were, but these were cold, unmeaning and cheerless as the aspect of the town itself; and although, in one or two instances, the hand of an old school-fellow was held out to me, it lacked energy, warmth, vitality. The animal spirits of the man appeared to have been withered up and the decadence of the moral energy of the inhabitants to have been in proportion with the desolation that reigned around.

Richardson was dismayed at the lack of opportunities open to the young men. His two oldest half-brothers worked for the customs at Windsor, jobs provided by his uncle, Charles Askin, Commissioner of Customs. Henry Wellington Richardson, the dashing Captain, served in the Essex militia. The youngest, Robert Harvey Richardson, at fourteen revealed an intelligence which deserved an opportunity to develop.

As there was no house they could let in Amherst-

Return to Erie

IN EARLY May 1839, the Richardsons with their faithful Newfoundland Hector travelled up the St. Lawrence past the township of Fredericksburgh, where he had received 200 acres as an army veteran,[1] to the Charles Richardsons in Niagara, and then over Lake Erie to Amherstburg. His dream of returning home did not match what he saw.[2]

When we had crossed the bar, and drawn near to the river at the mouth of which the little town of Amherstburg is situated, the feeling of desolation which had been gathering in my mind, amounted to absolute painfulness. There was a stillness — a nakedness — a vacuity about everything, as we approached it, that, but for the leading features of the beautiful scenery, might have led one to doubt its identity.

The military had blighted the island before the town.

In order to deprive the patriots of the possibility of shelter in the dense cover of the tall and verdant wood, the military commander had caused

[1] Petition, J. Richardson to Lt-Gov. Arthur for land, Public Archives of Canada, RG1, Vol.436, bundle 21, No.23.
[2] *Eight Years in Canada*, pp.85-92.

burg, the Richardsons found accommodation twenty miles away, in Sandwich village, which is part of present-day Windsor. He described the house they rented, the only one available:

> The gable end of this house fronted the street, and was ornamented, at the angle of the sloping roof, with a suspicious looking projection and pulley that very much likened it to the residence of a hangman who does business on his own account. The two rooms below were just large enough to enable the body to be turned, without rubbing the coat or petticoat which covered that body against the white-washed, or rather yellow-washed, wall; but the twin brother or twin sister rooms above it required some dexterity, and not a little practice in the art of dodging and stooping to move in without bumpings innumerable on the cranium. In all, there were four rooms and an apology for a kitchen, the whole occupying the space of a moderate-sized drawing room. . .

He was left undisturbed to write. By early autumn, he finished revising his sequel to *Wacousta*, which he retitled, *The Canadian Brothers; or, the Prophecy Fulfilled*.

When he crossed the river to Detroit, he became a celebrity. *Wacousta* was known by the Detroiters through the American editions, and loved for its dramatic treatment of Detroit's history. In 1837, Dean and Mckinney's Theater in Detroit staged a long run of the New York stage adaptation of *Wacousta*, by Louisa Medina. A young actress, destined for international acclaim, Charlotte Cushman, played the role of Oucanasta.[3] The play attracted crowded houses in all the towns where the touring company stopped, but it was special for Detroiters because it helped commemorate Michigan's statehood granted that year.[4]

His introduction to Detroit society was made through the Brush family. Although Elijah Brush, who had married Richardson's aunt and became the Attorney-General for the Northwest Territories, had been dead for some years, his widow and her three sons lived in the Brush mansion on Jefferson Avenue where Richardson became a frequent visitor.[5] Also he was entertained by the officers of the American 4th Artillery Regiment, gambled at cards and drank pink gins in the hot summer days in their mess. In deference to his hosts, he refrained from expressing Tory sentiments, particularly as Detroit was a base for patriot attacks on Canada. In the previous year, 1838, when the English novelist, Captain Marryat, on a visit spoke out against the patriot invasions of Canada, a violent mob gathered outside his hotel and burned his books in the public square. Yet Richardson's enemies were always ready to stir up trouble.

In mid-July a letter to the Sandwich newspaper abused Americans for visiting Canada. Richardson heard of it on a visit to Michigan Governor Mason whose daughters told him that a Lieutenant stationed in the Amherstburg barracks assured them that Major Richardson was its author.[6] Richardson obtained a confession from the Lieutenant that he was merely repeating a rumour, and quashed it by showing the apology to people in Detroit.

Later in the summer an advertisement appearing in a Vermont paper was reprinted in Theller's Detroit paper; it began: "Hunters — Look out! Major Richardson, alias, Stevens the Spy" to be shot on sight as he moved along the frontier of New York and Michigan

---

[3] Friend Palmer, "Early Days Along the Border," Essex Hist. Soc. *Papers*, II, 96.

[4] Hemans, *Life and Times of Stevens T. Mason*, p.337.

[5] ALS, D. Beasley to Mrs E. Nolan, New York, Feb. 16, 1964 with marginal comments by Herbert Sherman Brush Jr; on file in the Detroit Public Library, Manuscripts Div.

[6] *The Guards in Canada, passim.*

and it described him as cowardly in a recent Montreal affair.[7] (In Detroit after escaping from prison in Montreal, Theller had instigated an attack on Henry Richardson to revenge his capture.) Richardson immediately sent Theller copies of documents on the affair in Montreal and got Theller to print a denial of the report in the next issue of his paper, thus assuring his safety in Detroit once more.

The writing of *The Canadian Brothers* was well along when he began soliciting for subscribers in August 1839. The Detroit *Daily Advertiser* reported that "at the urgent solicitation of several of his American friends" Richardson proposed to publish a sequel to *Wacousta*: "Mr. R. is a gentleman of close observation, possessing a fertile mind and well versed in the interesting history of this frontier."[8] Richardson in fact was disgusted with the manner in which Detroit seemed to have erased every trace of its history. Not only were the fort walls destroyed, it was impossible to tell where they had been. The flag-pole up which Wacousta carried Clara de Haldimar was dynamited in 1818 in spite of a plea from the city firemen who wanted it as a ladder because the wood was strong.[9] In October, after reading parts of his manuscript to an audience in Detroit, he obtained the signatures of 100 citizens who promised to buy the book.[10] He set off alone for Montreal immediately and arrived in the first week of November.

Armour and Ramsay, the Montreal printers, agreed to bring the novel out in two volumes. Richardson wrote to Sir John Harvey, defender of the Canadas at Stoney Creek in 1813, and introduced himself as the brother of Robert Richardson who had worked under him at headquarters in Quebec. [11] Harvey, now Lieutenant-Governor of New Brunswick, promised to make sure the book sold well in the Maritimes. The officers in the garrisons of those provinces received subscription lists and were strongly advised to sign. But aside from Detroit, only Brockville and Cornwall in Upper Canada responded with enthusiasm to the subscription lists.[12]

One of Richardson's subscriptions agents was William Hamilton Merritt of St. Catharines, boyhood friend of the Hamilton boys, who gained prominence as promoter of the Welland Canal. Richardson wrote to him concerning the Montrealers:

The people here are too much of pounds, shillings and pence men to care much about polite literature. Give them a newspaper with their own advertisement of flour, wine, etc. and that is all they learn to require. It is not very flattering to an author but there is no such thing as converting a sow's ear into a silken purse, as we all know.[13]

He wrote again in a frustrated mood:

I have seen but too much of the Canadians, not to be quite sensible that they would far more rejoice in a grand distiller of whiskey than a writer of books and their pride in the one would be in equal proportion... The first consideration is — will his writings put money into our purses? No, but the distiller can put whiskey into our stomachs, and that is a much more agreeable luxury.[14]

[7] *Eight Years in Canada*, p.96.

[8] *Detroit Daily Advertiser* (Aug. 16, 1839).

[9] Forgotten until 1873 when its stump was discovered and taken to the public library as the only testament to two centuries of human activity.

[10] *Eight Years in Canada*, p.105.

[11] *Ibid.*, p.106.

[12] ALS, J. Richardson to W.H. Merritt, Montreal, Dec. 17, 1839, Public Archives of Canada, Merritt Papers, MG24, E1, Vol.14.

[13] ALS, J. Richardson to W.H. Merritt, Montreal, Nov. 21, 1839, Merritt Papers, *op.cit.*

William Hamilton Merritt.

If he thought this way, why did he bother to publish in Canada at all? From a practical standpoint he hoped that a Canadian edition of *The Canadian Brothers* would make an English edition possible.[15] Also, he hoped the past which he captured in his novel at a time when Canadians defended their right to be independent, might yet inspire his countrymen to change their direction from materialism toward a sensitive and enduring culture. Toward this end, he aimed to circulate the novel throughout the country and sent circulars to at least fifty towns:

> ...for a time will come when the people of Canada less devoted to the mere matter of fact relations of life, will have more leisure to give to that which will then in a degree have become obsolete.[16]

In January 1840, he sent the first volume to editors of newspapers who had printed his prospectus and asked them to draw attention to it in their editorials before the second volume appeared in February.[17] He received a surprising number of names, only a third of whom reneged later. When he shipped copies to Harvey in the Maritimes, he asked a favour on behalf of his youngest half-brother, Robert Harvey Richardson. Harvey secured the boy the post of clerk in the Education Office for Upper Canada.[18]

Since Charles Poulett Thomson, the new Governor-General had just travelled by sleigh from Toronto to Montreal, a distance of 360 miles in 36 hours, to record the fastest journey over Canadian winter roads, Richardson decided he could do the same in the opposite direction. He bought a sleigh, black with red stripe, and two black ponies. His description of the ponies shows his love for animals:

> Both were about thirteen hands high, and the horse — a very strong and sturdy animal — had a round full carcase, a short but arching neck, and a shoulder that required a collar nearly as large as that of an ordinary English dray horse.

[14] ALS, J. Richardson to W.H. Merritt, Montreal, Dec. 17, 1839, *op.cit.*

[15] *Ibid.* "Another object in publishing in Canada — a very natural one is that I shall thereby more readily make my own terms with a London publisher for an English edition." It was not published in England.

[16] *Ibid.*

[17] ALS, J. Richardson to Dr Christie, Jan. 18, 1840, Christie Papers, Public Archives of Canada, MG24, 19, Vol.4.

[18] *Eight Years in Canada*, p.107.

He was an excellent draft animal, and although his speed was not equal to that of his companion, there was scarcely any load which could be drawn by a horse that he could not drag after him. The mare, rather slighter in figure, but an excellent match notwithstanding, had more quickness and intelligence — an extremely lively eye — much sensitiveness to the whip, which she never required to stimulate her exertions, and could not endure to be passed on the road. Owing to her great impatience, she was always in advance of the horse, whose absence of ambition, induced by his comparative sluggishness of character — a fault common to horses as well as men — she used invariably to rebuke by a spiteful bite at the head, which he, seemingly conscious of his offence and the punishment that was to follow, used most amusingly to dodge or turn aside, the moment he observed the ears of the mare wickedly thrown back in earnest of meditated mischief. The ponies had never been together until they came into my possession, but their friendship became in the end so great, that they could not endure even five minutes' separation, and if one happened to be in the stable and the other out of it, there was no end to their neighing and whinnying until they were again united. They were very great pets, fed from the hand, and although they had never been regularly led to the baptismal font, answered freely to the name of 'Pony.' If at the close of a hard day's travelling I but uttered the word "Ponies," either in an encouraging or a reproachful tone, their spirits were sure to be aroused, even if their speed was not, from exhaustion, materially increased.

Richardson either hired or adopted a young boy whom he nicknamed "Tiger," in remembrance of his years in Regency London. This stoic little figure who braved all the dangers inherent in accompanying Richardson is unnamed in the pages of Richardson's *Eight Years in Canada* which described the journey, but he makes an indelible impression as a terrified little boy who never let his terror be known.

An incredulous crowd gathered to watch Richardson depart. In spite of warnings that the snow was sure to thaw, Richardson was determined to experience the exhilarating speed of runners over the snow once again. His sleigh carried a cargo of his new novel adding the necessary weight for a smooth passage.

On the first day, as the sleigh started down an icy slope, the ponies' hoofs struck the front, exciting them to great speed. The cahots in the snow upset the sleigh, throwing Richardson onto his left arm which had suffered the wound in Spain. It swelled and pained excruciatingly. He reached a friend's house at Coteau du Lac where he stayed in bed for two days. The arm grew worse. Richardson dreaded returning to Montreal because his enemies would make fun of him. There being no doctor, his host persuaded him to let a French-Canadian herbist look at his arm.

He was a venerable looking man, apparently between sixty and seventy years of age, without any of that forwardness or pretension which are so common to the medical empiric; and notwithstanding his bronzed cheek was marked by hard lines, there was an expression of quiet benevolence on his countenance, which insensibly won the attention.

The old man bathed his arm with a brew, then turned to Tiger whose arm also hurt. Tenderly and firmly, the old man put it right, for it was dislocated. In three days Richardson was well again.

The accident had cost him valuable time; the snow was thinning. At Cornwall, he stayed with his old friend from the Portsmouth Barracks, George Jarvis, now a judge, who warned him to convert his sleigh to a wagon because wet snow had fallen and the wind would melt it. But Richardson insisted on pushing ahead as if he could not bear to have his dream of gliding over the snow disrupted. Within a few hours the runners dragged through mud. Richardson and Tiger had to walk beside the sleigh for 65 miles in two days before reaching Brockville where he checked into the only hotel and went straight to bed. He silenced a ventriloquist who was keeping some comrades in fits of laughter, by stepping into the hall and demanding "to know who it was who presumed to raise such a disturbance in the house at that hour of the night, to the great annoyance of those who preferred sleep to being tormented with their blackguardism."

When he awoke next morning, he discovered to his indignation that the walls of his room were planks spaced so that he was able to see in to the next room which appeared to belong to a woman of pleasure. This condemned the town in his eyes. He ventured out in a black mood, which was somewhat lightened when the ventriloquist and his friends apologized for making a racket. Some little attention never failed to strike a response in him, and since this town subscribed for more copies of his book than any other place in Canada, he began to change his mind about it. Brockville was prettily situated on the St. Lawrence, the fertile country round it was cultivated, and inland there were hills and lakes of great beauty.

Richardson called on Alex Grant, whom he had not seen since schooldays, and found him to be a happy bachelor, a retired officer, and in comfortable circumstances owing to the fortune left him by a Montreal merchant. Grant adopted the same line of argument as Jarvis to convince Richardson to settle in Canada. This was the place to start a newspaper. The one already established comprised politics and gossip. The people of the district were hungry for literature

and would be proud to have a famous author living amongst them. Moreover, they were Loyalists.

Grant took him to the home of the Customs Officer, a Colonel, who often confiscated wagons at the border and sold them, so that Richardson was able to fit the box of his sleigh onto one of the Colonel's confiscations. While the work was being done, the Colonel spoke engagingly about a piece of property for sale in the neighborhood. Unknown to Richardson, he was also secretly a front man for an American real estate agent who bought land on the Canadian side and resold it at a high profit.

Richardson, quite taken with the house and property on the river bank, trustingly accepted the Colonel's price of five hundred pounds as its worth, though later he found the true worth to be only two hundred. The Colonel talked Richardson into signing a contract for the fourteen acres calling for installment payments at short intervals in small print, which Richardson did not notice. His inattentiveness to detail may have been caused by his listening to the Colonel talk about the forthcoming County elections, for which Richardson appeared to be an outstanding candidate. Other prominent citizens echoed the Colonel's sentiments, and Richardson, who saw a role for himself, bought the property. He left instructions with the Colonel for changes and improvements to be made and continued through Upper Canada.

His romantic notion of dashing through the snow had been thoroughly dispelled by the interminable bouncing of the carriage and the long stretches of deep mud. The inns were as unattractive as the roads, and as for the fare they offered:

Let the reader imagine to himself — sour, homemade bread — tea which resembles in flavor, a decoction of hay, and sweetened with what I never could endure, the maple sugar of the country — a rasher of bacon or ham exceedingly salt, and oftener rancid than sweet, and as thick as a beefsteak ought to be, but never is in this country — potatoes infamously cooked — eggs fried and overdone in grease — a saucer or two filled with preserved apples embrowned in the same eternal maple sugar — a few other fruits, such as raspberries, currants, etc., spoiled in the same manner — a couple of large plates of potted butter, with huge particles of salt oozing from them like drops of hoar frost from a damp wall — cheese resembling hard prepared bees' wax, and tasteless and tough as leather — let the stranger, I repeat, imagine this galimatias of eatables, (he must not forget to add huge slices not of crisp, but soddened toast) and he will know what sort of breakfast or supper he may expect to find in Canada, should he ever be induced to travel through it.

In Toronto he attended a ball given by Chief Justice Beverley Robinson who had just returned from a long stay in England where he had done his best to hinder the acceptance of the Durham *Report*. Richardson dropped off copies of his book for Torontonians, left some with Merritt for subscribers in St. Catharines, and posted some to his brother in Niagara. Instead of driving through the peninsula which he already knew well, he took the inland route over the escarpment through thick wooded areas and across the marshes for Brantford where his brother, William, was postmaster.[19] The picturesque scenery and stimulating air, famed for its salutary effect on consumptives, charmed

[19] Richardson never mentioned his brother, William, whose activities as postmaster at Brantford received attention in "Report of the Commissioners appointed to inquire into the affairs of the Post Office in British North America," Canada, Legislative Assembly, *Journals*, 21 (1846), App.F, p.26ff.

him. Brantford, built high on the river banks, was in the centre of the Six Nations Reserve which stretched along the Grand River and although the Indians had cultivated the land, their tribal presence gave the area that mystery which had excited him in his youth. Promising to return with his wife, he set out for London on the banks of the Thames River.

London was the centre of the Windsor-rebel trials the year before. Six patriots had been executed and many were deported. His cousin, James Hamilton, was Sheriff here, a conscientious and popular man who gave Richardson a spirited welcome. Insisting that Richardson stay at his home, he had Richardson's ponies taken from the hotel stable and lodged in his own. The fresh, long, rapturous Canadian spring, the forests in bloom, and the fragrance of the wilds conjured up scenes from the past that made Richardson fall in love with the country again.

Tecumseh's spirit seemed to belong to the forest, and, as Richardson drove along the banks of the Thames, visions of the warrior as he had known him, sprang to his mind. The red-coats, the smell of gunpowder, and the sight of death, seemed to have been enclosed forever in the solitude of the woods.

At the Moravian village, the scene of surrender on that late autumn day came back to him. With the experienced eye of an old soldier he regarded his surroundings and saw that Procter had made the troops fight in advance of a naturally defensible position. The Thames on the left, a morass on the right, and a ravine in front would have hindered the American advance, and made their cavalry practically useless. But such was the frustration of hindsight; such was the pain of recollection. A deserted, weather-beaten house stood alone by the roadside. It was the Inn where the British officers had been taken the night after the surrender. A faded sign reading "Sherman's Inn" still hung on the porch. When he came to the battleground, he walked over it and tried to recapture the feelings of the Gentleman Volunteer aged 17. The nation's character was undefined, but assuredly the Battle of the Thames was a part of its development; the dead men whose ghosts haunted this place, British, Canadian, and Indian, needed a man with power of language to give meaning to their deaths.[20]

Now near the end of their journey, the ponies struck the wagon with their hoofs as they had against the sleigh and dashed crazily ahead. Powerless to stop them, Richardson remembered his previous experience in Waltham Abbey and rode the wagon against the stumps at the roadside. The impact flung Richardson and Tiger like stones from a sling. Richardson, unhurt, stood up.

> A few paces from me lay my unfortunate Tiger, with his face downwards, and apparently without sense or motion. A dreadful presentiment that he was dead came over me, and, with a beating heart, and a cheek that I felt to be blanched, I approached and turned him over.

Tiger was unhurt, but suffering from shock. The axle of the wagon was broken. Richardson had seen Spaniards correct a similar accident by strapping a plank under the wagon, and so with a prayer for deliverance from this wilderness, he sat by the roadside, until two woodsmen carrying axes came along the road and fashioned and nailed two slim trees to the length of the wagon. Gathering up their fallen belongings, Richardson and Tiger were able to reach Chatham, the furthest port of call upriver for steamers from the Great Lakes, where, with the ponies and their cargo of books, they took ship for Windsor. It was the beginning of April when he greeted Maria.

Since the lease was up on the Sandwich house, the Richardsons accepted the Brushes' invitation to spend some weeks in Detroit. Before leaving Sandwich, however, Richardson tried to help his brother, Henry, who was released from the Essex militia. He asked Lieutenant-General Arthur as a special favour to employ his brother as a Captain in the force which was to be continued indefinitely, and preferably near him at Brockville where, he explained, he had been "strongly solicited to stand" for election.[21] Unfortunately Henry died at age twenty-six the following year.

Richardson, not suprisingly, got involved in a duel after he took up residence in the Brush household. He was challenged by George Meredith, the estranged husband of Richardson's first cousin, Semanthe, the daughter of Richardson's Aunt Adelaide Brush. Meredith, a good-for-nothing, suddenly appeared in Detroit near the end of May and demanded that Semanthe come back to him. When Semanthe refused, Meredith wanted to take their son. Semanthe turned to the courts for a separation and custody of the boy. An excerpt from the correspondence of the daughters of Governor Mason gives a lively depiction of the scene. Kate, who recently married Mr. Rowland, Semanthe's lawyer, is writing to her unmarried sister, Emily:

> By the way, you must know that *Meredith* has *challenged your friend, Major Richardson* (the re-

---

[20] Richardson's letter signed "Gwell augan new Cuwilydd," to the *United Service Gazette* (rpt. *Albion*, March 28, 1846) clearly reveals this sentiment.

[21] ALS, J. Richardson to Sir George Arthur, April 17, 1840, Arthur Papers (1480), Toronto Public Library. A mistake in the published volume gives the date as Sept. 17. Henry Richardson dueled over a lady with Arthur Rankin, later famous as a wild west showman and explorer of minerals, on Nov. 23, 1836 in which Henry was wounded in the thigh. On Feb. 22, 1841 he was Justice of the Peace in Windsor before whom Sam Clay, James Cotter and James Carlo were arraigned to be extradited to Detroit on a charge of rape. (Woodbridge Papers, Detroit Public Library). This incident may have been a subconscious influence in the creation of *Westbrook*.

nowned author of Wacousta), because he thinks he is too *attentive* to Semanthe — and a duel is every moment expected. A young Lt., by the name of Wooster, who has been very attentive to Semanthe this winter, acts as Major Richardson's second — and E.J. Roberts is Meredith's. Brush is in *actual* distress — and is moving about doing all in his power to prevent it. Mr. Rowland and Brother Tom are his principal friends and advisers — and they have all three been together today. Meredith and Roberts were out yesterday *practising* with *rifles*. Of course all *Detroit* is interested and excited; but I think it a great farce. You know what a bully Major Richardson is — and Meredith is a great coward. I pity poor Semanthe — it is placing her in such an awkward predicament, and making her so conspicuous. . .[22]

If Meredith hoped to impress his wife by challenging a renowned visitor, he had made a serious mistake. On the day of the affair, Richardson borrowed duelling pistols and strolled with American officers to the rendezvous on Fighting Island, located on the Canadian side of the river. The sun filtered through the trees on the warm spring afternoon as they awaited the irate husband. Just as they decided the man was not going to turn up, a Canadian Justice of the Peace walked up and informed them that the duel was illegal. Richardson explained they were just bird-hunting and returned with his friends to Detroit.

Meredith wrote an apology for his rudeness, but Richardson considered him beneath contempt.

Immediately after this affair, Governor Woodbridge invited Richardson to join a party of Detroiters attending the Whig convention at Fort Meigs on June 11 where William Henry Harrison was to be nominated

[22] ALS, Catharine Rowland to Emily Mason, Detroit, June 7, 1840, Mason Papers, Burton Hist. Coll., Detroit Public Library.

to run for President. As it was also to celebrate the anniversary of the Fort Meigs battle, an attempt would be made to recreate the battle in Harrison's honour. Lines of fair maidens waved the conventioners goodbye as the steamers pulled out of Detroit and the booms of a twenty-six gun salute resounded over the water. The flag-decked vessels churned over Lake Erie to the Miami River. Bands constantly played music on deck. Ships were plying from all directions to join the convention upriver.

Richardson leaned against the railing and stared at the scenery, its primeval beauty erased by the creation of industry, roads, and rows of houses. He would have liked to have seen the wild turkeys fly up from the shore just once, to hear the breathing of the forest from boats gliding noiselessly through the water. Instead, he heard the band music and the loud gaiety of the partymakers. The land seemed to despair now that it was in the grip of pragmatists, and as if to symbolize its deprivation of soul, a passenger leaping from the upper deck was churned by the paddle wheel out of sight.

His party pitched its tent in the field where the centre of the fort had been. The celebrations and fair hardly interested him. He was introduced to General Harrison sitting in a carriage and preparing to review the marchpast of troops and delegates:

> He had removed his hat, and, as he held in his hand an umbrella, which slightly cooled while it protected him from the ardent rays of the sun, his venerable grey and scanty hair, attenuated features, and stooping person, seemed to claim a respect and attention which a more youthful candidate for popular favour might not have commanded.

They spoke only briefly of the battle, then the band started up, and Richardson retired to watch the review.

Bored, Richardson spent much of the time in the tent. But on the last evening, as he reclined hot and exhausted on his buffalo robe and meditated on the "humbug of the whole celebration," he heard

...several sharp cracks of the rifle, which momentarily increasing in number, were answered by the independent fire of musketry, occasionally broken in upon by vollies, and by discharges from one or two field pieces. I jumped up, and thrusting my head through the opening of the tent, beheld a sight that did indeed recall to me the scene of the past. The whole side of the camp which bordered on the ravine where we had constructed our light battery, had suddenly assumed an appearance of great brilliancy, as if the largest description of fire-flies were playing in myriads around, while the cries of combatants and the report of firearms, reverberating through the woods, and multiplied by echo, gave an air of vraisemblance to the manner of an Indian attack, which amply repaid me for what previous disappointment I had experienced.

Then always the perfectionist, he added, "the only thing wanting was the correct delivery of the scalp-cry..."

His spirits revived. The next morning he accompanied his party on the steamer with colours flying and bands blaring back to Detroit. He was playing cards one day in the mess of the 4th Artillery, when word was brought to him that his hotel in Windsor was in flames. Since he had moved everything he owned to the hotel after giving up the house, he dashed like a ruined man to the ferry and urged it across the river. As he approached the Canadian shore, he saw that the hotel was untouched but the barn where his ponies were kept was afire. A woman on shore seeing his alarm called out that Tiger had saved both ponies and

carriage. Shaken, he commended the proud boy, who luckily had been playing near the barn when the fire broke out.

His departure for Brockville was delayed to give the mare pony time to recover from a birth in May. Unfortunately, the colt, too young to travel, would have to be shot. Richardson was loath to do this, so, finally, near the end of June, when the colt was barely a month old, he decided to wait no longer and let the colt take its chances for survival. Sending the heavy luggage to Brockville by steamer, he attached boxes to the back and front of the wagon to carry their clothes, a box of dishes, a box containing all sorts of meats, and a five gallon of cider, wine and brandy, and cigars. Thus he, Maria, and Tiger picnicked under the sunny skies, and spent the nights in inns en route. They followed the road to London, where they stayed with his relatives, the Askins, then to Brantford, and by the main route, to Brockville.

The hearse-like wagon was quite an attraction:

The people as we passed, ran to the doors to admire the ponies, the curs ran after the colt, whom they seemed not much to admire, and Hector ran after, and upset right and left, the curs who had the temerity to insult his little friend and charge.

Hector took good care of the colt which quickly went off a milk diet onto oats giving it the strength to finish the journey in good health, an amazing feat considering they travelled 25 to 40 miles daily.

They arrived at Brockville early in July and claimed their haven, Rock Cottage, to which the flattering Colonel had made no improvements. Harvesting the vegetables and fruit, tearing down the ugly barn, Richardson set about improving the place. He made a fish pond, landscaped the grounds,[23] built an icehouse, and purchased a pleasure boat.

Meanwhile, he cast about for some means of pur-

124

chasing a press. He decided to sell his Lieutenancy and use the money to finance a newspaper. "I had neither the habits, taste, nor aptitude to become anything that had not some connection, more or less, with literature."[24]

[23] *Eight Years in Canada*, p.182. Richardson's interest in agriculture is reminiscent of his grandfather Askin's agricultural experimentation at Michillimackinac in the 1760's. Although Richardson stated that he intended to return to England after a sojourn in Canada, the house and property he bought in Brockville belied any intention of a short sojourn. The price he paid was 500 pounds, very high for those times. The "Indenture of Bargain and Sale" between William Hayes and John Richardson, March 7, 1840 in the Brockville Register Office has been reproduced in: Desmond Pacey, "A Note on Major John Richardson," *Canadian Literature*, No.39 (Winter 1969), pp.103-4. From it we learn that the name of the engaging Colonel was Richard Duncan Fraser.

[24] *Ibid.* In his Petition to Queen Victoria for a pension as reward for his literary achievements, Richardson stated he was forced to dispose of his Army Commission ("his sole means of existence") to satisfy claims incurred in the publication of *The Canadian Brothers*. (Brockville, Jan. 20, 1842). Sir Robert Peel as First Lord of the Treasury replied (Feb. 19, 1842) that the Government had 1200 pounds yearly for literary and scientific merit but could not hold out the prospect of success for his application. Incidentally, in his Petition, Richardson laid claim to being the first Canadian author: "That your Majesty's Petitioner is known and acknowledged as the only Author this Country has hitherto produced — indeed the only writer who has attempted to infuse into it a Spirit of Literature." Peel Papers, Vol.cccxx. B.M. Add. MS.40, 500, pp.278-82.

Brockville

RICHARDSON was unlike the British settlers of first-class, who brought servants, and particular breeds of English dogs, had private fortunes and simply began in Canada where they left off in England. At first the Brockville citizens believed him to be rich, but when he fell into debt, they readily criticized him. Richardson looked down on them as crude wastrels who took no more delight in living than that provided by the local tavern.[1] But this mutual disillusionment took many months to run its course.

Again he was settled in Brockville for only a short time before he was inevitably engaged in an affair of honour. This particular incident was worthy of comic opera. The details, which become too involved to describe in this book, may be found in two pamphlets: *A Brief Statement of the Facts. . .* by Colonel William Williams, Richardson's opponent, and *Major Richardson's Reply to Colonel Williams' Gasconade.*

Apparently Colonel Williams, a short spare man who was the Commander of the Brockville Garrison, took a room in a Brockville boarding house where Richardson, two Brockville gentlemen and young officers

[1] After returning to Canada Richardson began to give the name poison to whisky in his fiction, viz. *The Canadian Brothers* and *Westbrook*.

The Riverside, Brockville.

gambled at cards until 3 in the morning. After the young officers returned to their stations, Williams forbade them to see Richardson again, and wrote a provocative note on the subject which, of course, soon reached Richardson. "If Major Richardson wishes to keep a gambling house, he had better make one of his own," could be laughed off, but "Why does he not go home to Madame sa femme?" was too provocative to be overlooked.[2] In spite of his recent experiences Richardson allowed his hot temper to embroil him in a series of

exchanges of notes which led to the intervention of a local magistrate, a public challenge to Williams on placards, a challenge to Richardson to shoot it out at five paces and finally the placarding of Richardson as a coward with posters left over from the Montreal affair.

The successor to Colborne as Commander of the British Forces in Canada, Sir Richard Jackson, ordered that no officer associate with Richardson as a result of the affair. In a vain effort to justify his conduct, Richardson sent copies of his *Reply* to all the regiments but they were returned to him. Only his friends from Waltham Abbey, Major Jessup and his wife, dared the military wrath by visiting with the Richardsons.[3]

The *Reply* shows Richardson at his pettiest. Assuredly Williams' pamphlet was a mean little production and the affair of honour was just the opposite, an affair of dishonour, so that the *Reply* had to begin at a low level, and continue to refute each of Williams' charges against him. But the task of defending his reputation in communities dependent on the favour of the military for their prosperity was insuperable; sentences such as "If, as he facetiously observes, I am a writer of fiction, I yield to him the honour of being a fictitious fighter," are the rare gems of humour to come from this production.

An egoistic tendency to put himself at centre stage is revealed in it and seems to have developed from his quixotic portrayal of himself in his *Personal Memoirs*. Moreover, there is an indication that he somewhat enjoyed the buffoonery of the affair. Its wide publicity and the vicious rumours spread about Richardson, however, seriously injured his reputation.

That very August in 1840 he wrote to Governor-General Thomson, now Lord Sydenham, to ask for a

[2] ALS, J. Richardson to Lt-Governor Arthur, Brockville, Oct. 6, 1840, Public Archives of Canada, RG5, C1, Vol.49.
[3] *The Guards in Canada, passim*: W. Winters, *Centenary Memorial of the Royal Gunpowder Factory, Waltham Abbey* (Waltham Abbey, Essex: 1887), p.145.

government appointment, specifically as Commander of a Permanent Canadian Corps if one were to be raised.[4] Sir George Arthur had written to Sydenham to recommend Richardson for such a post. After the notoriety of the Brockville affair, however, Sydenham would have found it unpolitic to appoint Richardson as the Corps Commander, or even to a Secretaryship "of trust and importance" which was Richardson's second choice.

The money from the sale of his Lieutenancy reached Richardson in late November.[5] He immediately set out for New York City to purchase a printing press. Maria, unfortunately, had to remain behind. She felt she could not endure Richardson's absence for two months, and made him promise to return by New Year's Day. Meanwhile Hector stood guard over the property and allowed none but friends to enter.

Sailing his yacht across the river to Morristown, Richardson went by sleigh to Utica. The first snowfall had blanketed the land of Upper New York State, and the solitary crags and silent forests reminded him of the atmosphere in Cooper's novels. From Utica he went by rail to Albany, and down the Hudson by ship.

After he had installed himself in the Globe Hotel near the Battery, a young lawyer showed him the sights of New York. Through his new friend's introduction, he attended a lavish ball at a private home. He was told that a grey-headed gentleman across the room was James Fenimore Cooper. His host promised to introduce him. Richardson, excited, patiently waited, but by the time his host got round to this duty, Cooper had gone. But there were other compensations.

> Most of these with the loveliest faces that can be imagined, and of pure soft delicate complexions, were yet sadly wanting in that fulness of contour of person — that seductive embonpoint which gives to woman a charm far surpassing that of mere beauty of feature, and awakens emotion where the other only commands the admiration, and yet, there were two or three exceptions to this too general deficiency in the American style of beauty. These were in the full meridian of womanhood. While their rounded proportions fascinated the attention, and insensibly awakened feelings of adoration for the Masterhand from which has issued the most splendid work the human imagination can conceive.[6]

The eldest daughter of the host, a lovely young girl, undoubtedly with "embonpoint," persuaded Richardson to stay after the party and entertain the family with stories. He gave in to her enthusiasm until he noticed the eyelids of her parents drooping!

He purchased a good printing press and arranged for a compositor to accompany it to Brockville. He spent three rainy days as a guest in Westchester, and experienced the comfortable life of a successful businessman with his guns and books. His host had purchased a number of plates by Audubon and proudly permitted Richardson to study them. The painter's love for nature won Richardson's deep admiration. A few years later he met Audubon when the painter visited Kingston to find subscribers to his book of plates

---

[4] ALS, J. Richardson to C.P. Thomson, Brockville, Aug. 21, 1840. This letter reveals as a falsehood Richardson's assertion (made in *Eight Years in Canada*, p.184) that he "could not endure the thought of running to seek favour from a new Governor."

[5] Richardson arranged his transfer to the active list, taking the place of Lt Gray in the 92nd Reg., sold his commission to Ensign Swinton and resigned all on the same day, June 12, 1840, *vide Army List* (July 1840), pp.92-3. The purchase of a Lieutenancy on the active list cost about 700 pounds, but if the demand were great, which appears to have been the case, the price could have been much higher.

[6] *Eight Years in Canada*, p.170.

on birds.[7]

During his three weeks in New York he encountered much hospitality. The speed of city life was exhilarating. On Christmas Day he entered St. Paul's across the street from the Globe Hotel and stood near the stove at the back of the church. Presently the beautiful young girl to whom he had told stories after the gala ball, appeared with her parents and welcomed him into their pew.

When he started back by stage for Canada, he was gloomy; he pictured with dread the muddy little town of Brockville and a sedentary existence awaiting him. The St. Lawrence was frozen a distance out from shore, so in order to launch his yacht, he had wooden runners built to carry his boat over the ice and into the water. He arrived back in Rock Cottage at four in the afternoon of December 31st, keeping his promise to Maria.

Richardson expected the press to arrive by stage coach a few weeks later, but he learned in February, that it could only be transported through the Erie Canal after the ice had melted. It was a blow to his hopes for political office as he planned to write editorials advocating his cause and publicizing his candidacy for office in the March elections. He explained his predicament to Arthur who wrote: "the disappointment respecting your newspaper happens most untowardly."[8]

There were other ways to win elections in Canada however. Stewart Derbishire, because he won election to the House of Assembly in Bytown became a successful rival to Richardson for government appointments. The plump, sandy-haired Derbishire, a former lawyer and editor of London newspapers had worked for Durham and edited the Quebec *Mercury* during Durham's administration. The returning officer, whose four sons wore Derbishire's badge during election day and whose daughter made a flag for Derbishire, not only cheered and sang "Rule Brittania" at the top of his voice when he claimed victory for Derbishire, but took an active part in the triumphant procession.[9] Derbishire's opponent complained that the returning officer reported votes contrary to the law, administered oaths to the intoxicated, and allowed Derbishire's henchmen to assault his supporters.[10] His complaints were in vain because Derbishire enjoyed Governor-General Sydenham's support.

The press arrived finally in early June. Richardson began his weekly newspaper, *The New Era: or the Canadian Chronicle*, which signified the new political climate of Responsible Government that Sydenham initiated. His avowed purpose was to introduce polite literature into the province, though the literature was almost exclusively his own. He began volume one with a serialization of *Jack Brag in Spain*. The remainder of the eight-page folio issues carried excerpts from English and American papers, which was common practice. Richardson's editorials ran the gamut from scathing attacks on the Americans to informed commentaries on the Afghan War. He counted on two pages of advertising, but could get no clients — an ominous portent.[11]

The Literary Garland applauded the *Jack Brag* story as "full of laughable incident and caustic remark dictated by personal dislike of Evans."[12] Although the story was printed so that it could be detached and bound separately for preservation, no one seems to

[7] *Ibid.*, p.168.
[8] ALS, Arthur to Richardson, Toronto, March 8, 1841, Arthur Papers (1815).

[9] Lucien Brault, *Ottawa Old and New* (Ottawa: Ottawa Hist. Info. Inst., 1946), pp.143-4.
[10] A.H.D. Ross, *Ottawa Past and Present* (Toronto: Musson, 1927), p.115.
[11] Richardson did not mention the probability that the merchants in town who were particularly anxious to have the trade of the military, would not be likely to advertise in a paper whose editor had been black-listed.
[12] "Our Table," *Literary Garland* (July 1841).

have done it — no file of Volume I can be found. Richardson would have been disgusted at its loss. He took special care to wrap and address all copies of the newspaper himself.[13]

His hopes were high and his days idyllic on the sunny banks of the St. Lawrence. He wrote his editorials for an hour or two every morning, then fished on the river for pike and took along a double-barrelled manton in case he should chance on wild duck. He worked hard in his garden and began growing watermelons, the West-Indian fruit which was unknown in Canada. His orchard comprised apple, plum, and cherry trees. His land had wild strawberries, raspberries, huckleberries and grapevines. The property was a paradise but it presently became a question as to whether he could afford to keep it. His paper could not compete with the dailies, papers of strong political bias and passionate invective. Subscribers did not pay their bills; indeed there were not enough subscribers. He foresaw his difficulties and petitioned Sydenham in July 1841 to create a pension fund for needy artists as was common in civilized countries.[14] Of all Governors-General, Sydenham was by nature the most sympathetic to the arts. He read widely and was friendly with some of the literary figures in England. He was, however, a politician. The idea of giving sinecures to such unnecessaries as artists and writers in a country of pragmatic-minded people, who dedicated the public purse to road and canal building, was too risky to propose. Sydenham simply replied that there was no fund for such a purpose.[15]

Richardson wrote again, requesting financial support for his newspaper. He also sent copies of Durham's letters so that Sydenham would be obliged to

Lord Sydenham.

notice just how much he had sacrificed.[16] This time Sydenham asked to see him late in August.

The meeting went smoothly. Richardson understood that Sydenham was forced to give many offices to the Reformers to attain his own ends and believed him when he promised to find a post for him. Richardson had his heart set on the job of Queen's Printer.[17] A week later Sydenham was thrown from his horse. His broken leg would not mend and he lay in fever for two weeks before dying on September 19 at the age of 42.

[13] *New Era* (May 13, 1842).

[14] Petition, J. Richardson to Charles, Baron Sydenham, n.d., Public Archives of Canada, RG7, G20, Vol.4, 414.

[15] *Ibid.* Sydenham scratched a six word reply on the petition which was officially answered on July 20, 1841.

[16] *Eight Years in Canada*, p.184.

[17] *New Era* (March 2, 1843).

Richardson, remembering how his Colonel brought him watermelon when he was ill with fever in the West Indies, sent Sydenham a 17 pound watermelon from his garden. He learned later it was the only food Sydenham had been able to eat.

Sir Richard Jackson, Commander in Chief of the Forces, the man who had forbidden any officer to associate with Richardson, took over the Government until another Governor-General could be sent out from England. Jackson made a number of appointments. Stewart Derbishire was made Queen's Printer which brought an outcry in the newspapers from aspirants to the post who complained that he was not Canadian. Richardson, swallowing his pride, defended Derbishire's appointment and praised his work for the Government in the past: "Although we may entertain disappointment that we should not have been admitted to a participation in the 'feast of places,' that, we repeat, is no reason why we should feel regret Mr. Derbishire has been more fortunate."[18]

Richardson's prospects looked bleak. He had no one in higher places to turn to: Durham was dead, and Arthur had left the country. The new Governor-General, Charles Bagot arrived in Kingston in January 1842. An ill-fated little man with a bad heart, Bagot, though disgusted with the mentality of the members of his Assembly, felt somewhat helpless against the Radicals.[19] Richardson went to see him, and, according to his account, won the promise of the first suitable office.[20] Bagot later denied this. In three separate petitions, Richardson used the same arguments: the desire of the late Lord Durham that he be recompensed for his sacrifice on behalf of Responsible Government, his newspaper which was aimed at "the improval of the moral conditions of the Province," and his family's

military services — all in vain.[21] The office of Treasurer in his district of Johnstown was denied him: then, he encountered the greatest insult when the Registrarship of Johnstown was awarded to one of the invaders of Prescott under Von Schoultz in preference to him.[22] Although there were many office seekers to placate, it was incongruous that a man of his ability, education and intelligence was continuously overlooked. Bagot wrote: "Out of 84 members of the House of Assembly, not above 30, as far as I can judge, are at all qualified for office, by the common advantages of intelligence and education."[23]

Richardson was in debt to the local merchants and had fallen behind on payments for his house. Charles Buller wrote from England that he was unable to help him secure a post in England, but suggested they wait for a chance happening.[24] Richardson's despondency increased.

There were moments when the idea of being buried alive, as it were, in this spot without a possibility perhaps of ever seeing the beautiful fields and magnificent cities, and mixing in the polished circles of Europe, and of matchless England in particular, came like a blighting cloud upon my thoughts, and filled me with a despondency no effort of my own could shake off.[25]

Hector died shortly after Richardson returned from New York. The dog had been poisoned by "ruf-

---

[18] *Ibid.*
[19] *Eight Years in Canada*, p.201.
[20] *Ibid.*, p.200.

[21] Petition, J. Richardson to Sir Charles Bagot, Sept. 21, 1842, Public Archives of Canada, RG7, G20, No.1805.
[22] *Eight Years in Canada*, p.199.
[23] Letter, Bagot to Lord Stanley, Sept. 26, 1842 in J.L. Morison, "Sir Charles Bagot, an incident in Canadian parliamentary history," *Queen's Univ. Bulletin*, No.4 (July 1912), p.9.
[24] *Eight Years in Canada*, p.198.
[25] *Ibid.*, p.159.

fians" in the neighborhood. Richardson cried bitterly at his loss, and, although he offered a reward, he did not discover Hector's murderers. His fondness for animals stemmed from his ability to draw out their intelligence. He was convinced that certain animals "possess a reason, feelings, perceptions, prepossessions and recollections, which far exceed those attributes in the merely animal portion of the human family."[26] At this time he captured a young deer weakened by swimming against the current in the St. Lawrence and tamed it so that one of his servants led it through town on a leash.

At the end of February 1842, he closed off Volume I of the *New Era*, and decided on a change of policy. Canadian readers had not been interested in the British Legion activities in Spain, but they would be in the War of 1812. By taking "A Canadian Campaign," editing it and inserting authentic documents which were lent him by Dr. Winder of the Legislative Library at Kingston, he printed a uniquely written first person narrative in Volume II beginning in March 1842. His closeness to the Americans through blood-ties and neighbourly contact, coupled with his youth, when rancour had not biased him, gave his writing a refreshing objectivity. As a soldier who fought the battles he described, he had an advantage over other historians for whom postures of prejudice were more easy to assume. He included "Recollections of the West Indies" which Canadians would have found interesting for its realistic descriptions of Barbados and Grenada. The new look and subject matter attracted more readers. Many citizens took an interest in the history of the Right Division as the serialized version of *The War of 1812* appeared week after week. It was suggested to Richardson that he should write the histories of the Centre and Left Divisions of the army during the war. Winder, who had been an officer under General Brock, promised him documents from a treasure house of

historical information in the library. Bullock, a minor hero in the War, who was now Adjutant-General of the Upper Canada militia, offered his papers. John Harvey offered his as well. The educators were eulogistic. All the schools in Canada were using the American texts with their chauvinistic interpretations and firebrand righteousness because none other was available. It was time that Canadian children were given the opportunity to understand why their fathers had fought the war. The Superintendent of Schools for Upper Canada recommended that the history be published as a separate book and purchased for the schools.

When *The War of 1812* terminated as a serialization in the *New Era*, Richardson continued with a serialization of his poem "Tecumseh" up to the last issue on August 19, 1842. His farewell editorial was not bitter:

> We shall enter with confidence upon a far more arduous and important undertaking — that of a correct detail of the Operations of the Centre Division of the Canadian army, during a period rife with incident and of the most stirring character, yet requiring diligent research and the closest attention, not only in following correctly the consecutive events, but in investing them with that fidelity which it is the great object of History to attain.[27]

He asked that newspapers inform their readers that he intended to precede the three volumes of the series with an historical sketch of the country, and to advertise for first-hand accounts of the war.[28]

Meanwhile *Wacousta* became available to Canadian readers. As early as October 1841, Richardson notified the newspapers that he was shipping a handsome

---

[26] *Ibid.*, p.178.

[27] *New Era* (Aug. 19, 1842).
[28] *Ibid.*

edition from London because the cost of producing a Canadian edition was too great.[29] He had tested production costs in Upper Canada that month by publishing his novelette, *The Miser Outwitted*.[30] When *Wacousta* arrived in February, *The Literary Garland* carried a long excerpt from the chapter "Escape" to boost sales.[31] Richardson advertised the five volume set of *Wacousta* and *Canadian Brothers* for $5. He explained that *Wacousta* never sold for less than $7 in England. As a special offer, purchasers of the set could buy *Tecumseh* in the English edition for half-price, the last number of which was to be placed under the foundation stone of the monument to be erected to the warrior.[32]

Despite all this promotion of his writings, Richardson had come to the end of his resources. His property was being reclaimed, after he had made all the improvements. He tried once again to secure a government post by asking Bagot to appoint him Civil Secretary at a reduced salary, but received an abrupt answer from the Military Secretary. He replied directly to Bagot:

> It has on mature reflection occurred to me that the recommendation to the office in Question being one of special election by Your Excellency, I may not have been strictly correct in asking for it. Should it appear to your Excellency that I have erred against etiquette in the matter, my application will ever be to me a source of profound regret.[33]

[29] ALS, J. Richardson to Dr Christie, Brockville, Oct. 26, 1840, Public Archives of Canada, Christie Papers MG24, I9, Vol.4.

[30] *Journal* (Chatham, Ont., Oct. 23, 1841) "in pamphlet form at the low price of 15d."

[31] *Literary Garland* (Feb. 1841).

[32] *New Era*, II (1842).

[33] ALS, J. Richardson to Sir Charles Bagot, May 16, 1842, Public Archives of Canada, Bagot Papers, Vol.3, pt.2, pp.309-10. Enclosure: ALS, J. Morris to J. Richardson, May 13, 1842.

He reminded Bagot that in two interviews with him he had been led to expect preferential treatment, but he was told that his claims for office were treated in common with other candidates "in repellant terms, imminently calculated to inflict a wound upon my feelings, I am not conscious of having deserved." Then he closed his letter on a gloomy note:

> Before the weight of that other ruin, which by reason of the sacrifices I have made in support of the Administration of this country, is already fast crowding upon me, and which will moreover be painfully accelerated by the communication just made to me from Your Excellency, I can do no other than humbly and submissively bow.

Now that he was ruined, the people of Brockville showed him no respect. Local fishermen set their nets in a small bay of the river which was Richardson's property and which he had stocked with fish. He chased them from his "pond" repeatedly and threatened legal action. The youths of the district annoyed him beyond endurance. They plunged naked into the river above his property and drifted by shouting to attract the attention of his female servants; then climbing out on a rock (appropriately called Devil's Rock) just beyond his property, they cried obscenities. Richardson shot near them, but could not frighten them away.

In the last issue of the *New Era* he warned these nuisances who disturbed his Sunday rest:

> We shall make it a point to take down the names of all persons found bathing within view of our own premises after sunrise, whether in or out of the limits, and this list we shall submit to the Magistrates, at their next Session, and to the public if circumstances render it desirable.[34]

[34] *New Era* (Aug. 19, 1842).

But this was no more than a threat because he was making plans to move to Kingston.

When *The War of 1812* appeared from his own press in book form, it had typographical errors, for which the Reformers damned it.[35] The Reformers who feared a return to sentiment for the British, were against the book's distribution. The School Council of Johnstown was informed that it did not have the right to vote money to purchase copies for the schools. The Wardens of other districts suddenly lost interest in the book. The Superintendent of Education said nothing more on the subject, and Richardson was left with a large number of unsaleable copies.

Kingston, the new capital of the two Canadian provinces, was the proper place to become involved in politics. Maria probably looked forward to the more sophisticated and entertaining society it offered in comparison with complacent Brockville. The town was pro-Loyalist which suited Richardson. It had a theatre, grand buildings, and was a stop-over for visitors to America.

Charles Dickens stopped there in May 1842. Richardson at the time was printing extracts from the American papers of Dickens' attempt to secure legislation for an international book copyright. He called Dickens: "Nature's purest and most faithful painter."[36]

He bought a small cottage on the outskirts of Kingston and moved his household by steamer in the late summer.[37] The pet deer caused the only difficulty; terrified by the noise of the steamer's motor, it shed its horns. Typical of his resourcefulness, Richardson used the horns as inkholders. His press was held by his creditors. But he was not defeated. Since his enemies used politics to hurt him, he would use politics to defend himself, and perhaps turn the tide.

Politics

OWING TO THE ORIGINAL ENTHUSIASM for the publication of *The War of 1812* Richardson recognized that there was a body of citizens who wanted Responsible Government, but wished to emphasize Canada's distinctness from the United States. If he could gather these people into a political body, perhaps he might create an effective and responsible opposition to the powerful Reformers; he felt that responsibility in government came only when the citizens recognized their obligation to the past.[1]

From his new home in Kingston he petitioned Bagot in September 1842 to consent that the Assembly appropriate a sum of money to finance the writing of the next two volumes of *The War of 1812*.[2] Bagot refused to consider the idea, because its publication might offend the Americans.[3]

Richardson turned to the Loyalist war-horse, Allan MacNab, to represent his petition in the Assembly. Although MacNab's Tories were now a minor representation, MacNab's strong support and the praises he read about the work from the Superintendent of Edu-

---

[35] *War of 1812*, p.294. Richardson wrote in an advertisement at the end of the 1842 ed. that the errors would be "obviated" when the work was stereotyped: "in which case all to whom the publication is now gratuitously sent shall be furnished with new copies."

[36] *New Era* (May 13, 1842).

[37] *Eight Years in Canada*, p.202.

[1] The prospectuses for "The Native Canadian" and the *Canadian Loyalist and Spirit of 1812* enunciate this view.

[2] Petition, Richardson to Bagot, Sept. 21, 1842, *op.cit.*

[3] *Eight Years in Canada*, p.202.

The Hon. (afterwards Sir) Francis Hincks.

cation and others, convinced the members of its worth. Richardson lobbied the French-Canadian members and won their support. In a few days Bagot signed the bill, on the recommendation of the House, that 250 pounds should be given to Richardson to carry on his historical series.[4]

The Reformers were unhappy, especially one of their most vociferous and conspicuous leaders, Francis Hincks, called by some an "unscrupulous man, with a tongue like a two-edged sword."[5] Hincks, appointed Inspector-General by Bagot, insisted on doling out the amount to Richardson over a length of time. When Richardson threatened to take the matter to the Governor-General, Hincks paid the amount in full. From this moment onwards Hincks became Richardson's *bête noire*.

Hincks feared that Richardson would spend the grant on a newspaper to attack the Reformers. As early as November 1842 Richardson had advertised for subscribers to a newspaper he had intended to call "The Native Canadian."[6] In January 1843 he reclaimed his press, set up his newspaper office on Queen street in the centre of Kingston and began publishing the *Canadian Loyalist and Spirit of 1812*, a weekly of four pages, the policy of which was to uphold the claims of Loyalists and older settlers against government preferment for newcomers.[7] Hincks in partnership with Derbishire had secretly bought the *Kingston Chronicle*, a newspaper known for its conservative outlook, and tried to mold public opinion in the Reform point of view. The *British Whig*, edited by a young English doctor whose liberal ideas had once caused his press to be smashed,[8] was a popular Kingston paper. And as if this were not competition enough, the *Kingston Statesman* was a conservative paper edited by Ogle Gowan, an Irish Protestant immigrant, who was revered by the Protestant Irish as the father and founder of the Orange Lodges in America.

Richardson was fated to spend his next two years in a political maelstrom with these men. For the most

---

[4] Canada, Legislative Assembly, *Journals* (1842): McNab moved on Oct. 4 that Richardson's petition be considered by a Committee of the Whole House. Discussion on Oct. 6. Motion to encourage publication of "War of 1812" made by MacNab, seconded by Hamilton and passed, in spite of a motion to postpone the voting, on Oct. 8.

[5] James A. Roy, *Kingston: the King's Town* (Toronto: McClelland and Stewart, 1952), p.216.

[6] *British Whig* (Nov. 4, 1842).

[7] Prospectus, Nov. 1, 1842, *Canadian Loyalist...* (Jan. 1843).

[8] James A. Roy, *op.cit.*, p.160.

part, the sarcastic Gowan and the vitriolic *British Whig* were Richardson's editorial allies.

The *Canadian Loyalist and Spirit of 1812* began like a bugle call to war which clearly indicated that Richardson's days spent establishing a Canadian literature were over:

A crisis having arrived in the affairs of this Country, not only alarming to its best interests but threatening to subvert those strong ties of union and attachment to the Mother Country, for which the Loyalists of the colony have ever been remarkable, and which had, in times of great peril and difficulty, been freely tested with their blood, it becomes the imperative duty of every Canadian, who has the power of wielding a pen in the field of politics, to throw himself into the breach..?

The moderate *Montreal Courier* deplored going back to 1812 which would divide people when the present demanded that they be brought together. Since the early issues of the *Canadian Loyalist* have not been preserved, the *Courier* account of its first issue is interesting:

The manner in which the Canadian Loyalist makes his appearance is, to say the least of it, singular. As admirers of the fine arts, we can scarcely enter into the spirit of the very original engraving which is intended we suppose to illustrate the motto and throw light on the proceedings of the Loyalist. Two stiff-looking military heroes standing on each side a monument, convey to our minds nothing in keeping with the actual state of things in this Colony at present whilst the drawing is in itself so ridiculous as to be a perfect caricature. Were it not for the explanation afforded

by the Editor himself, we would never recognize fame in the uncouth-looking figure who is handing what may be for ought our senses inform us, a string of red herrings to a raw recruit, who personifies, as the motto informs us, 'Loyalty Triumphant', whilst we still remain perfectly ignorant of the species of the singular-looking thing with four legs, a tail and whiskers, which serves as a foot stool to recruit no. 2, whose business, we learn, is to "crush rebellion." If these are fitting illustrations of 1812 and 1837, all we can say is, that they offer most interesting subjects to the naturalist; and as far as Fame is concerned, if one of the figures introduced is Fame to the public, it must be death to the artist.[10]

Such ridicule could not deter Richardson who vowed to Derbishire that his newspaper would continue until Hincks was pushed from power.[11]

To pay creditors Richardson put all the remaining copies of *The War of 1812* (after thirty copies were sold) on auction; only one copy was sold — for seven and one halfpence: "the liberal purchaser thereby redeeming his countrymen from the charge of utter neglect of literature."[12] As for the two volumes he was to write about the Centre and Left Divisions in the War, he considered that grant by Parliament as payment only for the first volume, and argued that the Canadians showed no interest anyway.[13] His two hundred acres in Fredericksburgh were auctioned for the benefit of a creditor.[14]

[10] "Extract from the Courier," *Chronicle and Gazette* (Jan. 14, 1843).

[11] *Eight Years in Canada*, p.208.

[12] *Ibid.*, p.205.

[13] Both Reformer and Tory suddenly became cautious about stirring up American resentment. John Harvey's letter to Richardson, Feb. 1, 1842, reveals a perplexing disengagement from the project (*Eight Years in Canada*, p.204).

[9] Prospectus, Nov. 1, 1842, *op.cit.*

His first task was to unmask the editors of the *Kingston Chronicle*. Since members of the Government were not supposed to be running a political newspaper. Hincks and Derbishire, as Inspector-General and Queen's Printer respectively, would not admit to the editorship. By attacking Hincks in his editorials, Richardson roused the *Chronicle* to respond, and thereby deftly flushed out some of its radical political views. Within a few months Hincks left most of the writing to Derbishire in order to rekindle the fire of the Reformers which seemed to be dying out.

By June 1843 the battle lines were clearly drawn. Hincks stirred up the Roman Catholic Irish who were referred to as the Hibernians and whose spirit was attuned to the cries for repeal of the Corn Laws in the English House of Commons. Many of these repealers favoured joining Canada to the United States, and there were rumours that armies of Hibernian Irish, drilling in New York, were preparing to march across the border. Confronting them, Ogle Gowan, the Grandmaster of the Orange Lodges, kept the Protestant Irish on the alert. Richardson, although not an Orangeman, supported the Orange cause because "it watches the repealers."[15] The Reformers under their youthful leaders, Baldwin and Lafontaine, exhausted Bagot and forced him to resign. The new Governor-General Charles Metcalfe, at one time an administrator in India and a man who understood the prerogative of the crown, had relieved him in April. Bagot died before he could leave the country.

Metcalfe, "the jolly-faced Englishman," was loathed by the Reformers, but respected by the Tories because he alone seemed strong enough to protect the freedoms of the minority. Richardson liked him immediately, his attraction increased, no doubt, by the fact that Metcalfe had a letter from Charles Buller recommending Richardson.[16] Metcalfe was not the man to disappoint him; he promised he would do what he could, but Richardson had to gain support in the Assembly first, a seemingly impossible task at the moment.

When Metcalfe laid the cornerstone for the new city Hall in June, there was a dinner at the major hotel afterwards where accomodation for one hundred and two gentlemen was made. To spite Metcalfe, the Radicals who bought tickets did not turn up; Richardson accused them of "wanton violation of decency" in his editorial the following week.[17]

The assembled dignitaries included the Commander of the Forces, and a young Alderman, John A. Macdonald. The wine was strong and the toasts were numerous; Richardson reported on the behaviour of "the responsible editor of the Chronicle," meaning Derbishire: "We can safely aver that, when we left the room, he was in that state of sweet oblivion which defies all powers of the recollection." Derbishire poking fun in the *Chronicle* quoted from Richardson's description of the banquet:

Such indeed was the insinuating power of the Champagne that, during the speeches that were subsequently delivered, it seemed to play the gambols of the "will o' the wisp" stealing away the train of idea from a given subject, and compelling it to wander, at its provoking pleasures, in the most intricate mazes of incoherency and confusion. The effect of this we were made to feel ourselves. On being called upon unexpectedly to rise to some remarks made by Thakarowante (Col. Kerr) who had alluded to the evening as being the anniversary of the affair at Stoney

[14] "Lt John Richardson vs Isaac Carscallan," *Chronicle and Gazette* (Dec. 31, 1842).
[15] *Canadian Loyalist* (July 20, 1843).

[16] *Eight Years in Canada*, p.223.
[17] *Chronicle and Gazette* (June 10, 1843).

Creek, we ran into a wild, discursive, and unconnected speech which had not more to do with the subject than with Gallow's Hill.

Derbishire then commented:

The Champagne and Claret, the Wines of Old France were in fact found too potent for the Spirit of 1812 — the brain even of the Loyalist underwent a revolution, a sort of vinous fermentation, became incoherent and confused and he raved about Gallow's Hill. Had not the good and honorable feeling of the Company, sensible of what was due to the presence of His Excellency, and of the impropriety of at any time turning a merely convivial meeting into an arena of political dissension, marked the "loyalist's" departure from the established rule of the evening's proceedings, there is no saying into what topics he would not have wandered. The individual who voluntarily placed himself in a position for which he deemed this explanation and apology necessary, can hardly be qualified for lecturing others upon the same occasion for wanton violation of decency and absence of respect for the Governor-General. In this fix we leave the gallant editor of the Loyalist for the moment.[18]

But this witty sparring was merely the prelude to a more serious confrontation. Tension had been building between the Hibernians and the Orangemen. One of the Hibernians, arrested on the charge of murdering an Orangeman, was awaiting trial. The Orangemen began to feel that Hincks and his followers were taking over the country by staging beatings and small riots to distract the attention of the public from the true political issues. When the Hibernians came out to watch the Orangemen celebrate the historic July 12, a drunken Orangeman announced to the crowd that he was "King Billy," which enraged the Hibernians. The Orangemen closed in on the Catholic Bishop, whose bodyguard sprang into action. A young boy belonging to the Orange crowd was killed by an Hibernian volley. One of the Hibernians seen brandishing a sword and calling on his followers to charge, was jailed the following day for the murder of the boy.

Richardson, whose office was in the vicinity of the shooting, walked home at three o'clock in the morning and found all was quiet. He was convinced that the lenient attitude of the Government to the repealists was to blame for the riot. But Derbishire took the opposite view in his newspaper, even exonerating the Hibernians of the death of the boy. When Derbishire visited the accused murderer and those arrested along with him, Richardson charged him with acting under Hincks's instructions, which he had to obey because he owed his appointment as Queen's Printer to the Reformers. According to Richardson, Hincks feared that the prisoners would reveal his political intrigue if they felt deserted.[19] Gowan joined Richardson in his attack on Derbishire, which angered the editor of the Chronicle into printing an attack upon Gowan. Gowan asked for an apology. Derbishire pretended that he was not the editor of the Chronicle and was not therefore the author of the attack. Richardson entered the fray, describing Derbishire's career in journalism in Spain, how he had switched from the Carlist to the Christino cause, and had illustrated a pattern of inconsistency which he was obliged to reveal because Derbishire was now defending the Catholic element whereas in Spain he had been opposed to the "monkish bigotry" of the Spanish church.[20]

Derbishire answered by writing a letter to the

[18] Ibid.

[19] Eight Years in Canada, p.216.
[20] Canadian Loyalist (Aug. 10, 1843).

editor of the *Chronicle* (whom he still pretended not to be) in which he denied Richardson's charges:

> Nor could a more baseless fiction, in point of fact, have entered into the dreaming brain of a romance writer. The Editor of the Loyalist is evidently but a poor hand at political writing, and you would do himself and his readers a service in recommending him to confine his future editorial labours to the single task of culling choice extracts from his own novels.[21]

The controversy continued while Richardson revealed more of Derbishire's character, by claiming that he was working for the Reformers secretly because his constituents in Bytown were Conservative. Gowan barked his support. Derbishire retaliated:

> And here we may inform those two gentlemen that their maniac tantrums move us no more than would the incessant barking of a dog serenading the moon. Could they but see their own distempered visages morally in a glass, swollen with impotent rage, every feature distorted, it would be a caution to them for the rest of their lives if it did not frighten them out of existence altogether.[22]

Answered Richardson: "Wast thou mad, that thus so madly thou didst answer me?"[23] Though Derbishire was enslaved to the Executive, he did not need to lash himself to anger. "Keep cool," he advised, "these are the dog days, and too much excitement may occasion apoplexy."

One upshot of the controversy was the general

21 *Chronicle and Gazette* (Aug. 3, 1843).
22 *Canadian Loyalist* (Aug. 10, 1843).
23 *Ibid.*

recognition that Derbishire was the editor of the *Chronicle*, which dimmed his popularity with the Bytown constituents considerably. The final provocation which caused Derbishire to challenge Richardson was probably very slight.

On October 17 at 3.30 in the afternoon, they faced each other with duelling pistols. The terms required Richardson to stay on the ground until Derbishire was satisfied. Richardson, who claimed he had no ill-feeling toward Derbishire, said he would fire low. In the exchange his shot landed inches from Derbishire's feet, ploughing up the earth and spattering him with mud. Derbishire's second, a fellow member of Parliament, took the gun from Derbishire's hand. Seeing this, Richardson's second asked, "Are you about to reload?" The answer being "No", Richardson's second approached and said that Richardson felt that their disagreement was occasioned strictly as political writers and wished to offer his hand in friendship. Derbishire refused and seized on this as an apology, so that Richardson's second had to withdraw the offer immediately. Richardson called out: "Recollect this proposition comes from Mr. Low, not from me." But Derbishire's second insisted that it was a sincere avowal, in which case the world would not permit them to line up again because the affair was terminated with honour to both parties.

Another subject seized the headlines. Led by Hincks, the Reformers drew up a Secret Societies Bill which outlawed all unauthorized meetings and stipulated that no Orangeman could hold public office. This would have virtually crushed the opposition which was just organizing effectively, had not Metcalfe refused to sign it. Although it sailed through the Assembly with a large majority, Metcalfe claimed that there were laws against breaking the peace and that further legislation was unnecessary. The members of the Executive Council denounced him and the Reform press attacked him. The Executive took the stand that the Governor-General had to sign whatever it advocated, particularly when it recommended persons for public office. When Metcalfe stood up to them, they all resigned, save the Provincial Secretary, Dominick Daly, the epitome of of the bureaucratic clerk, who had no private source of income. Although it appeared that the Council was acting from strength and forcing Metcalfe's recall, it was really taking a desperate step to kill a mounting opposition.

Richardson's editorials supported Metcalfe, and began a strong movement of sympathy for the man throughout the country. Even many Reformers rejected this precipitate action of the Executive Council. At a meeting in Kingston, Richardson proposed, and J.A. Macdonald seconded, a statement of support for the Governor-General whose action gave "the advocates of British connection a sufficient guarantee of protection against the encroachments of evil and designing men."[24]

Richardson was largely responsible for the resurgence of the Conservatives. He set the tone for the attack, gave a strong and critical voice to the opposition, and attracted readers to his newspaper by his descriptive writing and colourful personality. He had rejuvenated the Loyalist spirit in Kingston to the point where the Reformers wanted to move the capital to Montreal. Richardson made up a 'Black List' of Assembly members who voted for the move. It included Derbishire, about whom he noted wryly that since his Bytown constituents opposed the move, he was saved from having to stand for re-election by a clause in the Bill precluding the Queen's Printer from holding a seat in the Assembly. This meant that Derbishire was permanently appointed to the post and that Richardson's hopes of winning it from him at the next election were dashed.[25]

By advocating the move to Montreal the Reform-

ers hoped to win support from the French-Canadian members. Not only were the Quebeckers sick of the English meals and alien atmosphere of Kingston, they were pleased by the prospect of economic riches which would come with the establishment of the capital city in Quebec province. To the English-Canadians the Reformers made the excuse that the archives would be safer in Montreal than in Kingston which was on the border and could easily be invaded by the Americans. Richardson then suggested Bytown (now Ottawa) as the logical site for a capital.[26] He, of course, faced personal ruin by the removal of the Government; his Loyalist newspaper would find none of the support it enjoyed in Kingston; besides, he had just laid the groundwork for the political support necessary to win him some public office.

Hincks and Derbishire sold the *Chronicle* newspaper in November 1843 to a moderate Reformer.[27] This was a pleasant victory for Richardson, but his chief satisfaction came from bringing political defeat to important Reformers in long battles through the printed word.

The popularity of the *Canadian Loyalist* reached its high point in the autumn and winter of 1843/44 when members of the Assembly complained they were not receiving copies. But the confusion and uncertainty in Government worked against his ambitions: he had become so politically controversial that Metcalfe could not risk further dissension by giving him an appointment. As a result, his political thought, as expressed in his editorials, grew increasingly sharp. He advocated an Order of Knighthood and listed 32 names for it. He favoured the creation of a government arm like the House of Lords and to that end suggested

24 *Chronicle and Gazette* (Dec. 13, 1843).
25 *Canadian Loyalist* (Nov. 16, 1843).

26 *Canadian Loyalist* (Nov. 9, 1843).
27 S.B. Harrison, a liberal reformer, purchased it (*Can. Loyal.*, Nov. 2, 1843) and immediately its tone became more conciliatory to Metcalfe, as Richardson noted (*Can. Loyal.*, Dec. 21, 1843).

that the Legislative Council be appointed by the Governor-General to act as a check on the House of Assembly. He felt that the wants of the French-Canadians were misrepresented by pseudo-Reformers like Daly. He wanted Papineau, the leader of the Lower Canada rebellion of 1837, brought back from exile and placed at the head of his party. He advocated that a French-Canadian regiment be drawn up within the British army "composed of native-born officers and soldiers."

He tried to bring the spirit of the outside world into the Canadian capital by reprinting stories from European and American magazines, and publishing letters from army friends abroad; for example, a description of the defence of the 44th at Cabul. Adjutant-General Bullock's "Operations of the Army under General Wolfe" was serialized as "a valuable addition to Canadian history." He stirred interest in the arts. But the exhibit of a South African gazelle and the performance of Signor Blitz, who hypnotised his canary, remained the popular choice of entertainment despite his enticing reviews: "As Mrs. Chatterly, in the Widow's Victim, she looked and acted like a blooming girl of 18 — full of life, fun, and frolic, and yet Mrs. Noah, we should say, has arrived at the full, ripe, luxuriance of meridian womanhood."

Despite his efforts, and despite Kingston's new City Hall, new churches, an Assembly House with seats said to be plushier than those in the British Parliament, and a busy harbour crowded with high-masted schooners, agitation for removal of the capital to Montreal increased.

Hincks moved to Montreal in January 1844. Until he formed his own newspaper, the *Pilot*, he constantly attacked Richardson in pseudonymous letters to the *Brockville Recorder*:

When we look at the *high* eminence which the editor already occupies in the world of letters,

140

and the *fame* which he has won for himself as a warrior, not only in his native land but in a foreign country 'Where flashed the red Artillery,' it is neither astonishing nor wonderful that he should frown contempt upon so humble and unpretentious an individual as myself. On the contrary (pardon my egotism) I think it betokens no small degree of moral courage, for a mere pygmy, like myself, to assume the unparalleled audacity of gainsaying anything that should emanate from the giant intellect of the truth-telling editor of the Canadian Loyalist.[28]

Hincks, refusing to reveal his identity, carried on abusing Richardson in this manner, as if out of frustration at having been toppled from power, and as if admitting that the Reformers' defeat was partially owing to the sharp and diligent reporting in the *Canadian Loyalist*.

In the Montreal elections of April 1844 Hincks's ruffians clubbed away the voters opposing the Reform candidate, a fact which Richardson recorded in his newspaper.[29] The battle between the two was far from over.

Richardson quietly and hopefully waited for the Conservative nomination to run for the Kingston Assembly seat in the forthcoming elections, but when it appeared that Macdonald was the overwhelming choice, he signed the petition for Macdonald's nomination, and noted in his paper: "The qualifications and claims of a gentleman so universally known and liked as Mr. Macdonald, can need no eulogy from us."[30] It is tempting to surmise how much influence Canada's first novelist had upon the Dominion's first Prime Minister.

[28] "Letter to the Editor...Strabo," *Brockville Recorder* (Dec. 21, 1843). Hincks followed with two more abusive letters signed "Strabo."
[29] *Canadian Loyalist* (April 18, 1844).
[30] *Canadian Loyalist* (March 21, 1844).

Richardson kept alive Durham's thought for a federation of the Canadian provinces by discussing it in his newspaper.[31] Little did he guess that Macdonald would be the architect for such a scheme.

Possibly Richardson laid the basis for the Conservative Party in his formation of the United Empire Association. At a public meeting in May 1844, one hundred and thirty Conservatives and a few Reformers resolved "to counteract open attempts to organize people of the Province against H.M. the Queen."[32] Richardson was named Corresponding Secretary for the Association with the power to transact business for the Midland District and to begin similar organizations in other districts. He was already selling his newspaper at reduced rates to societies which he had encouraged to form, and thereby had a ready-made network which needed only to be drawn together. He was enthusiastic about it, calling it "provincial in essence, which will form one of the most memorable epochs in Canadian History."[33]

His youngest brother, Robert Harvey Richardson, lost his salary of 175 pounds a year in the Education Office for Canada West when the new Superintendent of Education brought in his own clerk. A year later when Robert was in "dire necessity" Metcalfe appointed him Surveyor and Landing Waiter at Port Colborne on Lake Erie at 50 pounds a year.[34]

Metcalfe was fond of Maria and gave her special attention in public.[35] Such small considerations won him Richardson's eternal gratitude. As for loyalty, Metcalfe could not have doubted the Richardson family; when he was attacked by his Council, Charles Richardson led a deputation to Kingston to present him with an address of support from the citizens of Niagara.[36]

At social functions, such as balls and afternoon teas, Metcalfe entertained lavishly, and the distinguished Richardsons were invited. Regattas in summer, parties in Daley's Hotel during winter and the meetings of various guilds and societies comprised the entertainment. It was a society in which a good conversationalist, such as Richardson, shone. Although he had achieved a certain prominence in politics by taking a conservative stand (he once recommended that half-pay officers be struck off the rolls for attending a Reform Party meeting censuring Metcalfe) fundamentally he was a Liberal. When the editor of the *Fredericton Loyalist* was imprisoned for publishing the speech of a Parliamentarian attacking the Governor of New Brunswick, Richardson strongly defended the freedom of the press. In this instance he noted that the editor was popular: ". . . new subscribers to his paper, *Who Pay* are flocking around. . ."[37]

The emphasis revealed his own predicament. As the Government prepared to remove to Montreal, the *Canadian Loyalist* began to feel the change in its affluence. In April 1844 Richardson complained that some gentlemen did not pay for his newspaper, and even returned it without acknowledgement when postage was prepaid. It shut down in early summer.[38]

The psychological effect of the move on Kingston was devastating. The fall in property values and business obliged the town to borrow heavily from the bank

31 *Canadian Loyalist* (Sept. 7, 1843).

32 *Chronicle and Gazette* (May 4, 1844).

33 *Canadian Loyalist* (May 2, 1844); apparently the Association served as a political platform to launch Macdonald and faded away *vide* D.G. Creighton, *John A. Macdonald: the Young Politician* (Toronto: 1952), p.97.

34 ALS, D. Daly to R. Richardson, Dec. 16, 1845, Public Archives of Canada, RG5, CI, Vol.882, 12268.

35 ALS, J. Richardson to Lord Elgin, Montreal, May 10, 1847, Public Archives of Canada, RG5, CI, Vol. 196.

36 *Canadian Loyalist* (Jan. 18, 1844).

37 *Canadian Loyalist* (March 14, 1844).

38 Richardson wrote that it "was published for about eighteen months only," *Eight Years in Canada*, p.208.

and use scrip certificates signed by the Mayor and Treasurer to pay its creditors.

The Richardsons had to follow the Government to Montreal if they hoped to make a livelihood. The ponies, the pet deer and the dogs had to be sold.[39] And the compositor, whose name appeared on the *New Era* and the *Canadian Loyalist* as J. Corbier, could no longer be retained.

In the last months of the *Canadian Loyalist* there was only one truly bright moment in the atmosphere of impending ruin, and even that was culled from tragedy. A fire at the Globe Hotel in Kingston destroyed Derbishire's large cache of Champagne and Burgundy. With great wit Richardson imagined the scene in a poem, after the satirical style of Pope, called *Miller's Prophecy Fulfilled, in the Destruction of the Globe*,[40] to the delight of his readers. The *double entendre* of the poem's title was clear to his contemporaries. William Miller from New York State prophesied the end of the world in the spring of 1843. He attracted tens of thousands of followers who formed a Millerite sect. When the world was not destroyed in 1843 Miller set October 24 1844, as the final day.

The poem, though, was an expression of Richardson's political rivalry with Derbishire whom he depicted giving a sumptuous party to his friends of the Reform Party. When engulfed by fire, Derbishire desperately tried to save his books and bribed his guests with a cache of wine in the cellar if they would rescue his library. The ensuing confusion and wreckage of "Darby's household gods" is made to appear as if it were the work of unpredictable fate.

In the face of his own adversities, Richardson clung to a naive faith that chivalrous behaviour received its just reward. On the occasion of a presentation of a trophy at a regatta in Kingston he informed his readers of

> those bright days of the preux chevalier... It was generally under the lustrous eyes of his mistress, that the young belted knight, or the grim warrior chief, did homage to the Sovereign in the manner we have shown, and all the perils of the past were repaid tenfold by rewarded ambition with the one, and by gratified love with the other.[41]

Welland And The Police

AFTER CAMPAIGNING for John A. Macdonald, who won election to the Assembly in the autumn elections of 1844, Richardson hoped for some recognition of his services by the Tories who ruled with a slim majority. He was in Montreal shortly after the New Year of 1845 when the new Parliament was in session.[1] In February

---

[39] The deer made the trip by boat over the rapids to Montreal (*Eight Years in Canada*, p.184).

[40] Rpt. *Papers of the Bibliographical Society of Canada*, 10 (Toronto: 1971), pp.19-28.

[41] *Canadian Loyalist* (Aug. 17, 1843).

[1] Richardson had shifted his political stance slightly. He took the view that the country should not be governed by one party, but rather by a combination of moderate Conservatives and Reformers for "the furtherance of the general good and interests of the country." He now attacked the ultra-Conservative clique in Toronto for withholding support from Metcalfe until Conservatives should be appointed to Government as strongly as he attacked the Radical clique under Hincks, Baldwin and Sullivan. He outlined his position in a letter to the Kingston *Chronicle and Gazette* (May 22, 1844) which indicated Metcalfe's intention to form a coalition ministry. His involvement in politics had reached its deepest level. If he hoped to survive he had to be on hand to apply for Government posts which he believed he had now a better opportunity of gaining. His opposition to the ultra-Conservatives, however, brought him new enemies, such as James Fitzgibbon who wrote of Richardson: "I know not how to characterize him without using terms which I will not write." (ALS, J. Fitzgibbon to F.B. Tupper, Montreal, May 13, 1846, Ontario Archives).

he applied for the post of Inspector of Customs for the Midland District of which Kingston was the centre.[2] Aware of all the rumours about posts to be filled, Richardson, like dozens of fellow-office-seekers, tried to track down the truth and discover the particulars before applying. In this case the post was for Inspector of Licences, but his mistake was inconsequential as he had no real hope of an appointment.

In April he desperately wrote for help to Draper, the leading Tory, who promised to do what he could,[3] yet only Metcalfe was sincere. Metcalfe's difficulty was finding some post in which Richardson's suitability could not be questioned. A new law, calling for the establishment of police forces along the Canal Works under the supervision of a Superintendent, was passed. Metcalfe, now seriously ailing, carefully planned for Richardson's appointment to the post of Superintendent.

An M.P., George McDonnell, who said that Richardson was a stranger to him, recommended him for the Chief Commander of the Police Forces in Ontario. "I feel I am only doing a common act of justice in recommending him."[4] Dominick Daly, the Secretary, pencilled two exclamation marks after Richardson's name.

The Council members vehemently opposed Metcalfe's choice of Richardson for Superintendent. Daly notified Richardson of his appointment in May, with the subtle warning that the post was temporary. Richardson took this to mean that it was a step to something better, for the post was hardly a plum. The pay, ten shillings a day, was equivalent to an army Captain's. But he had not been at such a low level of economy since his days in Paris.

As he lacked the funds to buy passage for the 400 miles to his Headquarters in the small town of Allanburgh near St. Catharines on the Welland Canal, he asked the Government to advance him the money. The Council refused and also denied him expenses, which considering the inflated salaries and expense accounts of its members, seemed unreasonable. Fortunately he was able to borrow thirty pounds from an army friend who was in business in Montreal with the understanding that he would pay it back from his first salary cheques. Now able to purchase the necessary equipment, he and Maria prepared for a new and challenging life. Metcalfe pressed Richardson's hand affectionately when he said good-bye: "Go; this is the only appointment I have been enabled to obtain for you at present; but acquit yourself of your duty as I know you will, and it will only be the opening to something better."[5]

However well-meaning were Metcalfe's wishes, the situation into which Richardson headed was explosive. The state of unrest amongst the canal workers was serious throughout the forties. When the canal project began under the Board of Works, the labourers toiled from six in the morning until six at night for five shillings daily. Conditions were deplorable, men were laid off without notice and if it rained there was no work. Some lived in shanties which they put together with cheap plyboard slabs on a square of rented land. The others boarded in hovels constructed for the purpose. When the Board of Works leased sections of the canals to contractors, conditions worsened. Payment was reduced to two shillings daily, hours were lengthened from five in the morning to eight in the

[2] ALS, J. Richardson to D. Daly, Montreal, Feb. 28, 1845, Public Archives of Canada, RG5, C1, Vol.882, No.9848.

[3] ALS, W.A. Draper to J. Richardson, Montreal, April 15, 1845, Public Archives of Canada, RG5, C1, Vol.882, No.16720.

[4] ALS, George McDonnell to D. Daly, Montreal, March 1, 1845, Public Archives of Canada, RG5, C1, Vol.882, No.9881. McDonnell revealed that he knew nothing of Richardson's past when he wrote: "...many (especially in Upper Canada) were of the opinion he was overlooked as not having been employed in the Incorporated Battalions during the late troubles."

[5] *Eight Years in Canada*, p.223.

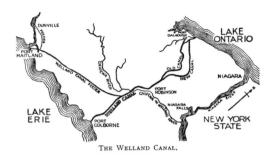

THE WELLAND CANAL.

The Welland Canal

evening; the contractors charged exorbitant rents for lodgings which were supposed to be provided free; they paid the men only once a month thereby forcing them to buy on credit at stores owned by the contractors which sold only expensive food, such as bread, butter, coffee, etc, which the labouring classes could never afford. Because of the rain or ice or a breakdown in the machinery, the labourers could expect to work only 20 days a month during the most favourable season. They were unable to supplement their income as they had to stay near the works which were far from town, otherwise another would be hired in their place, and their wives, who might have been able to contribute by working in town, became an added burden.

In 1843 the labourers on the Beauharnois and Lachine canals struck for the higher wage of three shillings. Maddened by starvation and misery they descended on the homes of the contractors, one by one, and tried to force them to promise to pay the higher wage. Soldiers were called out and fired into the crowd of unarmed workmen. They killed several and pursued the remainder with bayonets. As the official report worded it:

Whether a Magistrate can legally order troops to

144

fire into an assembly of men who are not at the moment engaged in the perpetration of any Act of violence against persons of property and when no more than four minutes have elapsed after reading the proclamation contained in the Riot Act is a question which with various others of minor importance arising out of the occurrences of that fatal day is left for the consideration of the Executive.[6]

Conditions were as bad on the Welland Canal, but the labourers were skilfully turned against one another. The majority of them were Irish, either new immigrants or from public works elsewhere in Canada and the United States. The riots between the men of Cork and the men of Connaught broke out after they struck for higher wages and were idle for some weeks. Some newspapers charged that Hincks was behind this rioting which caused a number of deaths, and which put the lives and property of persons living near the canal in constant jeopardy.[7] Since Hincks was one of the members of the Executive Council who controlled the Board of Works, he may well have had a hand in dissipating the strike in this way.

The Welland Police, under a local man called Benson, seemed unable to control the workers; only the coloured corps under Captain MacDonald from Port Robinson on the canal route could stop the rampaging. Now in 1845 after repeated rioting and bloodshed, Parliament created the Montreal Rifles whose men were to be stationed at strategic areas wherever canals were being built. It was really a device to bring all the local police groups under the command of one Super-

[6] Canada, Legislative Assembly, *Journals*, 7 (1843) App. T.

[7] "Letter to the Editor" from "Hugh MacGregor," Kingston *Statesman* (Dec. 27, 1843); Richardson wrote that the police force was raised to suppress violence "on the part of Mr Hincks' canallers" (*Eight Years in Canada*, p.223).

intendent.

As soon as Richardson's appointment was announced, the Radical press attacked him. Hincks wrote in his newspaper, the *Pilot*: "We wish his Lordship much luck with his friend the Major, who will get him into scrapes enough before he is done with him, or we shall be surprised."[8] He printed a letter to the Editor (which he probably planted), calling the appointment a disgraceful act: "The very appearance of the fellow is enough to excite disgust. He is fond of notoriety and generally contrives to obtain it wherever he goes, as he is universally admitted to be the most quarrelsome and disagreeable person in every society into which he obtains admittance." The *Montreal Courier* berated the *Pilot* for using such bad language about Richardson and warmly supported the appointment.[9]

The man who felt most injured by the appointment was William Benson, who had been nominally in charge of the Police on the Welland Canal for over two years. Killaly, the Chairman of the Board of Works, and other influential politicians assured Benson that his appointment would be made official. On the strength of this promise Benson took a house in Allanburgh, the centre of the works in progress, and moved his family there. When informed that he was to take up the post of Lock Tender and Deputy Collector in Broad Creek at half the pay and less respectability he stormed up to Montreal. Killaly pacified him, raised his salary and may have given him instructions to dislodge Richardson.[10] Benson returned to Allanburgh with the story that Richardson caused his misfortune, thus creating an atmosphere of hostility before the Richardsons arrived.

Meanwhile Daly notified Richardson as to his duties, such as writing official monthly reports directly to Lord Metcalfe. When Richardson reached Allanburgh on the first of June 1845 he found the police in the last stage of disorganization. Since Benson told the constables that the Government had opposed Richardson's appointment and the new Police Act gave the Superintendent no power to deal with insubordination, the first roll call was openly hostile. Two men refused to answer when their names were called and one, George Stoker, dared Richardson with open disdain. He promptly dismissed them which left him with only fifteen men on the force, thus saving the Government 200 pounds yearly, he reported to Metcalfe.[11]

He began laying the foundation for a disciplined force. He ordered that each man should procure a plain uniform, comprising a fur cap, frock coat and two or three pairs of strong riding pantaloons as summer clothing, and a military great coat and trooper's boots for winter, the cost of which the men were to pay in six months installments on the understanding they were to be reimbursed by the Board of Works, according to the terms of the Act. He bought a uniform of finer texture for himself which he wore on official occasions. As he molded the force he asked every man to buy a horse which they all did by autumn. It was a promising beginning, in spite of pressure put on the labourers to show Richardson no respect, and the uncooperative attitude of the local employees of the Board of Works.

The most unco-operative official was the Chief Engineer of the Works, Sam Power. On Benson's recommendation, he hired the men whom Richardson dismissed, as constables for his special force. When

---

[8] *Pilot* (Montreal, June 7, 1845).

[9] *Pilot* (June 17, 1845), excerpt from the Montreal *Courier*.

[10] Killaly, supposedly apolitical in his role as chairman, was really a Reformer who could not have failed to see an opportunity to use the ultra-Conservatism of the "Tory" Benson against the liberal-conservative Richardson. The *Pilot* (July 1, 1845) quotes Tory newspapers differentiating between the politics of Benson and Richardson.

[11] *Correspondence (submitted to Parliament)...* Letter, Richardson to Killaly, Allanburgh, June 6, 1845.

Richardson objected, Power replied that he had done so on grounds of their good character.[12] Two local magistrates were American born and openly opposed to Conservative politics. Understandably, Richardson, who was a magistrate for his district, wrote to the Attorney-General for instructions as to the limits of his jurisdiction so that he would not interfere with the other magistrates. But the Attorney-General would not reply, in spite of repeated queries from Richardson. It seemed that Richardson would have to tread very carefully in order not to be caught out on a technicality.

The village of Allanburgh today comprises about a dozen houses with farmland on the Welland Canal. In 1845 it was a prosperous village of 60 houses which enjoyed the patronage of the canal ship traffic between Lakes Erie and Ontario. Port Robinson lay two miles to the west and St. Catharines about seven miles to the east on Lake Ontario. A coach road led through a twenty mile stretch to Niagara.

Maria stayed with the Charles Richardsons in Niagara until Richardson found a home. The board of Works failed to provide living quarters for them, and the Police Office at Allanburgh was a shambles. Daly recommended the Roman Catholic priest at St. Cath-

arines, the Reverend Mr. McDonagh, as an important contact because of his influence over the Irish labourers.[13] The priest, a rough and ready man, whose brother was one of the contractors on the canal, rented rooms in his house in St. Catharines to the Richardsons until they should secure private accommodation. The Chief Constable, Ed Wheeler, who had been with the force longer than Benson, gave Richardson the necessary guidance during the first weeks.

The pressure upon Richardson to make a good job of his post to vindicate Metcalfe's choice and prove the Reform press wrong became keener every week. He earned Metcalfe's praise when his force apprehended a wanted fugitive,[14] but this success was soon undermined by Benson and his fellow conspirators. Since Richardson knew that Benson's men were watching him, and counselling the constables to disobey his commands, he stayed alert. One evening, one of his men in a drunken condition, pushed into his office and cursed him to his face. As it was rumoured that Richardson had a quick temper, his enemies hoped to provoke him. But Richardson quietly took the abuse, and arranged for the constable to be transferred to a distant post. Richardson complained of Benson's activities to Metcalfe, who unfortunately, was powerless to act, other than to intimate to Benson that he knew of his involvement.

The constable, unhappy in his isolated post along the line of the canal, filed suit against Richardson for both endangering his life and threatening to burn down his house while he was away. The charge was hatched by a local lawyer who did not care if it sounded unreasonable as long as it served the purpose of putting Richardson under arrest.[15] A magistrate in a village far along the canal from Allanburgh issued the

---

12 ALS. S. Power to T. Begley, Secretary of the Board, Jan. 10, 1846, Welland Canal Papers, St Catharines, Jan. 10, 1845-Jan. 2, 1848 on microfilm. "George Stoker is a man whose equal in integrity, intelligence and industry can rarely be found."

13 An example of W.P. McDonagh's influence is given in Ernest Green, "Upper Canada's Black Defenders," Ont. Hist. Soc., *Papers and Records* 27, p.365ff: McDonagh stopped a confrontation between the Coloured Corps and canallers by drawing a line across the road and threatening the ban of the Church on whosoever should cross it. According to Hugh G.J. Aitken, *The Welland Canal* (Harvard Univ. Press, 1954) McDonagh was a scholar. By Oct. 1845 McDonagh was able to congratulate Richardson on the admirable order and appearance of the police force.

14 *Correspondence...* letter, Daly to Richardson, July 19, 1845.

15 *Ibid.*, letter, Richardson to Daly, July 22, 1845.

warrant and stipulated that Richardson be brought to him for trial. These men gloated in anticipation of the humiliation of Richardson as the Superintendent of Police arrested by an ordinary constable.[16]

Benson's resentment overshadowed all other considerations. A reactionary Tory, he plotted with Captain MacDonald, head of the coloured corps, who was a Reformer. MacDonald was so well-connected politically that he was able to have his rival for the contol of the coloured company dismissed, although that rival had filed 13 charges against him.[17] Benson and MacDonald arranged for a third friend, the pugnacious George Stoker, in his capacity as District Constable, to make the arrest at noon one day in the third week of July. Fortunately, Richardson was warned of the plot early in the day by another magistrate from Port Robinson who advised entering into "volontary recognizances" which would free him of having to be brought along the line of the Canal to the magistrate who had issued the order.

Stoker strode into the Police Office at noon when Richardson was eating with some of his men, dragged him from the table, and pushed and pulled him into the street in front of a crowd of people. In spite of the indignity, Richardson remained calm. Stoker made him get into a rail car which was drawn alongside the canal, with the intention of taking him in review past the labourers. Lighting his pipe, Stoker blew smoke in Richardson's face, then, when that brought no reaction, he mocked him. One of Richardson's men rode

Port Robinson, enlarged canal.

ahead to inform the magistrate of Port Robinson, who prepared a bail order and intercepted the car half-way to its destination. But Stoker refused to give up his prisoner until the magistrate persuaded him that his refusal would be a grievous oppression.

A mob of spectators, following the action, filled the Port Robinson courtroom. Among those who crowded in the doorway was Capt. MacDonald, who shouted his disgust as the list of names supplying Rich-

[16] By taking Richardson as a prisoner along the line of works, his enemies expected to undermine his authority and effectiveness.

[17] Ernest Green, "Upper Canada's Black Defenders," Ont. Hist. Soc., *Papers and Records*, 27, p.365ff.

[18] These schemes, against which Richardson depicts himself as politically powerless, cry out for some explanation beyond the antagonisms of party politics which Richardson gives. Similarly it is unbelievable that Richardson's person-

ality could have aroused such hostility. Obviously the members of the Board of Works feared Richardson's presence on the Canal. Possibly an answer may be found in the issuance of a Parliamentary report of the Board shortly after Richardson was dismissed, which revealed the corrupt dealings of its members with the canal contractors (for whom Power had responsibility) and their joint exploitation of the workers. The Board understood that a police superintendent not in complicity with it could be dangerous to it.

147

ardson's bail was read. As Richardson walked away from the courtroom, he considered asking that a court-martial try MacDonald for undermining his authority with his men. It was the only weapon he had.[18]

It might seem strange that the Board of Works would have condoned this methodical plotting against Richardson, who was acting on the orders of the Governor-General, but when one considers that four of the five members of the Board were traditionally on the Executive Council, and the Council had opposed Metcalfe's appointment of Richardson, its attitude can be understood. When Richardson wrote to the Board of Works for instructions, he was abruptly told to address himself only to Lord Metcalfe through the Provincial Secretary. Metcalfe was very ill; cancer had disfigured him; he had to have a hole bored through his cheek so that he could masticate his food; consequently he conducted all his business from his room through the wily Daly. Hincks was eager to hurt Richardson, and the President of the Board, Killaly, who all this time was misusing the funds,[19] was not the kind of man to show sympathy.

The arrest of Richardson was certainly illegal, as no other party could intervene between an officer and his men. Richardson's cousin, Robert Hamilton Jr. of Queenston, took his case, and, showing the groundlessness of the charges, made his accusers drop them with ignominy. Meanwhile Richardson was able to have MacDonald tried in a military court at Niagara by applying to the Major General of the Militia for Canada West.[20] But this unexpected turn of events did not deter his enemies.

George Stoker was posted by the Board at Stone Bridge, a point on the line where the majority of Rich-

ardson's men were stationed. He tried to turn them against their Chief, and when this failed, he was instructed to stir up the canal workers in the usual fashion of turning the Catholics against the Protestants. Bolstering himself with drink, Stoker stood out on the line and shouted: "To hell with the Pope and Father McDonagh!" He had reason to hate McDonagh, as the priest had asked for his dismissal long ago. Stoker's blasphemy caused a riot all right, but it was the workers who almost murdered him. Ironically he had to be rescued by Richardson's police. So far Richardson had been lucky to confound his adversaries. But another attempt to bring him to trial effectively ended his luck.

On August 6, Richardson had a trying day as magistrate in the St. Catharines police court. A lawyer named Burns, cousin to Benson, who made himself obstreperous in Richardson's court on several occasions, provoked Richardson to threaten him with contempt. Burns let it be known that he would "serve Richardson out."[21] That evening as Richardson was walking to the office of the Board of Works with one of his men, Burns walked against them. As the sidewalk was too narrow for the three men, Burns was forced off. He immediately filed a charge against Richardson for assault — "walking violently against the complainant and turning him half round."[22] Richardson, having finished his business at the Board office, and giving the incident no thought, returned to Father McDonagh's residence where he and Maria were staying. Two other clergymen were invited to dinner. As the five of them were at table, George Stoker burst into the house, rushed into the dining room, and, dramatically slapping his hand on Richardson's shoulder shouted that he was under arrest. The effect on the company was that of pure shock. Maria almost fainted. She had been

[19] ALS, H.H. Killaly to W.H. Merritt, Dec. 21, 1845, Public Archives of Canada, Merritt Papers, pp.3206-3210.

[20] Maj.-Gen. William Elliott had fought beside Richardson in the 1812 War, and their families knew each other well.

[21] ALS, J. Richardson to Lord Elgin, Montreal, May 10, 1847, Public Archives of Canada, RG5, C1, Vol.196.

[22] Ibid.

badly upset by the first arrest; the brazeness of this one which seemed incredible in civilized society, shattered her nerves.[23]

Richardson was taken before the magistrate issuing the warrant and remanded for trial the following day. This magistrate was, as Richardson called him, "Yankee-born," and very recently appointed to the magistracy, though he was an "unlettered" coach-driver and tavern keeper.[24]

At the trial, Richardson's companion, the police constable, who was the only witness, testified that no physical contact with Burns was made. But Richardson's judges, the magistrate who issued the warrant, and a fellow magistrate, who was also "Yankee-born," found Richardson guilty and fined him the humiliating sum of one shilling.[25] Their purpose was obvious. They wanted to advertise Richardson's rumoured reputation for violence, and show that their power was such that they could treat him with disdain. Consequently the Superintendent of Police was exhibited as a powerless functionary. This conviction for assault was sufficient cause for his removal from office, if the Board of Works so wished it. Richardson requested an appeal.

Maria pretended to treat the whole affair lightly and laughed at the comic gestures of Stoker, though Richardson noted that behind this facade she was deeply disturbed.[26] She suffered the humiliation of the last few years uncomplainingly, keeping her worries from him just as he tried to keep his fears from her, until drawing further into poverty, uncertainty, frustration and unhappiness, she may have doubted that Richardson would ever succeed. She must have been overwhelmed at the abuse shown this sensitive and talented man. The police appointment had given them hope, but the insidious and ubiquitous opposition Richardson encountered convinced her that his enemies were too numerous and too relentless. The shock of the arrest brought her to bed with fever on the following morning.

For the ten days of her illness Richardson had to ride daily to the Court of Enquiry on Capt. MacDonald in Niagara where he was the prosecutor. If MacDonald were found guilty, Richardson would strengthen his position immeasurably and win back respect for his office. On the seven mile stretch of the winding, tree-lined road back to St. Catharines in the evening, Richardson planned his case for the next day. After seeing to his police and magisterial duties he had little time left for the sick Maria; consequently, he did not realize how sick she really was.

On the last day of the Court of Inquiry in which MacDonald was found guilty, a messenger from St. Catharines rode up to him with the news that Maria was dying. Heart in mouth, he galloped the seven miles like a madman and dashed to her bedside, but she was dead. The catastrophe overwhelmed him. Cursing his enemies, he blamed them for her death. This tragedy, in his words, "rendered my after life desolate and without hope."[27]

Some newspapers reported her death as a result of epilepsy; one said bilious fever. Her obituary was carried in *the Gentleman's Magazine*,[28] England's most

[23] *Ibid.* Maria had been greatly upset at Richardson's first arrest and must have been apprehensive for his safety in a society where he alone represented order opposed to rioting workers and scheming officials on the political left and right.

[24] *Ibid.*

[25] *Ibid.*, *St Catharines Journal* (Aug. 14, 1845): "...the Major apprehended and brought up in the morning for examination when he was nominally fined... a warrant, we understand, was executed with great rudeness"; Hincks commented in the *Pilot*: "Has the Major been looking fierce at him?"

[26] "She affected to treat with levity the inhuman action of the ruffian... but the effort was a forced one." ALS, J. Richardson to Lord Elgin, *op.cit.*

[27] ALS, J. Richardson to Lord Elgin, *op.cit.*

[28] *The Gentleman's Magazine*, NS24 (July-Dec. 1845), 665.

fashionable periodical. Richardson arranged for a grand funeral, in which she was borne from St. Catharines to a grave in the illustrious Butler Burial Ground at Niagara. There are only a half-dozen graves in this small graveyard, which today is still cared for, on the fringe of the town of Niagara-on-the-Lake. A visitor can barely decipher the epitaph on Maria's tombstone:

> Here reposes Maria Caroline. The generous-hearted, high-souled, talented and deeply lamented wife of Major Richardson, Knight of the Military Order of Saint Ferdinand of the First Class, and Superintendent of Police on the Welland Canal during the Administration of Lord Metcalfe. This matchless woman died of Apoplexy and to the exceeding grief of her faithfully attached husband, after a few days' illness in St. Catharines on the 16th of Aug. 1845 at the age of 37 years.[29]

Richardson, who had just paid back the loan from his friend in Montreal, was now almost penniless, but as he had collected a fair sum from fines as magistrate, which he was to turn over to the District Treasurer at the November sessions, he borrowed this money to pay for the funeral. He knew that with parsimony he could soon pay the amount back from his salary.

To help him save, he rented a small cottage at Allanburgh at nine pounds a year and spent twenty pounds to make it habitable, which was to be deducted from the subsequent rent. In other words, he paid his rent for over two years in advance by which time he imagined that the canal work would come to a close. He lived frugally and kept himself apart from the community, entering no private home for the next six months.

[29] Janet Carnochan, "Inscriptions and Graves in the Niagara Peninsula," Niagara Hist. Soc., *Pub.* No.10, p.3.

In a desperate attempt to raise money he again tried to sell his secret on preventing dry-rot in timber, this time to the Executive Council, and enclosed copies of his 1833 correspondence with the British Admiralty on the subject.[30] He recommended that his treatment be applied to the rail lines which were to be built from Quebec to the Maritimes. Thus wood could be used for rails instead of iron. The subject was sent to a legislative committee.

As magistrate he judged cases of petty theft, trespassing, breaking the Sabbath, and assault with sentences from about five shillings to two pounds, the alternative being two months in the Niagara jail. He intended to donate the petty fines he collected from those who broke the Sabbath to the relief of distressed labourers until he discovered that even these fines were payable to the Treasurer of the District.

Charles Richardson recommended a book-keeper, whom Richardson relied upon not only to keep the accounts but to copy out much of the correspondence. In this regard the local office of the Board of Works refused to certify his vouchers for stationery, pens, ink, stoves, wood, candles and so on until he explained that his work was different from his predecessor's as he had to answer the many reports which came from along the line. Power also opposed his requisitions for the establishment of a Police Office at Allanburgh, the central point of the Works, because of the cost, which turned out to be only twenty-five pounds including rent. The need for a place to try prisoners at this point, however, convinced the Board to construct it.

The police force was gradually assuming a smart and well-disciplined look, now that Benson's elements were weeded out and experienced men took their place. There was Chief Constable Wheeler, an ex-militia

[30] ALS, J. Richardson to J.M. Higginson, Allanburgh, Dec. 1, 1845, Public Archives of Canada, RG5, C1, Vol.169, No.12266.

officer, who was a dependable and courageous man; on the recommendation of Father McDonagh, Richardson recruited a surgeon as a constable; he hired an ex-N.C.O. of the King's Dragoon guards who was an excellent driller, so that he was able to drill the police twice a week on two separate sections of the line. These men were taught to use the broad sword, and other useful cavalry movements. The force still comprised 15 men plus Wheeler and Richardson, but its effectiveness began to awe the labourers. When Richardson first began as magistrate he was faced with a gang of Sunday rioters in court every Monday morning, but now the number had greatly decreased.

In September, Richardson sent a note on mourning paper by two of his men to the Military Secretary in the party of the new Commander of the Forces, Lord Cathcart, who was stopping in St. Catharines. He offered the services of his men, who knew the territory well, as guides for Cathcart's passage through the Niagara frontier. The Secretary's abrupt rejection implied mistrust of Richardson's motives.[31]

Just as Jackson (who had died of apoplexy in June) was opposed to him, so apparently was his successor, Cathcart. Cathcart received the result of the court martial on Captain MacDonald but did not act upon it.[32] One reason for his journey through the area may have been to investigate the matter, for MacDonald had powerful political backing and it was becoming evident that Cathcart would have to replace Metcalfe as Governor-General soon.

Meanwhile Richardson's appeal for the decision in the Burns assault case was being prepared by his lawyer for the autumn assizes. Burns who came from an old family in St. Catharines, was well-known locally. As the trial got underway Burns chatted and joked with

the jurors who were openly hostile to Richardson. The two magistrates were the same "Yankees" who had judged him previously when there was no jury.

The police constable who had testified on Richardson's behalf in the first trial, now appeared as chief witness for the prosecution. Richardson had discharged this constable shortly after the first trial for remarks he made on the management of the police which Richardson considered deliberately impertinent. He then learned that the constable had been given a month's pay in advance by Power and a better post in the office of the Board of Works. No one was surprised that he changed his testimony, but Richardson was surprised that anyone would believe it.[33]

Although it was obvious that the verdict of guilty was contrary to all the evidence which could be relied upon, Richardson heard the jury uphold the verdict, and in frustration referred the case to Lord Cathcart, who had just succeeded Metcalfe as Governor-General. He asked for the interposition of the Attorney-General, but Cathcart refused. Some other magistrates of the District, scandalized by this kind of justice, referred the case to the Court of the Queen's Bench in Toronto, which, however, would not interfere with the proceedings of the Quarter Sessions.[34] All of these appeals cost Richardson money, which he was ordered to pay under penalty of imprisonment in the common jail at Niagara. Consequently he used up most of the money he collected in fines as magistrate and was unable to pay the Treasurer the amount due at the Quarter Sessions. Fortunately the District Clerk at Niagara arranged for him to settle the full amount at the Winter

[31] ALS, Lt-Col F.A. Fraser to J. Richardson, Sept. 1845, Public Archives of Canada, c ser., Vol.60, pp.287-9.

[32] *Correspondence...passim.*

[33] ALS, J. Richardson to Lord Elgin, *op.cit.*

[34] *Ibid.*; The Court of the Queen's Bench may have refused to hear Richardson's case owing to the influence of a leading member of the Bar and a Judge of the Queen's Bench Court, Hogerman, a former law partner and close friend of Robert Burns, Judge of the Home District Court, brother of Thomas Burns who was charging Richardson with assault.

Sessions.

Richardson's insistence on proving his innocence in these suspect circumstances was typical of him. He shared with the Knight of La Mancha a naive belief in the justice of providence. If there were ever a symbol of a windmill, this court was it. Richardson tilted his lance against the hypocrites and came out of the battle much the worse for wear. Maria's death shocked and saddened him, but it did not destroy him; rather he became more determined to scatter his enemies and survive by means of the chivalric code. Her death, though, made him feel that his days were numbered. When he began living in his small cottage he worked at an autobiography every evening. It was eventually published as *Eight Years in Canada*, historically valuable for its accounts of the Durham, Sydenham, Bagot and Metcalfe administrations and as the main social commentary on the Canada of that day.

Escape as he might into the world of the artist in the evening, he faced the bitterness of the day without flinching. Warned by Chief Constable Wheeler that the fever days which kept the labourers subdued from July through October were coming to an end, Richardson asked Power to construct quarters to hold a large force of men at a point in the line between Port Robinson and Port Colborne on Lake Erie, where the major work was to be done during the winter. He had three men at this point, "the junction," who were insufficient to control 475 workers. Also the Major-General of the Militia issued an order for twenty of the coloured troops to be stationed there as soon as the Board of Works rented or constructed the accomodation. But Captain MacDonald of the Coloured Corps opposed the order. He called the place unhealthy although this was disproved by the doctor of the Coloured Corps. Power, agreeing with MacDonald, refused to act on

Richardson's request, and insisted that the Montreal office of the Board of Works rule on the order.[35]

Colder weather caused a slow-down in the canal works and many labourers were laid off. To offset the inevitable rioting after payday, Richardson placed his men in several posts along the line for purposes of communication. He worried that the small force at the Junction would be overpowered before help could be summoned from Port Robinson which was fourteen miles away. Throughout this tense situation the Montreal Board of Works maintained silence, and Richardson became angrier with Power. Just then, he made a bold decision which intimidated the workers and probably did more than any show of troop strength to dissuade them from rioting.

In December four workers tried to kill a Port Colborne citizen. Three of them were caught and sent by Richardson to the Niagara jail, but the fourth escaped over the U.S. border, a trick which had always brought them refuge from Canadian police. This time Richardson sent Wheeler over the border to Lockport where he obtained the permission of the authorities to make the arrest. Encountering the escaped man on the street, Wheeler put him in a carriage and drove him back to police quarters at Stone Bridge, much to the amazement and consternation of the workers. For the next

[35] *Correspondence...*, letter, J. Richardson to S. Power, Dec. 18, 1845.

[36] The ms., which became *Eight Years in Canada*, was entitled at that time "Seven Years in Canada." The passage referred to concerned Killaly's caustic remark to a woman friend about Richardson's clothing and his subsequent humble apology. It eventually found its way to Hincks who commented in the *Pilot* (May 21, 1846) about Richardson's "peculiar winter dress calculated to attract observation and which caused its wearer to cut a very grotesque figure" in an attempt to throw the onus off Killaly should the passage appear in print. (Richardson cut it from the published work). Richardson described his travelling dress as a Spanish zamarra or fur jacket, and a tasseled velvet cap (*Eight Years in Canada*. p.67).

months there was peace on the Welland Canal.

Meanwhile Richardson's bookkeeper was acting strangely. He was repeatedly drunk on duty, and he sent an unflattering paragraph about Killaly in Richardson's manuscript, which he was copying, to Killaly, the Chairman of the Board of Works.[36] Richardson discharged him, only to see him immediately employed by Power who urged him to give reasons for disbanding the police force. Since there now was peace on the canal during the inclement season when usually there was much rioting and destruction of property, Power claimed that the police were no longer necessary. His official letters to the Board Secretary reveal that this idea had been in his mind for months, dating from the time Richardson became Superintendent. By mid-August he had written: "Fortunately the number of labourers now employed on the Canal is so small that the preservation of the peace cannot be a matter of great difficulty. If it were otherwise, and the united effort of all were needed I fear that it would scarcely be possible for the officer of the Board and the inhabitants generally to act in concert with this Gentleman."[37] Now in December aided by the bookkeeper's testimony he wrote an official report asking for the reduction of the force.

Power's machinations were unknown to Richardson until Power, in a boastful mood, told Father McDonagh on December 17 that Richardson's force was to be disbanded. Richardson wrote an angry letter to Power:

You, I believe, are an Irish-American — at least your home is in the United States — and much of the public monies you have amassed to yourself in Canada, have gone, if I am correctly informed, to the improvement of your property in that country. Most of the contractors employed by you are also Americans and the large sums paid to them are ultimately taken out of the Province. With such absence of inducement, to feel anything like interest in the successful defence of this country in the event of a war between England and the United States, which is now looked upon as a certainty, it cannot afford matter for surprise that you should deem a Police Force unnecessary on this Canal. What matter to you if the unchecked labourers should use the arms, you well know to be in their possession, to strike a blow in favour of the Americans, in this District, in which they will find too many heartily disposed to join them. Your home is not in Canada, and it is but to cross the Line to escape the evil you may have caused.[38]

Richardson's accusations were politically explosive. The Americans were pressing Britain in order to get control of the Oregon territory, indeed for all the land in the west up to the fifty-fourth parallel, a problem which occupied Cathcart to the utter exclusion of other governmental affairs. Richardson laid six specific charges against Power illustrating how he had deliberately hindered him in the discharge of his duties, and sent a copy to Daly with documents. This temporarily deterred the Board from taking any immediate action regarding the police.

Power wrote self-righteously to the Board office in Montreal to comment on his official request for the dismissal of the police:

In that report I carefully abstained from naming or alluding to the Superintendent conceiving that I was only requested to state my opinion as to the expediency of maintaining a force or not and that it would be improper for me unsolicited and un-

[37] ALS, Power to Begley, Aug. 19, 1845, Welland Canal Papers, op.cit.

[38] Correspondence..., letter, Richardson to Power, Dec. 17, 1845.

153

provoked to censure the conduct of an officer appointed by the government to an important charge especially as many of his proceedings (which are excusable only on the supposition that he is a lunatic) have caused such general dissatisfaction. It is proper that I should inform the Board that hereafter I will return all Major Richardson's letters and decline to hold any communication with him. This course may cause some embarassment to the service but cannot be disapproved of by the Board who would not wish that any officer should be exposed to outrage and insult — the necessary consequences of contact with this person.[39]

The Secretary of the Board asked Power for a further report. Power replied:

The statement which is appended, will explain the general distribution of the laboring force and will show that if the desire of the Board be the persecution of such riots only as may obstruct the progress of the works essential to the opening of navigation no Police establishment whatever can be required and with this view solely the Board would be justified in removing the force altogether. They would however in my opinion act more wisely in retaining the Chief Constable Mr. Wheeler and one or two men who in case of necessity could cooperate with him and might by proper vigilance prevent these trifling disturbances which often culminate in serious riots. They would also be very careful next season in preventing any attempts on the part of the labourers to interfere with vessels navigating the canal.[40]

[39] ALS, Power to Begley, Dec. 20, 1845, Welland Canal Papers, *op.cit.*
[40] ALS, Power to Begley, Jan. 2, 1846, Welland Canal Papers, *op.cit.*

When asked by the Secretary to comment on Richardson's accusations against him, Power defended himself at length; "Personally I cannot stoop to notice any act of the Superintendent of Police — he has fallen too low — his disgraceful conduct on a recent occasion, has removed him beyond the reach of such notice..." Power explained that he was not hostile to the police, but had tried to advise Richardson through Father McDonagh to reduce the force: "I do not mean to say that by persuing this course I was activated by any feeling of friendship towards the superintendent — such I never professed to entertain but neither could I have entertained any feeling of hostility — for that feeling is incompatible with unmingled contempt."[41]

The Board of Works, which is to say the Executive Council, with Cathcart's consent, advised Provincial Secretary Daly to disband Richardson's police force on January 31, 1846. Now that Metcalfe had returned to England, Richardson could expect no support from any part of the Government. Although it was usual to give militia men good notice so that they could find other work, and a month's separation pay, the Government disregarded these niceties, causing dismay and incredulity. The constables, who could not hope to find other work, some of them living in other districts of the country, were thrown with their families into great hardship.[42]

Richardson's creditors were prompted to sue him. The contractor for the men's uniforms journeyed from Toronto to Allanburgh to draw a bond on Richardson for seventy-five pounds.

At noon on January 31, Richardson and his men

[41] ALS, Power to Begley, Jan. 10, 1846, Welland Canal Papers, *op.cit.*
[42] Testimony of Frederick Wilkinson, "Minutes of Evidence (Question) 32," June 3, 1846, "Report of the Select Committee to which was referred the Petition of Major Richardson...," Canada, Legislative Assembly, *Journals* 9 (1846), App.ZZ.

trooped to the Board of Work's Office in St. Catharines and handed over their arms and ammunitions. Richardson made sure he received a receipt for every item. As he returned to Allanburgh, one member of his force told him that a jubilee was planned for that evening. There remained just Richardson and one other constable to keep the peace. The hate for this saddened lone knight was evident in the faces of the citizens.[43] His reserve might have offended many of the democrats who were settling the country, and his well-known dislike for the "Yankees" may have made him unnecessary enemies. Apart from this, Richardson was a convenient scapegoat: the poor citizens had to scrape through a long and cold winter of high prices, and the labourers who had been intimidated for weeks by his force, were angered when they found themselves being laid off work because of the cold and ice. He was not the man to speak of the treachery of Power and Benson beyond his official reports so that his police did not understand the feud between the Board of Works and himself; they may well have thought that the whole force was being punished because Richardson had been convicted for assault. An ugly mood was brewing.

It was Saturday, and at eight o'clock in the evening, Richardson, who was reading in his small cottage on the town's outskirts, noticed that candles were placed in the windows of some houses and the tavern across the way. The tavern belonged to a "Yankee ruffian" who allowed a great bonfire to be built in its backyard.

At 8:30 the sound of horns and trumpets, sufficient to tumble Jericho's walls, came from a mob which had assembled in the tavern yard and was moving towards Richardson's cottage. He set his pistols on the table and locked the doors. A band of boys and 12 men marched along the road and fronted to face the door of his cottage by command. They cheered three times and fired a dozen shots. When Richardson failed to appear they went away.

At nine o'clock the same procedure was followed, though the mob now was much larger. The gunshots continued in a deafening display in front of his cottage for some time, but Richardson refused to be intimidated. The mob called on him to come out, but he knew that if he did so he would be shot and little effort would be made to find the culprits. The act of breaking and entering Richardson's cottage, on the other hand, was dangerous because it revealed criminal intent, and the trespassers could be gunned down by Richardson quite legally. The mob retired.

At about 10:30 the shouting and gunfire resumed. Twenty-five to thirty canallers shouted for him to come out. "I had on this occasion taken the precaution to go into a dark room where I could see from the window without being seen myself, and I could distinctly make out the dress of one of my own policemen, although I could only suspect the party."[44] It was a contest of nerves. Richardson, the sole representative of law and order, was being challenged to assert his authority. This time the lone knight thought discretion the better part of valour.

At midnight, when it appeared that the assaults were abandoned for the night, Richardson wrote his last official report to Secretary Daly in which he described the events of that evening as a riot. He added that he had heard it rumoured that a new police force was to be drawn up under Power, about whom he had justly complained. Actually this was no rumour, but a fact. Killaly planned to keep Chief Constable Wheeler and four other police on the new force, two of the men as constables who had been discharged by Richardson, one of whom was George Stoker. But the cruelest stroke, which Richardson learned of

---

[43] *Correspondence..., passim.*

[44] *Ibid.*, letter, Richardson to Daly, Niagara, Feb. 20, 1846.

later, was the arrangement to pay Wheeler and Stoker the same salary that Richardson had received, though they had nothing like his responsibility.[45]

Richardson would not venture outside his cottage. The contractor's suit gave Power the right to arrest him for debt and cart him twenty miles to jail in Niagara, should he appear. But after a week, in the dead of night, he stole out to his stable, swiftly saddled his horse, and rode for his brother's house in Niagara.

Period Of Adjustment

SOME YEARS EARLIER, Charles Richardson introduced in the Upper Canada Assembly but failed to win approval for a bill to abolish imprisonment for debt. Now, ironically, his brother came to him with the baillifs at his heels. Only a technicality saved Richardson from jail: he refused to sign the paychecks for his men until a bond of indemnity from the contractor released him from having to pay for the uniforms. The fines he collected as magistrate and had spent on the cottage and Maria's funeral had to be paid to the District Treasurer at the winter Court Session in Niagara. Charles, as Clerk of the Peace, allowed him to forego payment until he should have the money — not an unusual occurence among the magistrates, Charles explained.[1]

Meanwhile Samuel Power had barracks constructed at the junction for a detachment of coloured troops under Captain MacDonald. That which he would not do for Richardson, he accomplished within days after the reduction of Richardson's force. His haste resulted from the riotous mood of the labourers who were unemployed because of a suspension of the Works.[2]

Richardson set out late in February for Montreal where his credit was good. First, he solicited and received a letter of praise from Metcalfe's former Private Secretary — for overcoming impediments

which he has thought were purposely thrown in your way and which tended to render your position more difficult and embarrassing and that his lordship was to the best of my knowledge satisfied with the manner in which you had encountered and overcome the obstacles opposed to you.[3]

Secondly, he petitioned Lord Cathcart charging that the sudden reduction of the force injured his character "for capacity to discharge a public trust" and that the Government had failed to support its servant in the pursuit of his duty. He asked for either a new post equal to the last or a gratuity.[4]

He appealed to Parliament and his case was referred to a Select Committee with the power to send for all persons, papers and records required.[5] His complaint came at a time of public concern over a "Report" of an official investigation into the Board of Works, which charged the members of the Board with irresponsibility in its operations and total disregard of every rule laid down for its guidance. The Board's engagements with contractors were fulfilled by extraordinary aid from the Government. It was concluded that the Board was a defective organization with poor bookkeeping and a disregard for the law.[6]

The Report of the Select Committee, presented to

---

[45] *Ibid.*

[1] ALS, Richardson to Lord Elgin, *op. cit.*

[2] ALS, Power to Begley, Feb. 16, 1846. Welland Canal Papers, *op. cit.*

[3] ALS, Higginson to Richardson, Mar. 17, 1846, Public Archives of Canada, RG, C1, Vol. 882, No. 16720.

[4] *Correspondence.... passim.*

[5] "Petition of Major Richardson, May 22, 1846." Canada, Legislative Assembly, *Journals*, (1846).

[6] "Report on the Board of Works, Mar. 28, 1846," Canada, Legislative Assembly, *Journals*, 5 (1846) App.O.

the Assembly on June 5, recommended that Richardson and his ex-constables receive payment for their uniforms and an additional month's pay as gratuity.

Your Committee are also of opinion that injustice has been done to the Petitioner, in dismissing him from his situation on the reduction of the Police Establishment, and continuing the Chief Constable at the same rate as that previously paid to the Petitioner. There appears to have been no cause of complaint against the Superintendent, and from all that appears he had discharged his responsible duties in a satisfactory and creditable manner.[7]

The Assembly voted 38 to 8 to reject the recommendations of the report. (Among the eight were Macdonald and Merritt.) By printing the pamphlet of his correspondence as Superintendent, and by hinting of widely distributing it, Richardson may have turned many members against him. He had written: "I trust to be enabled to make out of the publication of their own monstrous injustice, quite as much as they may feel inclined to accord to me, if they do accord anything at all."[8]

Hincks ridiculed the pamphlet in his paper, the Pilot, as a threat to the administration. Other papers carried Richardson's denial that he intended to publish the pamphlet, which he said was only for the understanding of the members of the Assembly.[9] "Surely," Hincks retorted, "the Major does not expect his minis-

terial friends to believe this."[10] He warned that Richardson was preparing the prospectus of a newspaper to oppose the administration and that he would edit it if he did not get another public office.

On June 9, days after the adverse vote of the Assembly on his petition, handbills were pasted on walls throughout Montreal announcing the publication of Correspondence (submitted to Parliament) Between Major Richardson, Late Superintendent of Police on the Welland Canal and the Honorable Dominick Daly, Provincial Secretary. . . . He dedicated to Lord Metcalfe this collection of official letters to Daly, Power and others, and charged that after Metcalfe had striven to find him a post against great opposition, his removal from that post was planned by the Conservative Government as soon as Metcalfe left Canada.

The attempt to put me quietly aside has, however, signally failed; and let those who have thus sought to make their authority subservient, not to the ends of justice or to the public good, but to their own private views, incure all the odium and censure of the public sense of right. They have spread their nets only to ensnare themselves and it must be confessed that they have made a bungling affair of it, not to have continued the execution of their designs in such manner as to escape detection.[11]

Taking a poke at Daly, he defended himself with something less than candour: "I am no toady; nor can I play the fawning truculent courtier to each succeeding Governor, and pay to all an equal homage."[12]

The money from the sale of the pamphlet provided the capital for Richardson's anti-ministerial news-

[7] "Report of the Select Committee to which was referred the Petition of Major Richardson..." Canada, Legislative Assembly, Journals, 9 (1846), App.ZZ.

[8] ALS, Richardson to John Simpson, Montreal, May 21, 1846, Public Archives of Canada, RG5, C1, Vol. 202, No. 15919.

[9] Pilot (May 23, 1846).

[10] Ibid.

[11] Correspondence.... passim.

[12] A soubriquet, the Perpetual Secretary, was applied to Daly.

Major John Richardson, Knight of San Fernando,
by Frederick Lock, 1848.

paper, the *Weekly Expositor or Reformer of Public Abuses
and Railway and Mining Intelligencer*, which began to
appear in August of 1846. Commented the Toronto
Globe:

It is throughout characterized by that delightful
self-possession, that happy tone of assumption,
that "*Whose dog are you?*" sort of air, which gives a
charm to every man or thing fortunate enough to
emanate from the city of Montreal.[13]

No copy of the newspaper remains, but excerpts
from it in the form of disclosures of frauds by Government officials and of bureaucratic mismanagement
were reprinted in other papers.[14] His intention, baldly
stated, was to embarass the Government and drive it
from office — an early example of muckraking.

At the close of September Richardson began to
serialize "Eight Years in Canada" in his newspaper; it
won praise from the Montreal *Courier*:

From the promise afforded by the first chapter we
should think that it will prove a very amusing
work, as the style, in the lighter parts, is very easy
and unaffected, and at the same time very in-
structive as a work of reference. . . .[15]

In 1847 it was published in book form in London
and Montreal. An autobiographical commentary from
the time of his arrival in Canada through the Metcalfe
administration, its analysis of the Canadian politics of
the day from the point of view of a participant makes it
a valuable record for Canadians.

About this time Richardson had his portrait drawn
by an itinerant Englishman; his eyes reveal his intelligence but they hold a sadness only faintly obscured
by a touch of humour; his carefully groomed mustache,
untidy hair, bold expression, and dangling eyeglasses

[13] Ms. notes tipped into the back of McGill University's
copy of *Eight Years in Canada*.

[14] *St. Catharines Journal* (Oct. 29, 1846).

[15] *St. Catharines Journal* (Oct. 1, 1846), excerpt from
Courier.

combine to give the impression of a clearsighted dreamer, a visionary whose medals at his chest are mere tokens of his experience.

The Niagara magistrates were still after him. They formed a Select Committee of three, one of whom was Chief Engineer for the Board of Works, to go over his accounts. They concluded that he owed over 37 pounds rather than 29.[16] Richardson's income from his newspaper now made it possible for him to pay, but he refused to consider a debt, one third greater than he owed. He was even less inclined to pay when he learned that the Attorney-General had been prowling the Welland Canal district to find complaints about his work as a magistrate. Fortunately his accounts and behaviour were above reproach. He wrote in a mood of frustrated anger and self-pity to the District Clerk at Niagara:

Had the Government — had the infamous Chairman of the Board of Works not indirectly countenanced every attempt that was made to insult and annoy me, the gross outrage offered to me in dragging me in the presence of my wife from the table of a Minister of Religion would never have been perpetrated, and I should not have been as I now am, desolate and writhing under the conviction that the false Government had by its conduct been instrumental in her death. True, the avenging hand of a just Providence has caused the immediate perpetrator to perish by a violent death, but the prime movers of the whole still live and have my unmixed detestation.

But the Select Committee rather than showing

sympathy accused him of "language disrespectful to the Government."[17] Finally, in April 1847 Richardson gave a detailed explanation of the items in question, which proved satisfactory to the Council in Niagara.[18] He was charged with owing 29 pounds.

But winter had brought a change in fortune. His newspaper had died in January. Cathcart was replaced as Governor-General by Lord Elgin. It was to this nobleman, brother-in-law to Lord Durham, that Richardson addressed a long letter of explanation of the Welland Canal affair and admitted his inability to pay.[19] Moved, Elgin quashed the charges.

The repercussions of the repeal of the Corn Laws and the return of the Whigs to Government in England brought the Reformers to power in Canada in January 1848. Richardson had the satisfaction of seeing his Tory enemies defeated, and found consolation in the fact that his writings were in part responsible — though a Reform government gave him no cause for celebration, especially when he saw an old enemy like Murdoch Morison win election to the Assembly on the Reform Party ticket.[20]

His life-long dislike for the merchant class which had become the dominant force in Canadian politics, helps to explain his apparent ambivalence between the

[16] ALS, Daly to Richardson, April 13, 1847. Public Archives of Canada, RG5, C1, Vol. 882, No. 15919.

[17] ALS, Richardson to Simpson, Montreal, Sept. 27, 1846, Public Archives of Canada RG5, C1, Vol. 882, No. 15919.

[18] ALS, Thorburn to Daly, Niagara, May 4, 1847, Public Archives of Canada, RG5, C1, Vol. 882, No. 16686. The accounts were withheld from Richardson until April, although he had asked repeatedly to see them.

[19] ALS, Richardson to Lord Elgin, May 10, 1847, *op. cit.*

[20] The reaction of the country to the bad Government of the Conservative-Reform moderate coalition (sabotaged by Tory and Radical alike) brought to power these Reformers whose previous term in office had been frustrated by Metcalfe. Eager to effect reforms quickly the new government proved tragic for the country. A piece in the satirical *Punch in Canada* (March 3, 1849) called Murdoch Morison a specimen of "spar" in a report of a debate on a geological survey in the Assembly.

two political parties. The Rebellion of 1837-38 had swung the capitalist bourgeois into power against which Richardson fought to preserve gentlemanly conduct and the expression of individualism. Like a true Saint-Simonian he sought a compromise between commercial development and the less selfish spirit of a by-gone age. But he saw that politicians, Reformers and Tory alike, were caught up unthinkingly in the utilitarian wave of capitalism which was conquering all opposition under the guise of Responsible Government. In this age of commercial development, beginning in the late 1840's following through several decades, the men in Parliament indiscriminately granted one another charters for banks and railroads which became the bases of Canadian family fortunes. Whether it was the Tory MacNab (later Sir Allan) or the Reformer Hincks (later Sir Francis) Parliamentarians got rich dishonestly in the name of capitalist enterprise.[21]

For example, Hincks, when Finance Minister in 1850, was quietly paid $250,000 by English contractors for giving them the building rights for the Grand Trunk Railway despite an Act of Parliament calling for its construction as a public work by the Canadian Government and the municipalities.

Richardson as a "Reformer of Public Abuses" in 1846 pointed out how Canada could be exploited by these shameless promoters. His political position, therefore, led him to fight corruption in Government regardless of party. He became an occasional correspondent for other newspapers, including the Montreal *Courier* of which Stewart Derbishire became editor in 1847. For this the *Courier* was reproached by Hincks:

Canada has produced two men who if they are

neither great nor distinguished, are certainly ambitious, and we may add, so far as regards Canadian society, a little notorious: Gugy and Richardson. . . . The Major is a man of rather less importance than the Colonel, but he is happy in having the same organ for communication with the public, vis: that talented and consistent journal, the Courier. . .[22]

Colonel B.C. Augustus Gugy was a Conservative whose contributions to the *Courier* were in the form of letters defending himself from the attacks of the Reformers.[23] A mixture of French courtliness and English practicality, Gugy clashed with the Reformers when as Adjutant-General of the Lower Canada Militia he sided with Lord Metcalfe against the Executive Council to prevent the Council from making Militia appointments. The Council abolished his post and the Reformers started a vilification campaign against him as they had against Richardson. Thus the two men having a similar outlook and personal characteristics became fast friends.

Richardson's contributions to the *Courier* included a series of letters under the pseudonym "Detroit" advocating that medals should be awarded militiamen for certain battles of the 1812 War. He encouraged militiamen to send petitions to their respective Colonels who would send them to the Adjutant-General who would then notify the Prime Minister of England — ". . . most assuredly Lord John Russell will not hesitate to redress

---

[21] Gustavus Myers, *History of Canadian Wealth* (Chicago: Charles Kerr, 1914), I, 154ff; ref. Hincks and Grand Trunk Railway, I, 170ff.

[22] "The Colonel and the Major," *Pilot* (April 9, 1847); the *Courier*, now called the *Morning Courier*, was reprinted in the evening until Sept. 1848 when it announced that the *Evening Courier* would be no longer a facsimile "but a literary and art newspaper entirely on its own." Richardson's talents would have been employed by this latter paper.

[23] *Morning Courier* (Montreal, Oct. 19, 1848). Gugy counted 81 articles vilifying him by Oct. 1848: 15 in the *Herald*, 22 in the *Transcript*, and 44 in the *Pilot*.

the grievance."[24] Other newspapers eagerly took up Richardson's idea. Also he again raised the subject of a monument to Tecumseh, for which various committees in Upper Canada had collected money, but which was forgotten over the years. He claimed that the Treasurer of the Montreal committee had used the money to make a road which benefited his property.

A close friend to Richardson, William M.B. Hartley, worked on the staff of the *Courier*. The interest in literature in Montreal, which prompted the citizens, including ministers of the Government, to form literary societies, owed much to his energy. He was the President of the Shakespeare Club and lectured on literary topics: for example, on "The Ancient Literature of England" for the Mercantile Library Association.[25] His interests are reflected in the theme of Richardson's novel written in 1848 about the Crusades in the eleventh century.[26] As its title, *The Monk Knight of St. John*, suggests, Richardson intended it to be popular reading. Here again, however, is the inevitable confrontation; it dealt with sexual love in a frank manner that, as Richardson must have known, was sacrilegious in his Victorian age. It was not pornographic; on the contrary, it was revolutionary. Yet, considering the socialist agitation in Europe and the Revolutions of 1848, Richardson was in step with the spirit of his age. His writing bursts with energy as if fueled by the revolutionary fervour of the period. At one point in the novel, he referred to the possibility of the public's adoption of the novel's free-thinking philosphy by an oblique allusion to Lamartine, the poet of free love, who in the spring of 1848 was chosen as the Premier of France by the "capitalists of the most intellectual city of the world."[27] Under the guise of Gothic romance, *The Monk Knight of St. John* represented a sexual emancipation that went counter to the moralistic thinking of its day, stood opposed to the mainstream of American literary conventions and expressed an intensity of emotion whose honesty could not be denied, yet could only be accepted after the "sexual revolution" of the 1960's. The novel dealt with the relationship of divine love to carnal knowledge at a time when American novelists associated sexual desire with sin and avoided describing the sexual act as if it were an irrevocable taboo.[28] In the novel, sex, whether it be homosexual love or adultery, is not wrong unless the result of licentious desire and rape: there are three crimes against God: murder, blasphemy and slander: the remaining crimes are "of human invention."[29] In this way Richardson dispensed with the standard stock and trade of the American novelist — for him, virginity is of no value and carnal knowledge leads to an understanding of God rather than to ignominy and hideous death. Richardson relied on the techniques of the Gothic to give rapid pace to his story, to introduce the unexpected and to avoid having to account for interludes of time in order to synchronize the action. But actually he turned the Gothic novel around. Instead of a background of church morality and hypocritical transgressors in which sexual desire was condemned as sinful without question, he set the novel in the eleventh century with the crusading Christian armies in

[24] "Correspondence. Militia Medals — No. III," *Morning Courier*, Oct. 30, 1847. Richardson wrote three letters from Oct. 15 - 30, 1847.

[25] On April 30, 1848. Practically nothing is known of this man who seems to have provided a literary spark in Montreal. He also was a returning officer for Montreal elections.

[26] *The Monk Knight of St. John* catches a sense of the Middle Ages through representing the mentalities of the personages rather than depicting castled scenery and armoured accoutrements.

[27] *The Monk Knight of St. John*, p.83.

[28] Leslie A. Fiedler, *Life and Death in the American Novel*, 2nd. ed. (New York: Criterion Books, 1966), *passim*.

[29] *The Monk Knight of St. John*, p.84.

Palestine when the grossest immoralities and the unrelenting slaughter of human life were committed as if by the command of God, and sexual expression was the divine right of the conqueror in whichever mode he chose. Against this background sin was no longer an issue, and Richardson could develop his ideas on love through inter-relationships among people rather than in juxtaposition to an anonymous and all-powerful morality.

In the manner of the Gothic novel he begins the book with his discovery of an old parchment in a deserted ancient Chateau in Auvergne. The parchment tells the story of three people whose likenesses are represented in the life-size statues of a noble knight-crusader, a beautifully-formed female, and a Monk of the Chivalric Order of St. John "grouped round a figure of Cupid, bearing a torch in his right hand." The parchment warns the reader against condemning the story: "Man is the creature of circumstances. . . make not evil where none exists."

The main theme of sexual tri-union is introduced right away. Alfred, the handsome, blue-eyed Baron de Boiscourt, is attempting to excite the imagination of the chaste Abdallah, a warrior Monk, by describing the voluptuousness of the Baron's wife, Ernestina. He is pleased to see by Ernestina's letters that he has been successful in stirring her passions for the Monk, and as for Abdallah, he watches his resolution to lead a life of chastity begin to weaken (as if Mephistopheles were taking pleasure in tempting Faust).[30] The reader soon interprets the Baron's motives as indirect homosexuality. This impression is reinforced by the recounting of his first meeting with the Monk Knight whom the Baron finds slaying some of his men as they are raping Saracen women, the most ravishing being Zuleima, one of the wives of Saladin, the Moslem leader. The

Baron, taking the Saracen women disguised as soldiers back to the Christian camp, encourages his sixteen-year old page, Rudolph, to sleep with the beautiful Zuleima during the night. In the morning he wakes Rudolph, sends him on an errand, and makes love to Zuleima himself. ("Have I not, in my turn, followed where you have led?" remarks the Baron enigmatically to Rudolph later).[31] Abdallah awakens, and looks into the tent:

Gently he raised one corner and stood almost transfixed with confusion at what he beheld. There was now no doubting the evidence of his senses. Rudolph was nowhere to be seen, but on the broad velvet couch, and faintly revealed in the dim light which burned in the distance, he saw the lady and the knight fast locked in each other's arms. Abdallah felt the blood to ebb and flow within his veins with a violence that threatened to destroy him. Quickly he dropped the curtain, pressed his hands to his aching brow, and sank upon his knees, praying silently, but fervently, that some dreadful scourge might not fall upon the Christian camp, as a punishment for so great a sin. Somewhat relieved by this prayer, he rose, moved back to the seat he had just left, and mused deeply. For the first time, the veil had fallen from his eyes, the sealed book of God's holiest mystery had been fully opened to him.[32]

Some time passes before Abdallah is finally overwhelmed by desire and with carnal experience breaks free from the trammels of narrow thought to a greater understanding of the world; but when he is overwhelmed, it is by the charms of Zuleima. Unfortunately, Abdallah, who is of Moorish origin, discovers that Zu-

---

30 *Ibid.*, p.12. Richardson's favourite play was Marlowe's *The History of Dr. Faustus.*

31 *Ibid.*, p.36.
32 *Ibid.*, p.28.

leima is his sister — a touch of Gothic, but of no significance to the story other than to persuade him to concentrate on Ernestina. For some critics such as Desmond Pacey writing in 1951[33] the novel represents "a sly, lascivious, lip-licking dirtiness" that reveals Richardson's mind as "affected." There may be some justification in viewing the Baron's action as unsavoury, but the honesty of Richardson's portrayal of the Baron should not be impugned. To deny that the characters of the novel should enjoy the sexual act according to their individual natures, is to adopt the Victorian attitude that disinfects love of its carnal relationship.

When, after the Knights are defeated in the Battle of Tiberias, and Abdallah, believing the Baron dead, journeys to Auvergne to meet Ernestina, the "divine" passion of love is described with a purity of intention:

> . . . so completely were their senses steeped in the all-absorbing love, which placed no limit to its indulgence, that their appetites failed them, and the common rest of wearied nature was denied to them. One only thought, one only image, one only desire filled their mutual and quenchless affection, which circulated keenly, exquisitely, stingingly through their veins, and produced an excitement that never slumbered. . .[34]

When the Baron de Boiscourt mysteriously appears on the scene, the exquisite love between Ernestina and the Monk leaves no room for him. Driven to fury by desire he imprisons them where they can barely touch each other. Under such torture Ernestina gives in to the Baron. But the mystic tri-union of hearts once achieved, presently is disturbed by the Countess of Clermont who lusting after the Monk Knight and jealous of Ernestina, gives Ernestina slow poison. Abdallah throws the Countess into a dungeon and swallows poison to die at the same time as Ernestina.

To create tension Richardson relies on the psychological characteristics of the individuals, who are motivated by impulse, beyond their ability to comprehend yet discernible to the reader; they all serve to make Richardson's central point about true love as "living in the soul" and distinct from gross sensuality. The novel glorifies Romanticism without reservation. Rousseau's philosophy is the breath of its creation.

> It was the triumph of nature over art — of truth over falsehood — of a hallowed and divine sentiment, over the cold and abstract conventionalism of a world, which, child-like, forges its own chains, fetters its own limbs, and glories in the display of its own bondage.[35]

Richardson's Rousseauist attacks on social convention, Christianity and private property serve to underscore the assumptions he makes about the true nature of man — capable of great creativity, understanding and love because he is part of God's divinity, man is crippled by his environment in the shape of modern civilization.

> But tyranny, then, under the name of society, had not framed its stringent laws. It had not yet accumulated fortunes, and grown arrogant by the humiliating sale of the most petty articles necessary to human existence. Men had not yet appropriated to themselves millions of acres of that globe which God had given in common to all.[36]

Yet Richardson is hopeful for the future: "But all

[33] Desmond Pacey, *Creative Writing in Canada* (Toronto: Ryerson Press, 1951), p.28.
[34] *The Monk Knight of St. John*, p.132.

[35] *Ibid.*, p.21.
[36] *Ibid.*, p.79.

these great atrocities will be no more when the millennium arrives. We feel that we live a century too soon."[37]

The great Lavater regarded the millennium as a theological reality, and the idea became an undercurrent in the pre-romantic movement. Nicholas de Bonneville, a pre-romantic, advocated universal religion and communism under the guiding divine principle of nature. Both ideas seem to have combined in this novel.

An early biographer of Richardson wrote that Matthew Lewis's *The Monk* was probably the inspiration for *The Monk Knight*.[38] Although Richardson knew Lewis's novel it had no more influence on *The Monk Knight* than it did generally on the development of the Gothic novel. Of course there are the underground dungeons and the inhibited Monk tempted by sexual desire common to both, but fundamentally they are at opposite poles: Lewis relates a series of picaresque adventures to shock the readers with the hypocrisies and unreasonable tragedies in the world whereas Richardson concentrates on the development of one theme (divine love) through the psychological working out of the inter-relationships of his characters. Moreover, Lewis's Monk is damned by sexual desire whereas sexual experience brings Abdallah closer to God. Rather, there were two great influences upon Richardson which burst forth with power and energy in *The Monk Knight of St. John*. Richardson mentioned one of them in the text: "What Rousseau has since been, his noble countryman, de Boiscourt, then was. . ."[39] The reader is reminded of Jean-Jacques Rousseau's triunion with Madame de Warens and Claude Anet as described in his *Confessions*. Rousseau's discovery of the connexion between the beauties of nature and the purity of sexual love underlies much of the description in the novel.

The other influence was Percy Shelley, the English poet most influenced by Rousseau. Shelley's high-flown sentiments of love, belief in the natural integrity of the individual, the humanizing of man through the teachings of nature, and evocative language — all these help *The Monk Knight of St. John* form its essential impression of an unfulfilled humanistic wish, such as Shelley himself represents. The phenomenal influence of Shelley on America after 1840 has been extensively described by Julia Power.[40] Shelley's influence on Richardson probably began in the twenties when Richardson was associating with the literati of London.[41] Rumours of the wild Shelley, Mary, and Claire Clairmont spread through the English communities on the Continent and into England with as much sense of bewilderment and outrage as those about Byron. Shelley's fascination with the *menage à trois* was widely known. His constant attempts to bring male and female friends together into his households, his living with Mary and Claire abroad, the affair of Claire and Lord Byron in which Byron professed no interest other than in the child she bore him — these together gave Richardson the fictional framework for *The Monk Knight*.

The blond, blue-eyed Baron de Boiscourt whose "generous and ardent nature" sought "indulgence, not in the grossness of sensuality which governed the mass, but in the refined and tender voluptuousness which lives in the soul rather than in the senses,"[42] is an idealization of Shelley. Abdallah, the inhibited Monk

---

[37] *Ibid.,* p.80.
[38] William Renwick Riddell, *John Richardson* (Toronto: Ryerson, (1923), p.61 Judge Riddell called the novel "senile and silly."
[39] *The Monk Knight of St. John*, p.41.

164

[40] Julia Power, *Shelley in America in the Nineteenth Century* (New York: Haskell House, 1964).
[41] Charles Ollier, one of Richardson's literary acquaintances after 1826, knew Shelley and published his poems in 1820. Cyrus Redding edited the Galignani edition of Shelley's poems in 1824 and wrote a biographical preface, some of the material for which he received from Mary.
[42] *The Monk Knight of St. John*, p.40.

Knight, has nothing in common with the reputation of a licentious Lord Byron, but he is an idealization of the dark and noble warrior about which Byron wrote and with whom he later became identified. And Ernestina? She was the ideal woman — the embodiment of love as dreamed by the nineteenth century man.

Yet one lady from "the Shelley Circle" seems to have been included in the novel: the Countess of Clermont who attempts to seduce Abdallah may represent the much-maligned Claire Clairmont who successfully seduced Byron; she is the idealization of the worst rumours about her.

A final point about this novel should be made. Novels of chivalry had degenerated to the reading fodder of that day, and popular reputations were made by authors who churned them out. *The Monk Knight of St. John* obviously gave the *coup de grâce* to those sentimental romances of fair ladies and their knights.

Meanwhile his *Eight Years in Canada* stirred public interest and brought forth the old stock criticism from his detractors. *The Guards in Canada; or, the Point of Honour; a sequel to Eight Years in Canada*, published in April 1848 served as a reply to his critics.

> . . . I cannot go down to the grave without leaving behind me this imperishable record of facts in which is illustrated, under the signature of my enemies, my proud adhesion to those principles of action which prevail in the modern world of chivalry, and by which my conduct has ever been regulated.[43]

Richardson, in spite of angry assertions that he did not

43 *The Guards in Canada*, p.51.
44 *Eight Years in Canada*, p.95. "...should a more refined and cultivated taste ever be introduced into the matter-of-fact country in which I have derived my being, its people will decline to do me the honour of placing my name in the list of their 'Authors'."

want to be canonized by any future generation of Canadians,[44] was certain that his importance as a novelist would be recognized some day. Beginning with a citation from Cooper, ("He who has a clamour raised against him by numbers, appeals in vain to numbers for justice, though his claim be clear as the sun at noonday.") he reviewed the affairs of honour he had fought in Canada and tried to show the political thread running through them all. His remarks on the army were incisive:

> But I know well from long experience that the army is a school of great tyranny, for not only is the body "cribbed, cabined, confined" by it; but the mind, the will, the judgment also; and it requires but a hint from a commanding officer, directing the course he wishes to have pursued, to ensure unanimity of purpose and of action. Habits of implicit obedience have too long influenced them to admit of the unchecked exercise of their own judgment, and "every duck waddles at the same gait."[45]

Half-hidden in this essay of self-justification lay an acknowledgement that his death was near at hand. Montreal had been one great death scene. In the previous summer, shiploads of immigrant Irish were attacked by cholera. Then in March 1848, Charles Richardson died at age forty-two in Niagara. This brilliant man, whose future had looked so promising, succumbed to alcohol.

With the publication of *The Guards*, Richardson burst forth like a meteor into the newspapers as a subject for gossip once more. And as if to add to his notoriety, in early May there appeared in the Montreal *Courier* a letter entitled "Signs in the Heavens" and signed "A Half-Millerite," indicating a sympathy for Miller's

45 *The Guards in Canada*, p.41.
46 *Morning Courier* (May 9, 1848).

belief in the imminent destruction of the world.[46] The writer, who was Richardson, had observed a phenomenon in the heavens from his doorway at 10PM on May 6; a stream of bright light spiraled from the upper horn of the moon in its first quarter for over ten minutes. "Will the Astronomers in Canada, if there are any such in this country, condescend to explain?" But most interesting was the writer's association of change in the Heavens with the series of revolutions taking place throughout Europe. And in another letter, which he signed " A Believer in Impending Doom to the Whole of the Present Human Race," he predicted the end of the world.[47] The Montreal *Transcript* quickly seized upon the letters as a subject of ridicule.[48] Richardson learning that a young poet, Charles Dawson Shanly was the author of the humourous attack, demanded an explanation. Shanly answered with an airy "under the circumstances I must avoid entering into any explanation whatever. . . ."[49]

Richardson's response typifies so well that simple directness of the chivalric manner whereby one man claims his right to take another man's life.

It therefore only remains for me to assure that the paragraph alluded to in my note, was written with your sanction and approval; and in the absence of that explanation which I conceive I have the fullest right to expect at your hands, I now demand from you, through my friend Captain Turner, who will hand you this, the appointment of another party . . . with whom that gentleman can enter into such arrangements as are now left open between us.[50]

Shanly, one of whose surviving books is entitled *Truant Chicken*, took this note to the police. Richardson was brought before the magistrate and charged with keeping the peace for six months.

Did Richardson really believe that the end of the world would come in 1852, a date which he quoted from the prophecy of a hermit named Bug de Milhas? He claimed that man's faculties had attained the highest power permitted by God, and that further understanding of the universe could only be gleaned by observing the supernatural, such as planetary movements in the heavens. The world was doomed to be destroyed by volcanic eruptions and falling comets as predicted in the Scriptures, he wrote, and the general disorganization in Europe which was happening simultaneously with the appearance of strange spots in and around the sun, indicated that the end was near. (Strange to say, Richardson died in 1852).

In mid-August 1848 an old friend from London, Nicholas Bochsa, visited in Montreal. For years Bochsa had had to tour the Continent giving concerts, because he had spirited the singer, Anna Bishop, away from her husband, the English composer. But now that revolutionary Europe was dangerous for travellers, Bochsa

[47] "Signs in the Heavens," *Morning Courier* (May 18, 1848).

[48] Richardson referred to the Editor of the *Transcript* as "a Hermaphrodite gentleman, who partakes of the double character of a small lawyer, and editor of a small print."

[49] Domina Regina vs John Richardson. Offence, Misdemeanor, May 21, 1848, Office of the Peace, Montreal.

[50] *Ibid.* Richardson's friend in this affair, Captain Turner, was commander of the Montreal cavalry. Shanly wrote for *Punch in Canada*, a periodical of satire, and worked as a clerk in the Board of Works. Since the editorial offices of *Punch* were on the floor below the *Courier*, he could easily have learned who wrote "Signs in the Heavens"; since Richardson had disclosed the circumstances of the Montreal affair of 1838 in his just published, *The Guards in Canada*, de Bleury, who still held his sinecure in the Board of Works, could have prompted Shanly to ridicule the Major in revenge. The Montreal *Herald* (May 22, 1848) under "Police — A Sequel to the Guards in Canada" described it as a theological dispute, but William Hartley replied in the *Courier* that it dealt with a more serious matter which he could not divulge.

and Anna were touring American cities. The review of their Montreal performance sounds as if written by Richardson: "... when the rich and melodious notes of this charming performer were heard pealing forth the beautiful Canadian air, so popular among our French countrymen, 'Vive la Canadienne,' the enthusiasm of the audience was unbounded."[51] About Bochsa, the *Courier* reported: "the greatest Harpist of this, or perhaps any other day."

Bochsa's great wit and zest for life was captivating. He undoubtedly told Richardson about the literary opportunities in New York City and caused him to think of emigrating.

On September 5 the Bochsa troupe set out for Canada West. Richardson also went west,[52] arriving in Windsor in the last week in September. Within two weeks he intended to join a Government party taking presents to the Indians of Walpole Island and Port Sarnia, possibly as a result of a note he addressed to the Prime Minister.

> Major Richardson presents his compliments to Mr. Baldwin and will be glad if he will enclose through the post office here the trifling amount due on his copy of *The Guards* forwarded to Mr. Baldwin a week or two ago since (price 5/) Major R. regrets the necessity for thus adverting to this subject and for such a trifle but unfortunately he has not the advantage arising from the possession of an office fat or lean under the Goverment.[53]

[51] *Morning Courier* (Aug. 31, 1848).

[52] *Morning Courier* (Oct. 19, 1848). Gugy speaks of "some communication" from Richardson in the *Courier* "only the other day."

[53] ALS, Richardson to Baldwin, Montreal, May 5, 1848, attached as front. *Richardson's War of 1812* (Casselman ed.) illustrated by Alf Sandham, Art Room, National Library, Ottawa.

The Hon. Robert Baldwin.

Baldwin may have considered that he was cancelling Lord Durham's obligation to him once and for all; it was just such a mission that Durham had offered Richardson in the first place.

Sensing this was his farewell visit to the land of his youth,[54] Richardson looked forward to visiting the Indians as it would give him the opportunity to see that race in the wild once more, a race which formed a strong part of his own nature.

[54] A.H.U. Colquhoun, *Tecumseh and Richardson* (Toronto: Ont. Book, 1924), *passim*.

Farewell

RICHARDSON was curious to see the changes wrought on the tribes on the reservations and eager to catch once more the excitement of the savage life. He wrote an article describing his trip which was published anonymously in the *Literary Garland* of January 1849 under the title: "A Trip to Walpole Island and Port Sarnia." It was "discovered" and republished as a monograph in 1924 by A.H.U. Colquhoun: *Tecumseh and Richardson: The Story of a Trip to Walpole Island and Port Sarnia.*

His travelling companions provided excellent company: the ship captain; two commissariat officers; a captain — a crack shot — on holiday from his regiment; and Cadot, a half-breed who had travelled to England with a Wild West show, married an English girl, and encountered much prejudice abroad. Although it had rained for the previous fortnight, the sky was bright and clear that October morning when the ship stopped at Windsor for Richardson. He soon came to be on good terms with his companions and brought Cadot to speak of his experiences in England. In writing of him Richardson might have been describing himself:

As is the case with many of those who have Indian Blood in their veins, Cadot has much of the polished manner of the courtier, and is imbued with high and honourable sentiments — sentiments

which may serve both as a lesson and a reproach, to those who make great hypocritical display of morality, and seem the very incarnation of virtue.[1]

The ship made its first stop at the wharf and provision store on Walpole Island in Lake St. Clair.

There was a handful of houses on this western part of the Island plus the Station, a two-storied building where the missionary instructed the Indians, and a white-steepled church which Richardson admired for its simplicity. The thick vegetation of the American shore seemed only a stone's throw away. About a thousand Indians from many miles around gathered to receive presents. With the utmost sobriety and good order, which, as Richardson commented, no similar group of whites was capable of, the Indians accepted the gifts with grace. Beautiful white blankets, cloth for leggings and breech-clouts, tobacco, thread, needles, shirts, linen, and so on were given to them, the better quality for those chiefs whose meritorious service with the British was recognized. Lastly they received three days' ration of pork and flour.

Richardson was fascinated and charmed by these colourful people. He explored their encampment, sticking his head into the wigwams of the Pottowattamie and finding men, women, and children lying promiscuously together, their feet to the fire. They appeared not to mind his intrusion and laughed in good humour at his attempts to speak their language. He was able to write that he found a complete lack of jealousy on the part of the man and a lack of envy on the part of the woman: "None but weak minds, and hearts, imbued with the most intense selfishness, are prone to jealousy. The greater the homage paid to a man's wife, the

[1] A.H.U. Colquhoun, *Tecumseh and Richardson* (Toronto: Ontario Book Co., 1924), p.50.
[2] Colquhoun, p.68.

higher the compliment to the husband's good taste."[2]
He considered the Indian woman superior to her civilized counterpart because she was sensible, never gossiping or envying her companion. He admired the Indians for sticking to their mores and language in spite of their mixing with whites. The missionary on the Island, having small success, called them pagans; these "pagans" had contempt for the creed and language of the white. Richardson thought wistfully of staying with them, but their way of life was vanishing. He sought out the Indian who was an aide to Tecumseh in the Battle of the Thames, and learned from him that the night after the battle the Indians had stolen Tecumseh's body and secretly buried it. Richardson obtained a signed statement from him to add to the material he was collecting on the subject.

During the day the government party organized events for general entertainment. Four braves had agreed to race small ponies bred on the Island. Richardson, the gambler, tried to find someone to take his bet. He and the Indian Superintendent held handkerchiefs on sticks a quarter of a mile distant to indicate the winning post and the race was on. Richardson's horse came first but he collected just a half dollar, the only bet he could obtain. There was another horse race, followed by a foot race, though it was hard to find Indians to compete. Only one older Indian and a young brave ran the foot race because of the half dollar prize money, and it was obvious at the start when they stripped for running that the muscular young brave would win. Indians scorned competition. Richardson was attracted to a young brave, Peter Phillip, whom he tried to persuade to enter the races in vain. This brave seems to have been the archetype for the "Wau-nan-gee" of his novels:

With the softest dark eye that can be imagined and a face formed in the true Grecian style of beauty — its whole expression being that of mild-

ness — my young friend had that air of independence, and dignified pride which is so peculiar to his race, and which seldom fail to arrest the attention of the beholder. We remember once hearing a well-known, and scrupulously consistent member of Parliament, state in his place, that he so hated the white man — the owner of the worthless acres of this worthless country — and liked the Indian, that if he had half a dozen daughters, he would give them to the latter in preference. Such was almost my own feeling on this occasion.[3]

His descriptions have a poignancy belying his deep regret that these colourful scenes were fading forever, that never again would a boy's imagination be captured by unforgettable Indian scenes. When the party left in early evening Peter Phillip, whom Richardson called his *fidus achates*, and some other braves accompanied the men to the ship and stayed with them until they weighed anchor. Richardson watched the shore from the moving ship as the Indians with wives and families, some on foot, others on horseback, disappeared from view. With their blankets and presents on their backs, in rich costumes, the Indians followed the winding of the road which skirted the river to left and right, leaving only a few stragglers behind. (Cadot left the party; he had purchased a horse and was riding home with the presents he received.)

The steamer quickly travelled the twenty-six miles to Sarnia and during the night moored off-shore. The following morning the Indians began to assemble in this hamlet wedged into their reservation by a few enterprising whites. Richardson found the majority of Indians (Chippewas) bearing the traces of semi-civilization which made them uninteresting to him, but a few wilder tribes in war paint had stern features and a generous demeanor in marked contrast to their "deter-

[3] *Ibid.*, p.65.

iorated countrymen."

The government party immediately acted like tourists; the army captain rushed ashore first and purchased a fine warclub which seemed to have been a part of the life-long equipment of the old Indian who parted with it. Richardson bought a stone pipe inlaid with a silver-like metal. Purchasing three feathers, he had an Indian drill holes in the pipe stem to fit them in. With a pouch and some Indian tobacco, Kinna-kin-nick, Richardson took great pride in his calumet which had a two and one-half foot stem decorated to imitate a winding snake.

But it was the women who caught his avid attention. A dash of white blood gave them an attractive beauty:

Many united to the dark long eye and hair of the Indian, a play of feature not usually seen in their race and assimilating them, in some degree, to the women of Southern Europe...and a good opportunity was offered for passing them in review, for they sat in three distinct rows from the edge of the bank and facing the road with plenty of room between each row, to admit of passing along without inconveniencing them. Under the plea of looking for Kinna-kin-nick which several of the squaws had for sale, I passed slowly along these rows, and then had an opportunity of gratifying my curiosity without rudeness. Nor, will it be supposed that I was alone in this survey.[4]

All too soon the party had to prepare for the return journey. The presents were distributed, the pretty Sarnia of main street, church, stores, and houses was inspected, and the visitors departed with their purchases. On his way to the streamer, Richardson met the old Indian who had sold his war-club. The Indian showed him a colourful mat for which Richardson offered to pay a quarter. Scornfully the Indian rejected the offer, and Richardson, with a sense of guilt for which he could find no explanation, went on to the ship.

Shortly afterwards as the steamer moved from the spot we saw him seated on the bank, in an isolated position, moveless as a piece of stationary, and with his classically costumed upper form, strongly defined against the sky. The shaved and plastered crown — the long and solitary eagle's feather stuck on the top — the red painted face — painted with a mixture of ochre and grease — the slight, very slight curvature of the shoulder, over which a sort of plaid mantle had been carelessly thrown — all contributed to form a *tout ensemble*, which it was impossible to look upon without inwardly acknowledging that there, in its rudest state, sat the impersonation of man in the true and unshackled dignity of his nature. So sensibly did I feel this myself, that I raised my hat to him and waved it gently. He was evidently looking at me, yet condescended not to make any sign of recognition. I repeated the salutation, but with no better result. There was something painfully solemn in the seemingly studied moveless-ness of person, and I was annoyed with myself for I recollected his look when I offered him the quarter dollar for the mat, and doubted not that I had deeply offended him. However, away went the steamboat, and soon the unbending figure of the old Pottowattamie was but indistinctly seen in the distance.[5]

After this confrontation of the two worlds, Indian and white, the one drifts away without conscience into

[4] *Ibid.*, p.88.

[5] *Ibid.*, p.88ff.

its own pleasures, while the other fades into oblivion leaving only the whisper of a reproach to be heard on the rarest occasions. On the way home the government party consumed the many good things on board, particularly the liquor, with gusto. The army captain proved his excellent marksmanship by providing quail, woodcock, and snipe.

Richardson as the anonymous story-teller distinctly separates the Indians from the whites and brings them together momentarily in such a way that the foibles of both are revealed. The civilized world is held up to sharper criticism because Richardson's sympathies obviously lie with the Indian, but he understands the white man's materialist nature, his spontaneous, almost unconscious power, and contentedly sets his own lot with civilization. The return to Windsor in the warm autumn weather with agreeable hard-drinking companions was for Richardson a memorable ending to a nostalgic journey.

He stayed in the West throughout October to witness the brilliant colours of forest foliage, to hunt pheasant and other game as he had done when a boy, and he took passage for Montreal in November before the lakes froze over.

While in Windsor Richardson read two accounts of the Indian massacre of the Americans at Fort Dearborn (now Chicago) at the start of the 1812 War.[6] They inspired him to undertake a trilogy — the first book to be called *Hardscrabble*, a clearing a mile or so from the

fort where the massacre took place; the second called *Wau-nan-gee* which would be concerned with the massacre; the third, untitled, to narrate the escape of the heroine. He intended to construct them as Dumas had written his musketeer series — each novel would be a complete story by itself, yet the three would be linked to make one all-encompassing story.

Richardson worked on these novels throughout the winter and spring in Montreal. The two which were published are masterworks. Perhaps William Hartley was the anonymous gentleman who in the March 1849 issue of the *Garland* reported on the progress of Richardson's writing: he compared the work thus far to *Wacousta*:

But the author holds his genius more in hand. . . witholds with a firmer wrist his imagination from passing beyond the sublime — and has paid more critical attention to the dialogue. From the commencement, there is a gradually increasing, but wholly unforced interest, which never relaxes except where familiar dialogues, appropriately introduced, serve to heighten by contrast, a succeeding crisis — and which occasionally dilates into breathless intensity. . . . I know not, of course, how the work will be carried through, for Major Richardson is one of those authors who, silkworm like, lay no frame, but spin from their heads as they proceed; but judging from that part of it which I have seen, and from the author's previous performances, it ought, I think, to produce a sensation, and to assume a place in the first rank of that department of imaginative literature.[7]

From this, it appears that *Hardscrabble* was almost completed in February.

In the *Garland* issue for May, notice was given that Richardson intended to read the first of three manu-

<hr>

[6] *Narrative of the Massacre at Chicago, August 15, 1812, and of Some Preceding Events* (Chicago, 1844). Although written by Juliette (Magill) Kinzie, the story was told by Margaret (Helm) Abbott, her sister-in-law, and added to by her husband, John Harris Kinzie Jr., who was about nine years old at the time of the massacre, and by her mother-in-law, the widow of John Kinzie. "The Account of the Massacre" by Lieutenant Helm (1814-15) was written for Judge Augustus B. Woodward of Detroit who undoubtedly allowed Richardson to read the ms.

[7] *Literary Garland*, 9 (March 1849), 144.

Place D'Armes, Montreal.

scripts at the Odd Fellow's Hall in Montreal on Saturday, May 12 and on the succeeding Monday and Tuesday evenings.[8] Readings by authors were becoming popular in America. Richardson obviously hoped to encourage subscription pledges from his audience to cover the cost of publishing. Unfortunately between the time the *Garland* issue was printed in April and the second week in May, the city of Montreal erupted in chaos making it extremely unlikely that the readings were held.

The fierce enmity of the Canadian Tories to the Rebellion Losses Bill, which would indemnify property losses by the rebels as well as the Loyalists during the Rebellion of 1837-1838, forms a tragic chapter in Canadian history. Richardson's sympathies would have been with the Loyalists who suffered private misfortunes in the defense of the country during the Rebellion.

In March effigies of the reform leaders were burned in Toronto and similar hostile demonstrations occured throughout Upper Canada. But on April 25 the devious manner in which the Governor-General, Lord Elgin, adopted to sign the Bill (pretending to leave Parliament for the day and then returning without the official observance usual for the signing of a bill) could not have failed to arouse Richardson's contempt. The crowds, which had gathered in suspicion, were driven mad when they heard the news.

Elgin was pelted with stones and eggs as he left the Parliament House; he lived in constant fear of his life for some days. Richardson must have been in the thick of the crowds. Some of the detailed and exciting reports of the events printed in the Montreal *Courier* bear the mark of his energetic spirit. At the burning of the Parliament that evening when the records of the colony and 20,000 volumes were lost, Derbishire[9] ran into the flaming Houses and tried to save the books. "Punch staggered upon the Editor of the Courier who, with anxious features and mustachios slightly singed rushed past in a whirlwind of smoke, with a portion of the Libraries of both Houses protruding from all his available grasps."[10] Since the Loyalists dearly valued the libraries as testament to their heritage, the arson was like self-immolation.

Elgin signed an order which armed the French-Canadian corps to suppress the British-Canadian rioters. The British armed themselves and at evening marched thousands strong to meet the French at Bonsecours Market. An English regiment under the Commander of the Forces aligned itself across Notre Dame Street between the two camps and warned that cannon charges with grapeshot would be fired into the midst of whichever faction crossed the limit fixed for it.

The British mob surged angrily toward the limit. Hundreds would have met the blast from the cannon if

---

[8] *Literary Garland*, 9 (May 1849), 240.

172

[9] Derbishire's action in this instance was consistent with his attempt to save his books in the Globe Hotel fire which Richardson described in his poem "Miller's Prophecy."

[10] *Punch in Canada* (May 5, 1849).

Colonel Gugy had not run forward and thrown himself into its midst. He scaled a ten-foot lamppost and talked to the infuriated people for two hours. With brilliant oratory, patience, and courage he persuaded the thousands to disperse and by so doing saved England's connection with Canada which might have been severed irreparably had the troops been forced to fire on these British Loyalists.[11]

The resentment of the Loyalists flared again when the Canadian Parliament made a show of support for Elgin. A movement to annex Canada to the United States was begun. The British Annexationist League swelled its members and long lists of Loyalists signed its manifesto. Hincks, the Inspector General, used intimidation against the annexationists, demanding that all civil servants, magistrates, and militia officers who signed the manifesto be dismissed. But the reaction throughout the country demonstrated that Elgin and his reformers had made a mistake.[12]

Where was Richardson throughout all this confusion? Aside from his disgust with the Reform Government and politics in general, he must have decided that all possibility of publishing his works had dissipated with political instability. Moreover England's free trade policy was visibly impoverishing Canada, making polite literature expendable. Probably Richardson did not actively favour annexation to the United States; his name did not appear on the Montreal Manifesto. As for himself, he made up his mind to emigrate to the United States. Publication of his manuscripts was his sole aim now.

He may have come to New York in October 1849. A special correspondent of the city addressed some letters to the Montreal *Courier* in that month on the American attitude to annexation.[13] It seemed incredible to Canadians but the Americans were too excited about the discovery of gold in California to think of annexing their northern neighbours. The correspondent implied that he had written an article in favour of annexation in a Philadelphia paper but it seemed a forlorn cause. The New York correspondent was not heard from again until December when he wrote a few reports on the New York scene signed "Ariel," the spirit freed on account of faithful service to his master.[14] Richardson, whose manuscripts had been accepted by publishers, had good reason to adopt the pseudonym. He had devoted his best years to a hard, unrewarding country to absolutely no avail. Now in the land of opportunity he was free to go where the elements might carry him.

Hardscrabble and Wau-nan-gee

These two short novels, the one continuing the action in the other, represent the transformation of Richardson's art from its European genesis to its American character. He portrays the decisions and actions taken by the American soldiers in Fort Dearborn and follows the movements of the settlers and the Indians before, during and after the massacre of the inhabitants of the fort on August 15, 1812. His depiction of ordinary living suddenly invaded by terror and defended hopelessly by men and women of great courage marks these novels as fore-runners of "realism" in American literature.

[11] J. Douglas Borthwick, *History of the Montreal Prison* (Montreal: A. Periard, 1886).

[12] In Gowan's case, the officers of his regiment from which Elgin and his cabinet had dismissed him held a public dinner for him. 15, 261 persons got up an address to Gowan which condemned the Government's conduct. He was elected Warden of Leeds and Grenville County (Montreal *Morning Courier*, March 25, 1850).

[13] Montreal *Morning Courier* (Oct. 20, 1849). The only reference to the length of his stay in New York City was in the *Sunday Mercury* (New York, May 16, 1852): "...for the last three or four years he has resided in this city...."

[14] Montreal *Morning Courier* (Dec. 24, 31 1849; Jan. 7, 1850).

HARDSCRABBLE;

OR,

THE FALL OF CHICAGO.

A Tale of Indian Warfare.

BY MAJOR RICHARDSON,

AUTHOR OF "WACOUSTA," "ECARTE," "MATILDA MONTGOMERIE," ETC., ETC.

Hardscrabble; or The Fall of Chicago,
(New York: Dewitt & Davenport).

Hardscrabble opens on the scene of a frontier farm on the Chicago River. Three men and a boy are sitting in the cabin and chatting: one is the owner of the farm, Heywood; the others, a Canadian, an ex-militiaman and the boy, are his servants. Richardson establishes the classless nature of the society right away:

174

At this early period of civilization, in these remote countries, there was little distinction of rank between the master and the man- the employer and the employed. Indeed the one was distinguished from the other only by the instructions given and received, in regard to certain services to be performed. They laboured together — took their meals together — generally smoked together — drank together — conversed together, and if they did not absolutely sleep together, often reposed in the same room.

Suddenly Indians enter the cabin and squat on the floor.

"Friendly Pottawattamies! no sare," returned the Canadian seriously, and shrugging up his shoulders. "Dey no dress, no paint like de Pottawattamie, and I not like der black look — no, sare, dey Winnebago."

The suspense increases as the scene shifts to a fishing party of soldiers who are unaware of impending war with the British and of any danger from the Indians.

Richardson develops authenticity by employing historical detail; for instance: "The mouth of the Chicago River was then nearly half a mile more to the Southward than it is now."[15] The vastness of the wilderness whose thick vegetation grows out over the wide-flowing river bathed in sunlight sets the novel in the limitless realm of the pantheistic. The Indians who appear suddenly on the opposite river bank are as much a part of the natural scene as the cou rouge ducks which the fishing party observes moving across the water.

Richardson is not above using tricks to enhance this impression as well as to sustain the suspense:

[15] *Hardscrabble*, p.15.

"... but dash me if it isn't temptin' to see them fellows there stealin' upon us, and we lookin' on, and doin' nothin.' "

"What fellows do you mean?" inquired the corporal, suddenly starting to his feet, and looking down the river.

"Why, them ducks to be sure. . ."[16]

The boom of a cannon from the fort warns the party of danger. Finding the bodies of Heywood and his servants, the men are besieged in the cabin all night by Indians until rescued by a party from the fort led by Lieutenant Ronayne. Disagreements between the cautious commander, Captain Headley, and his younger officers, and attempts by Mrs. Headley to patch up the differences become a secondary theme to the courtship of Maria Heywood by the dashing young Ronayne. An Indian brave, Wau-nan-gee, is attracted to Maria. There is a hint of a love triangle when Ronayne marries Maria. The fear of war, if not forgotten in the celebrations of the wedding and July 4, recedes into the background.

The second novel, *Wau-nan-gee*, opens at Fort Dearborn in early August with a message from General Hull at Fort Detroit requiring Captain Headley to evacuate and fall back to Fort Wayne. A friendly Chief warns that the Indians will attack the whites should they leave the fort. Indeed, the hostility of the Indians visiting in the fort convinces Lieutenant Elmsley, second in command, and his father-in-law, Mr. McKenzie, the first settler in the district, of the foolhardiness in following such an order. Headley, in spite of advice from McKenzie, is determined to be open and hospitable to the Indians to keep their friendship.

The link of *Wau-nan-gee* to *Hardscrabble* is reinforced by Mrs. Headley's narration to her husband of her fear that Wau-nan-gee had raped Maria. After

Mrs. Heald defending herself.

Maria is kidnapped by Indians, Ronayne refuses to believe that his wife has run off with Wau-nan-gee, although there are signs of it. His faith is rewarded when he learns that Wau-nan-gee tried to kidnap them both to save them from a massacre planned by the Indians. Meanwhile, Captain Headley has destroyed extra ammunition and food supplies, thus provoking the wrath of the herculean Captain Wells who arrives with a party of Miami Indians. Wells's appearance in the story brings a feeling of strength to the embattled whites, and hope that they might avoid a confrontation with the Indians.

Wells and his Miamis lead the procession along the Lake Shore. The Indians, separated from them only by a long range of sandhills, move parallel with them. Suddenly the Indians attack. Headley and his men form a square and move to meet them. But this allows other Indians to reach the baggage train and slaughter the women and children. Wells, spurring his horse for the Indian camp, swears to do the same but his horse is shot

[16] *Ibid.*, chap. 2.

175

from under him, and he fights off his attackers until his strength is gone.

Squatted in a circle, and within a few feet of the wagon in which the tomahawked children lay covered with blood, and fast stiffening in the coldness of death, now sat about twenty Indians, with Pee-to-tum at their head, passing from hand to hand the quivering heart of the slain man, whose eyes, straining as it were, from their sockets, seemed to watch the horrid repast in which they were indulging, while the blood streamed disgustingly over their chin and lips, and trickled over their persons. So many wolves or tigers could not have torn away more voraciously with their teeth, or smacked their lips with greater delight in the relish of human food, than did these loathsome creatures, who now moistened the nauseous repast from a black bottle of rum which had been found in one of the wagons containing the medicine for the sick — and what gave additional disgust was the hideous aspect of the inflamed eye of the Chippewa, from which the bandage had fallen off, and from which the heat of the sun's rays was fast drawing a briny, ropy and copious discharge resembling rather the grey and slimy mucus of the toad than the tears of a human being.[17]

The survivors are granted safe conduct when they surrender. Ronayne dies from his wounds in the presence of Maria and Wau-nan-gee. Then Wau-nan-gee and Maria ride to seek refuge in Fort Detroit. Richardson intended to depict their flight through the wilderness.

. . . and whether the third, on a different topic than

that of war, and which as we have just observed, is not necessary to the others, ever finds embodiment in the glowing language and thought of Nature, nursed and strengthened in Nature's solitude, will much depend on the interest with which its predecessors shall have been received.[18]

Hardscrabble and *Wau-nan-gee* created phenomenal interest; it appears, therefore, that the only hindrance to the publication of the third novel was its subject matter.

Love between Indian and white, when rarely written about, was glossed over with noble romantic sentiment. The inhibition about sexual intercourse in American writing became all the stronger on the subject of inter-racial sexual intercourse.

James Fenimore Cooper, for instance, was terrified of miscegenation.[19] His terror was a symptom of a psychological disease of national proportions. On the one hand, Richardson would have treated the relationship between the widowed Maria and the sensuous, though high-minded, Wau-nan-gee "in Nature's solitude" with realism. He knew the Indian's attitude to love, that it was practical and erotic, never sentimental.[20]

Unlike Cooper's novels whose characters discuss race and whose Indians might well be whites in disguise, Richardson's novels create a sense of racial difference through feeling and mentality. In *Hardscrabble* and *Wau-nan-gee* the racial difference between Indian and white is explicit from the moment when the Winnebagos invade Heywood's farm. Race is more significant in these two novels than in the earlier

---

[17] *Wau-nan-gee*, p.100.

[18] *Ibid.*, p.125.

[19] Leslie Fiedler, *Love and Death in the American Novel*, 2nd ed., rev. (New York: Delta, 1966), pp. 207-8.

[20] In his preface to *Tecumseh* he scorned Chateaubriand's depiction of love between Indians as sentimental.

Wacousta, which was set in the classic mould of revenge. Pontiac's Indians were motivated by the intensity of a European suffering from unrequited love, whereas in *Hardscrabble* and *Wau-nan-gee* the Indians attack the whites upon savage impulse. When they see suddenly at their mercy the whites, who had represented themselves as superior, they obey the primitive instinct of the strong to victimize the weak. A thirst for blood carries them to acts of bestial madness, guided only by the signs of racial difference. The extremity of the difference is quickly reached when the warriors eat the heart of Wells, whose bravery and strength they hope to transfer to themselves.

If Richardson chose the events of the massacre at Chicago for their spontaneity and unexpectedness to catch at a truer depiction of life in his novels, he owed a good deal to his sources — eyewitness accounts which had an existential quality about them.

The most obvious source, and the one most associated with Richardson's novels is *Narrative of the Massacre at Chicago, August 15, 1812 and of Some Preceding Events*, a pamphlet published in Chicago in 1844. Although written anonymously, the author was rumoured to be Juliette Kinzie, the wife of the son of the first settler at Chicago, John Kinzie, the McKenzie of the novels. Since she married into the Kinzie family long after 1812, she relied on the memory of Margaret Helm, the step-daughter of Kinzie, who is Margaret Elmsley in the novels. Richardson altered the names of the historical personages only slightly for his fictional account. McKenzie was actually Kinzie's original name; he was from Detroit and well known to the Askin family; when he had to become American, he Americanized his name. Originally Lieutenant Helm (Elmsley in the novels) was from Virginia, a fact mentioned in one of the sources, and used imaginatively by Richardson who recognizing the romantic sound in the word called the hero, Ronayne, "the Virginian."

Juliette Kinzie's *Narrative* has been called "fanciful and unreliable" by an historian,[21] and Richardson seems to have been aware of its weaknesses. Although he fashioned the characterizations of his personages after the impression given of them in the *Narrative*, he knew that the narration came from Mrs. Helm's experience and that she gave favoured treatment to her husband, Lieutenant Helm. For instance, she neglected to mention acrimony between Helm and Captain Heald (Headley in the novels) despite Helm's published report of the massacre which sharply accused Heald of blunders in judgement and stupidity in manoeuvres. As a result of the report Richardson characterized Elmsley as barely on speaking terms with Headley.

Another historical source, Henry Schoolcraft's *Narrative Journal*,[22] carried an account of the massacre told to Schoolcraft by John Kinzie. Kinzie's account alone mentions the Indians cutting out the heart of Captain Wells.

There is a similarity in character between Maria Heywood and Maria Drayson. Both were loyal, courageous, adventurous and steadfast in their love. The relationship between Ronayne and Maria Heywood gives the same feeling of trust and confidence as one feels about Richardson and his wife. Moreover, the use of his wife's name for the heroine of this trilogy suggests that it was she whom he had on his mind.

Fictional characters carry the personality of their creator to some extent, and in the portrayal of a major protagonist like Wau-nan-gee, particularly as he was to be developed in the third novel, alone with Maria,

[21] Milo Quaife, *Chicago and the Old Northwest, 1673-1835* (Chicago: Chicago Univ. Press, 1913), *passim*.
[22] Henry R. Schoolcraft, *Narrative Journal of Travels from Detroit Northwest* through the Great Chain of American Lakes to the Sources of the Mississippi River in the Year 1820 (Albany: Hosford, 1821), pp. 389-93. Also *vide*: Mentor L. Williams, "John Kinzie's Narrative of the Fort Dearborn Massacre," *Journal of the Illinois State Historical Society* (Winter 1953), pp. 343-362.

Richardson would have had to find the elements to create his Indian personality deep within himself, just as Ronayne was fashioned after the young and impetuous Richardson. Maria seems to be a catalyst between them, resembling the role that Ernestina played between de Boiscourt and Abdallah in *The Monk Knight of St. John*.

Miscegenation has not developed as a major theme in American literature as yet, but other aspects in *Hardscrabble* and *Wau-nan-gee* later became established themes in the Western Novel. The romantic hero who makes up for his impetuousness with his courage is standard to the Western as is the strong, experienced hero like Wells, who appears at the height of the crisis and engenders confidence in everyone. The women in Westerns are like Margaret Elmsley and Maria Heywood, who, sent to Eastern schools to learn the graces of being a lady, prefer to live in the rough pioneer life of the West when their formal education is completed. Given a choice, Maria cries: "Oh, yes, dear mamma! the Far West for me — no Europe. Give me the tall, dense forests of our own noble land..."[23] Also, the easy-going comradeship among the men, which the members of the fishing party depicted in *Hardscrabble*, is a trait of the Western's cowboys.

Mayne Reid, the other writer of that day who dealt with the West in an original way, began publishing his works about 1850. Reid's writing, though, accentuates the romanticism of action; it influenced the Western toward the fantasy of adventure rather than to the realities of inescapable conflict which Richardson presented in *Hardscrabble* and *Wau-nan-gee*.

The Knight in New York

IN PHILADELPHIA Richardson submitted *Hardscrabble* to the editor of the *Union Magazine*, Caroline Kirkland, popular authoress of backwood stories. The *Union Magazine* which was begun two years earlier was still struggling. Mrs Kirkland attempted to engage the big names of American literature such as Bryant, Longfellow, Duyckinck, but found they were under contract to other periodicals. The author of *Wacousta*, however, needed no introduction to the American public. Medina's stage adaptation of the novel was revived in New York in January 1849 and lasted almost a month. Another stage adaptation was playing in the smaller cities. When Richardson stepped into the American literary scene with *Hardscrabble*, he was like an exciting visitor from the past. The novel was scheduled to appear serially from February through June 1850. Mrs. Kirkland, known as the first lady of American letters, introduced it with a brief editorial statement: "Major Richardson has commenced a purely American tale of the settlement of Chicago, which for thrilling interest can hardly be surpassed."[1] It caught the attention of the public and sent the circulation of the periodical sailing upwards. In March the editor wrote: "We know not how to be sufficiently thankful to our kind friends, the writing and reading public, for the con-

[23] *Hardscrabble*, p.67.

[1] *Union Magazine* 6 (Philadelphia, 1850), 176.

stant increasing favour extended to the Magazine."[2] Finally, grudgingly, she had to admit that Richardson's story was the attraction:

We have been compelled, for a *third* time, to reprint the early numbers of the present volume. We feel certain now that we have enough to supply the demand. Those persons, therefore, who are still unsupplied, may send on their orders. The present volume ending with the June Number, will contain the whole of *Hardscrabble*.[3]

In the fall of 1849 Richardson preferred New York City because the journalistic opportunities were greater in that thriving commercial centre. It was a kind of thoroughfare where every remarkable character was seen once in his life. Artists and musicians from all over the country were migrating there. Many expatriate Englishmen lived there. As the poor immigrant Irish invaded the lower part of the city, the select area shifted northward to Chelsea on the west side from 27th to 30th streets. The city had the exciting quality of surprise, of the unexpected.

The city's pretentious attitude to art was typified by the construction of the Athenaeum, a meeting place for "artists." One room meant for "social interchange" had panelled oak walls and richly carved allegorical representations in the style of a Norman castle; another for chess players was built to represent an oriental tent with gorgeous decorations; a third in the style of Louis XIV had green wall panels in crimson frames edged with gold, was hung with large paintings of the miraculous inventions of the age in transportation and communication, and sported a huge chandelier and side lights beside comfortable sofas and chairs and racks of the latest newspapers from across the world.[4] The lone knight would have found the city to his taste. He could even have indulged his favourite pastime to the full; there were six thousand gambling houses.

Perhaps it was at one of Mrs. Kirkland's literary *soirees* in her New York home that Richardson met George G. Foster, the American poet now forgotten, who brought out the first American edition of Shelley's poems. At the moment he was famous as a journalist whose ups and downs had brought him into contact with all types of life. His *Gold Regions in California* had sold ten thousand copies in one week, and his *New York by Gaslight* was selling in astronomical figures. His publishers, two young men on Nassau Street, Dewitt and Davenport, began publishing in August 1848, and with a judicious and liberal system of advertising, were quickly established across the nation. They specialized in paperback books selling for twenty-five cents, the right price to meet the demand of the masses awakening to the delights of education.

The first manuscript Richardson handed them was *The Monk Knight of St. John*. While an older reputable publisher would have turned it down flatly for its hedonistic portrayal of sexual love, these young men brought it out under their imprint in the summer of 1850. Its success was not so much sensational as notorious. Dewitt and Davenport replaced their names on the title page in subsequent printings with the words "Printed by the Trade." There was no review, no word of it in the literary magazines, but Duyckinck, the most respectable literary critic of the day, mentioned it in his diary. He was travelling out of New York heat "like a cork from a bottle" bound for Fire Island in September 1851. Sailing from Islip, he commented upon the boatman: ". . . the old salt leans managing the sail, or coiled upon the lee, immersed in the delights of Major Rich-

[2] *Union Magazine* 6:244.
[3] *Union Magazine* 6:376.

[4] *Saroni's Musical Times* (New York, Oct. 19, 1850).
[5] Evert A. Duyckinck, Diary, Sept. 13, 1851, Ms. Div, The New York Public Library.

ardson's 'Monk Knight of St. John'."[5] If both the critic and the boatman enjoyed it to distraction, the novel must have had a wide readership.

Dewitt and Davenport also bought *Hardscrabble* in the summer of 1850, according to the editor of the *Union Magazine*, who noted its forthcoming appearance in book form.[6]

These two works established Richardson's fame. Although the drawing-room novel, much to the disgust of critics, had become the popular taste, Richardson's works revived interest in the adventure story. Novels of historical romance were being written by many authors, but the genre had not developed beyond the scenic framework used by writers such as Walter Scott. Richardson added another dimension by allowing the reader to identify with his characters. In the *Monk Knight* that identification was through sexual experience, but the work was so obviously an inquiry into the mystery of love in all its aspects that it could be called pornographic only by those who refused to recognize that inquiry. When Richardson wrote: "I believe He has given it only to a favoured few to realize the full fruition of that which we call desire, yet which, in fact, is a divine mystery without a name," who among his readers could refrain from following him through the labyrinths of love? His first-person preaching against the strict dogmas of the day expressed the thought of many men whose social conscience was being awakened by political movements throughout Europe. As for *Hardscrabble*, the people of the American West yearned for identification with the past. The Americans had reached the Pacific; now they needed to lay the spiritual foundations for constructing a culture in that vast land west of the Alleghenies. As early as 1839 a reviewer wrote:

The chief reading of the stirring men of the West,

is that which relates to stirring men. . . Western taste demands something which tells of men, of life, of battle, of suffering, of heroism, skill and wisdom; or else something which addresses man's highest nature, his holiest and deepest feelings.[7]

Richardson tried to do both.

George Foster found the romance and adventure that he loved in Richardson's work. *The Monk Knight of St. John* was in the tradition of Shelley's *Queen Mab*, and therefore warmly received by this describer of the wretched labouring masses whose voice cried out long before the Reformers:

The truth is, that the condition, both moral and physical, in which such a city as New York permits its poor to exist, is utterly disgraceful — not to the poor, for they deserve only our deepest pity, but to the community — the powerful, enlightened, wealthy community — which permits its unfortunate children, who know nothing but how to work, to become thus horribly degraded.[8]

Foster was living with Madame de Marguerittes, the colourful Julie Granville. Her husband, the Baron de Marguerittes, was in New York with her, but Julie preferred the exciting company of Foster with whom she became active in journalism as a music critic. Foster and Julie edited the *Merchant's Day Book* in 1850 which probably found place for unsigned articles by Richardson.

Julie, who fancied herself an actress and singer (at one time building an opera house in Albany), knew Anna Bishop who returned with Bochsa to New York in the summer of 1850 from a "triumphant" tour of

[7] *New York Review* 5 (Oct. 1839), 384.

[8] George G. Foster, *Fifteen Minutes around New York* (New York: Dewitt and Davenport, 1854).

[6] *Union Magazine* 7 (July 1850), 62.

Anna Bishop and Nicholas Bochsa, from
Anna in Mexico.

Mexico, and formed an enclave of expatriate Europeans to include their fellows in spirit, Foster and Richardson.

The young literary circle with whom Richardson's work was popular usually met in the home of Richard Kimball, a witty conversationalist and minor novelist. One of the young poets in the group, R.H. Stoddard, later to be hailed dean of American poetry, declared near the end of his long life that Major Richardson's writing had been a strong influence upon him.[9]

In August 1850, Barnum the impressario offered $200 for the best song welcoming the Swedish songstress, Jenny Lind, to America. Richardson was one of the hundreds who submitted a song to the competition. Three weeks later it was announced that Bayard Taylor, the young correspondent for the *Tribune*, was the winner, though a commentator wrote: "We anticipated this result when it was announced that an at-

tache of the *Tribune* and L.G. Clarke were members of the committee; but the whole thing is too transparent to impose upon the public the idea that Taylor has any of the essentials for either a song-writer or poet. . ."[10] Richardson asked Bochsa to compose music for his rejected song, "All Hail to the Land." It was published in the first week in October. "Its character," reported a critic, "is similar to that of *"Salut à la France"* which will insure it a proper appreciation among the masses."[11] Anna Bishop sang it in a new music hall, Tripler Hall, opened by Bochsa with the largest orchestra ever seen in New York, and a two hundred-voice choir as well. Referred to as the new national anthem by periodicals of the day, it seems to have been very popular. Encouraged, Richardson wrote a ballad, "Since Thou Hast Robbed Me of My Heart," for which the publisher of his first song, John E. Gould, composed the music. When it was published in the first week of January 1851, reviewers called it better than the generality of ballads published and a very beautiful air.[12]

That at the age of 54 he should have found himself starting a career as a song-writer must have been a surprise to Richardson. Unfortunately the two composers who had worked with him soon left New York. Anna Bishop, overshadowed by the hysteria created by Barnum for Jenny Lind, tried to compete giving concerts several evenings a week in Tripler Hall, and Bochsa introduced promenade concerts to the American public, but attendance dwindled and the Americans were shy to dance despite there being an "eminent professeur de danse" to direct them. Anna and Bochsa went to Philadelphia at the end of January. Young Gould sold his Broadway music business and moved to Boston.

Nevertheless, Richardson was writing contin-

[9] Hervey Allen, *Israfel; the Life and Times of Edgar Allen Poe*, 2nd ed. (New York: Farrar and Rinehart, 1934), p.522.

[10] *Saroni's Musical Times* (New York, Sept. 7, 1850).
[11] *Saroni's Musical Times* (Oct. 5, 1850).
[12] *Parker's Journal*, I (Feb. 1851), 44.

uously. A short story, "The Sunflower: A True Tale of the North-West," appeared in the November 1850 issue of *Graham's*. It told of the great love of a Saukie brave for Sunflower, the young wife of his guardian. After saving her life and running away with her, he is killed by a treacherous Chippewa. The beautiful Sunflower, heartbroken, kills the Chippewa and herself. A white man buries the bodies and narrates the sad tale to the old Indian who had been wronged by the young lovers. The sensitive atmosphere in which the Indian is depicted as a part of nature, and the awareness of a distinction between the Indian races, give the story its uniqueness. Richardson interposes at the beginning to set a spell-binding tone:

> The Saukies were the noblest looking men of all we have ever since beheld in any quarter of the globe we have visited. They were a collective impersonation of the dignity of man, as sent first upon earth by the will of God; nor were these characteristics of manly beauty peculiar only to a few, but general to all.

Later in a newspaper article[13] he developed his belief that the Indian races were native to the American continent, not emigrants from Asia as commonly thought. The Indian race formed separate nations like the European races, he argued; their physiques and languages differed just as among Europeans.

He prepared a new edition of *Wacousta*, cutting the descriptive introduction and scenes which tended to slow the action. Dewitt and Davenport published it in early 1851 with an autobiographical introduction. The lone knight was very much alive in him when he wrote: "Wacousta is not alone in his bitter hatred and contempt for the base among those who, like spaniels, crawl and kiss the dust at the instigation of their superiors, and yet arrogate to themselves a claim to be considered gentlemen and men of honor and independence." Duyckinck was among those who gave it a good review and commented on the attractive type of the compact volume, which had a very popular sale.[14] Medina's stage adaptation of the novel was revived in June at the Bowery Theatre and had a long run, giving Richardson an opportunity to see it at last.[15]

Richardson made an important contact in 1850: Rufus Griswold, editor and critic, who was the first to lay down principles for judging American, as distinct from European, writing. Griswold, the encyclopedic-mind, was said to be honest and open-handed by some and unscrupulous and vengeful by others. He is best known as Poe's literary executor who wrote an extremely controversial obituary on the poet's death in 1849.

Through Griswold Richardson made the acquaintance of some of the wealthy citizens of New York.

---

[13] "The North American Indian by Maj. Richardson, K.S.F." *Copway's American Indian* (New York, July 10, 1851). This was the first issue of George Copway's weekly newspaper, which listed Richardson among contributors such as J. Fenimore Cooper, Gilmore Simms, W.C. Bryant, Washington Irving, N.P. Willis and T.L. McKenney. Richardson dominated this issue as he also contributed "A Trip to Walpole Island and Port Sarnia in the Year 1848." Strangely in succeeding issues Richardson's name was dropped from the list of contributors and there were no more articles by him. Possibly he was too busy rewriting "Westbrook, the

Renegade" for the *Sunday Mercury* as he would have received it back from *Sartain's* at this time. Then again possibly his unorthodox and strong defence of Indian rights couched in such phrases as "arresting the hand of the insatiate destroyer of the North American Indian" was too inflammatory — not for Copway, who as an Ojibway Chief and writer of some distinction, carried the Indian cause to the American Congress — but for the distinguished gentlemen who lent their names though not their talents to the periodical.

[14] *Literary World* (New York, March 1, 1851).

[15] George C. Odell, *Annals of the New York Stage*, 6:33.

The New-York Historical Society, one of the intellectual circles of the communtity, honoured Richardson by asking him to give a lecture in its rooms in the New York University Building at Washington Square on April 1, 1851. Pleased, Richardson called it "a select body of men of the highest literary attainment in the metropolis of the United States."[16] He read a paper entitled "Incidents of the War of 1812 Embracing Particulars as Connected with the Death of Tecumseh." It was an unusual evening for the Society. The hall was so crowded that people had to stand in the aisles. One newspaper reported that "the narrative was of more than ordinary interest, and commanded almost breathless attention throughout."[17] The essay, which marked the culmination of years of research on the Battle of the Thames and the death of Tecumseh, gave a detailed summary of the life of the great Chief, exonerated him from all charges of brutality, and praised his character. Calling Tecumseh the greatest Indian who had lived, Richardson knew he was "treading on difficult ground, that it was no easy task to remove an impression suffered to take deep root with the masses." The paper also defended the actions of the British troops who were said to have abetted the terrorism of the savages. As for the American side,

> In relation to this affair (of Detroit) and the obloquy which has been cast upon General Hull, Major Richardson remarked that he held his own particular opinions which at some future time he might make public. He could never admit any American officer of the War of 1812 to have been

Rufus Griswold.

wanting in personal resolution.[18]

Although the paper was said to be a valuable addition to the Archives of the Society, Richardson took it away with him. It had cost too many years, too much energy, to hand over *gratis* at a time when he was one step ahead of starvation. His refusal to do so earned him the resentment of his wealthier literary colleagues. He had not understood that he was supposed to donate it; rather he had hoped to find a publisher for it.

Rufus Griswold was at the meeting. He briefly reported it in the journal he was editing and added in direct refutation of Richardson: "Certainly Tecumseh was not killed by Colonel Johnson."[19] In a later issue he noted that a debate had arisen whether papers pre-

---

[16] ALS, Richardson to Dr. Reynell Coates, New York, June 26, 1851. Philadelphia Historical Society.

[17] New York *Commercial Advertiser* (April 2, 1851).

[18] *Literary World* (New York, May 3, 1851). He had written about General Hull and Hull's reasons for surrendering Fort Detroit in "Wau-nan-gee", pp. 90-1, which was to be published in June of that year.

[19] *International Magazine*, 3, No. 1 (New York, April 1, 1851), 37.

sented to the society could be published, and came out strongly against publication. Somehow, however, he and Richardson became friends, perhaps because of Richardson's admiration for Griswold's efforts to found a national American literature.

The debate over the publication of the article which Richardson entitled "Movements of the War of 1812"was decided upon in an officious manner. *Sartain's Union Magazine* (Mrs Kirkland had sold her *Union Magazine* to the lithographer Sartain) offered prizes of $100 for the best essays and stories contributed to it that spring. Richardson accepted any opportunity to sell his manuscripts, especially at such a high price. The dollar then was worth just over three times what it is today, and it was *Sartain's* boast that it paid well in order to support American art against cheap reprinting of English writing. Richardson, who sold all the rights in his novels to his publishers, lived on any lump sum he received, making it stretch until he could publish something else and continue his precarious existence.

He sent the article with a story he wrote during the winter, "Westbrook, the Renegade: A Tale of the West." The Prize Committee was flooded with over four hundred pieces. From them it chose a handful of innocuous articles by unknown writers — with the exception of William Henry Herbert, whose "Hannibal Compared with Napoleon" was given a prize. A note from the chairman informed Richardson that his article on Tecumseh was not considered by the committee as the reading of a paper before a learned society was "esteemed"a publication; an article thus "published" could not enter into competition with articles written especially for the magazine. The chairman did not mention "Westbrook . . ." which prompted a disdainful reply from Richardson:

As that article was not read, in order to give it an additional value in the eyes of the public. . . it had not of course the same difficulty to contend with

as the mere fact of being entertained, and consequently remain among the rejected articles. But although of so little merit in the eyes of the committee as not to cause even allusion to it to be made, it is of some interest to myself, and I will therefore thank you as chairman to be good enough to acquaint me officially into its fate.[20]

Perhaps puritan America was penalizing Richardson for writing *The Monk Knight of St. John*; there is no doubt that *Westbrook* was one of the best stories contributed and that the committee could have accepted the Tecumseh article. This magazine, by overlooking the one writer who had given it a large readership, was bringing about its own death in the following year.

The reaction of the establishment to *The Monk Knight* was reflected by Griswold with an elliptical reference in a review of *Wacousta* at this time: "A later work from his hand, which we need not name, is more creditable to his abilities than to his taste or discretion."[21] But it was to Griswold, known for his soft heart towards needy artists, that Richardson turned for help. The following letter, written in June before he heard from Sartain's Prize Committee, reveals how desperately in need the very proud Richardson was:

Will you be amiable enough to do me a very *great* favour. Although I have arranged with my publishers for "Ecarté" and the "Prophecy Fulfilled," both of which I have sold them far below their value, the pecuniary settlement is delayed until I have made some slight alterations in the last named work — meanwhile I want some money. Will you lend me from ten to fifteen dollars until I receive wherewithal to return the amount from

[20] ALS, Richardson to Coates, new York, June 26, 1851. Philadelphia Historical Society.
[21] *International Magazine*, 3 (July 1851), 37.

them. It cannot be more than a fortnight hence. I write this in the event of not finding you at home when I call. Should you be out I shall call again either this evening, or tomorrow morning before eleven o'clock. No news yet from Philadelphia, nor I have any reason to believe, will any thing be known this month. Trusting that your Penates are safely entered in their new abode.Believe me Very Sincerely Yours."[22]

He seemed to be counting on good news from the Prize Committee.

The alterations Richardson made to *The Canadian Brothers; or, the Prophecy Fulfilled*, were more extensive than he implied in his letter to Griswold. For example, one personage, criticized for the unlikely Scotch accent Richardson had given him, was discarded; some descriptive passages were shortened, in particular that describing Mrs. Grantham's death; Sampson Gattrie took his real name, Simon Girty; all references unfavourable or offensively hostile to the Americans were either altered or cut — for instance, a British officer who originally said: "What glorious bayonet work we shall have presently" was made to say, "What glorious cannon work we shall have presently"; and the description of American troops being pushed over the Queenston cliffs was cut altogether. Although the changes led the theme away from Richardson's intention of creating a Canadian national novel, and lost some of the symbolism such as the suicidal result of war between Canada and the United States, the revised novel read more quickly and more clearly pointed out the revenge upon the de Haldimar family. The emphasis was now placed on the American heroine, and the title read: *Matilda Montgomerie; or, the Prophecy Fulfilled*.

A crisis appears to have confronted Richardson at this moment in June 1851. Not only had he sold two important novels simultaneously "far below their value," but he also sold *Wau-nan-gee*, the second novel of his Chicago trilogy, for serialization in a New York newspaper, the *Sunday Mercury*.[23] His keen disappointment on hearing from Sartain's Prize Committee was owing in part to a sudden need for money. In a hasty note to Griswold he offered the rejected article for publication in his magazine — he now called it "Life and Death of Tecumseh" — explaining it was "open to the highest bidder."[24]

He moved from a new building on Fourth Avenue at 20th Street to Wooster Street. His Fourth Avenue address was in the north of the city, three blocks south of the Bull's Head market for cattle and horses, an area which appealed to him. Beyond the market stretched farmlands with a dwelling here and there, and about his residence the houses were set apart with lawns and trees between them. He would not have given up this healthy atmosphere, far from the cholera areas of the southern parts of the city, unless he had to. The house on Wooster Street was owned by a straw merchant, an acquaintance of his publisher, Dewitt, and although still fashionable (Bryant and Parke Godwin were neighbours) it was in a congested district, just off Canal Street.

He may have wanted money for several reasons: first, he could have lost badly at cards; second, he might have wanted to invest in a project, say a newspaper (Foster and Julie began a newspaper in October but it folded within the month); third and most probable, he had to send money to his youngest half-brother Robert Harvey Richardson, who was very ill and alone somewhere in Missouri. Robert, who just turned 26, died

[22] ALS, Richardson to Griswold (1851), Griswold Manuscripts, Boston Public Library.
[23] *Sartain's Union Magazine*, 9 (Philadelphia, 1851), 79.
[24] ALS, Richardson to Griswold (1851?), Griswold Manuscripts, Boston Public Library.

there in 1851. Following the lead of his famous brother, he had left the underpaid customs post at Port Colborne in Canada to seek his fortune south of the border. Richardson went into debt to give his wife a decent burial; he might have done the same for his brother.

The announcement of the forthcoming appearance of his novel *Wau-nan-gee or The Massacre at Chicago* in the *Sunday Mercury* made it seem a major event in literature, which must have accompanied a fair-size payment to Richardson if one judges by the enthusiasm of the newspaper's editor. Hailing the "Unprecedented popularity" of *Hardscrabble*, the editor, Samuel F. Nichols, a close friend of George Foster's, concluded with a proud reference to Richardson:[25]

We presume that Major Richardson, as a writer, is sufficiently well-known to our citizens, to render any allusion here to his talents unnecessary. There may, however, be some, into whose hands this paper may fall, who are not cognizant of his abilities. To those, we will simply remark that he has received the eminent distinction from some of the best critics on both sides of the Atlantic, of being considered

The Best Living Writer
of
Graphic Indian Tales
surpassing James Fenimore Cooper.

The novel was carried on the front page for fourteen issues from June 1 to August 31, 1851. An enthusiastic readership spiraled upwards to a point where Samuel Nichols reported:

The demand for the paper, on Sunday last far exceeded our most sanguine expectations and we

almost regret that our first edition was exhausted, before the wants of all our regular agents could be supplied. That deficiency has since been made up, however; and we have now made ample provision to supply all those who may become subscribers to the *Mercury* during the run of the story, with the early numbers.[26]

Readers wrote in praise from various parts of the country — "one of whom, like the author of this tale, Major Richardson, was an eye-witness of the bloody massacre."[27]

Convinced that Richardson's writing was steadily increasing the newspaper's circulation, Nichols announced in the issue carrying the last installment of *Wau-nan-gee* that he intended to publish another of Richardson's novels, *Westbrook, the Outlaw; or the Avenging Wolf*. Richardson obviously had expanded the article rejected by *Sartain's*, perhaps more than the editor expected because he announced that it would run for no more than five issues, when it actually ran for seven — from September 14 to October 26 1851. Although Nichols prepared for an increased demand as a result of a large accession to his subscription list and a large increase in orders from his agents, he was caught short again and was forced to run off an extra supply of newspapers on Monday morning. He now reported that Richardson "has been classed among the most vigorous and fascinating writers of the age."[28]

Westbrook, the Outlaw; or the Avenging Wolf purported to be the story of Andrew Westbrook whose farm lay near the village of Delaware on the Thames River in Upper Canada in 1812. Bitterly resentful that the command of the local militia is given to the gentlemanly Captain Stringer, the young fiance of his

---

25 *Sunday Mercury* (New York, May 25, 1851).

26 *Sunday Mercury* (June 8, 1851).
27 *Sunday Mercury* (June 8, 1851).
28 *Sunday Mercury* (Sept. 21, 1851).

eldest daughter, rather than to himself, a yeoman, Westbrook takes his revenge on the Stringer family. When his eldest daughter dies in childbirth, he steals the infant and leaves him in a wolf's den. He covets the beautiful Emily Stringer, sister to the Captain, murders her lover, and keeps her in a hunter's cabin in the forest where he rapes her every night. When his acts are discovered he shoots Emily and deserts to the American forces for whom he acts as a scout on raids along the Thames valley. When the Americans encounter Stringer's militia, Westbrook pursues the wounded Stringer to the hunter's cabin and murders him only to be attacked by a vicious wolf which has been using the cabin to nurse the baby boy. Mangled and dying, Westbrook confesses his crimes to his American companions who leave the boy for an advancing party of Canadians.

"I cannot help thinking of the fiendish character of that Westbrook," ventured Lieutenant Holmes to the Captain, after the rapidity of their march had been somewhat abated. "In all my experience — and I think I have had some — I never knew the human heart was so desperately wicked. As you said to him, thank heaven he is not an American."[29]

A sub-plot of a love affair between Emily and a lay-brother, Anselmo, commences in a Montreal convent and continues in the forest.

In outline the story reads like a grotesque melodrama but the power of Richardson's writing gives it a stark credibility. The contrast of the beautiful, tender love of Emily and Anselmo to the vulgar lust of Westbrook becomes a personification of good opposed to cunning evil. In the voice of romanticism Anselmo tells Emily:

"In the forest we shall be free — no limit shall be there — the grass mantled earth, the womb from which we sprung, shall be our couch; the stars shall shed their mellowed light to show the shaded entrance to the grove of love; the sighing of the winds and the rustling of the forest leaves shall be our epithalanium by night, while the sweet songs of birds by day shall chaunt approval of our peerlessness of love."[30]

But evil in the form of Westbrook's envy destroys their dream. In this brute representation of evil foreclosing on the romantic dream Richardson embodies an overwhelming sense of realism.

From the fateful naturalism of *Hardscrabble* and *Wau-nan-gee* in which the characters are powerless to avoid their destinies, Richardson moves in *Westbrook* to the recognition that it need be only the peculiar psychological make-up of one man which brings tragedy to all. The lovers seek to express their love in its purest form removed from the society of men; yet the heightened sense of ideality they find through Nature, regardless how true it is for them, is superseded by the greater reality of Westbrook. Only Captain Stringer beset by one heartbreaking loss after another survives as a countervailing force to the close of the story when he too falls victim to that implacable agent of destruction.

As for the avenging wolf, it is the final form in which Richardson casts the theme of revenge. The wolf (as if acting for the innocent child) avenges the dead by killing their murderer. This interpretation is given by the American Captain in an attempt to rationalize the story in human terms. On close scrutiny, however, the ancient concept of destiny appears to be applied awkwardly in this case: the wolf is shot and the child "of idiotic expression" is synonymous with Na-

[29] *Westbrook*, p.72.

[30] *Ibid.*, pp. 42-3.

ture; neither can be said to be agents for revenge when they have no understanding. Rather they seem to illustrate the indifference of Nature to man. Indeed, this indifference of Nature is manifest throughout the novel when the finer sensibilities of man prove to be no match for the elemental forces that motivate Westbrook. When seen in this light Richardson's thought takes on a deeper significance pointing in the direction of existentialism where man has no place in the universe.[31]

Westbrook is void of conscience: even Anselmo and Emily never doubt the rightness of their love although it blossoms in a religious convent. Divinity seems present in their love, but that proves to be an illusion in a world where God is absent; how blessed is their love when the woman is raped and the man is murdered?

From the beginning of the story Westbrook appears as an aggressive, insensitive and selfish person whose desire for women is fed by his hatred for them — in short, he is a rapist.

> At the time at which we introduce him he was about forty-five years of age — stout, tall, robust, iron-faced and muscular, and with an expression of mixed cunning and revenge in his eyes, exceedingly unpleasant to behold.[32]

Thus Nature molded him and henceforth his actions are consistent with his character. He strives for no ideal — he has no self-doubts, he cannot be seen from the inside — he is an objective force with whom society in the form of Captain Stringer and his men must deal. Here is the mighty outlaw once again, but unlike Wacousta, he has no redeeming qualities — indeed, he offers no explanation for his crimes.[33] He is the outlaw stripped of romance and mystery.

Was the characterization true? Partially. Andrew Westbrook was born in Massachusetts and brought to Delaware on the Thames by his parents when a boy. At the outbreak of the 1812 War he was in his early forties. Red-haired, six foot two and powerful, he sympathized with the Americans, and though there is no proof of it, he probably served as a spy for them in Canada. He was reported to General Brock as one of those who disseminated the proclamation to Canadians to surrender when it was issued from Detroit at the outbreak

---

[31] Some of Richardson's contemporaries such as Nathanial Hawthorne and Herman Melville, were questioning the assumption that God had a special relationship with man. The transcendentalists led by R.W. Emerson equated God with Nature. By taking this concept one step further, Herman Melville came to the conclusion that just as evil was in Nature so was it in God (vide Billy Budd). In effect man's concept of a benevolent God was an illusion. In a different manner Hawthorne expressed the same injustice of God to man as illustrated by Nature's total indifference to man's suffering.

[32] Westbrook, p.1.

[33] An underlying motive for Westbrook, never explicit but always present, is the deep resentment of the lower class for the upper class. Westbrook, a yeoman, who feels that he is as good as, if not better than, any man, takes violent class revenge on the gentleman Stringer and his family. He restrains his show of hatred for Stringer only in the presence of his fellow yeoman. Sergeant Herbert, who represents that part of the lower class which is content with its position as a sort of inferior partner with the gentleman class in the maintenance of an orderly and just society. The passages of Socialist thought in the previously published The Monk Knight show Richardson's conviction about this subject. His association with G.G. Foster who was a Fourierist and his involvement with the workingmen's associations in New York City must have served to introduce him to Socialist literature: he could not have failed to have read the Communist Manifesto of 1848, for instance. This aspect of his thought when seen in conjunction with Westbrook's destruction of society could provide an interesting study into the effects of Socialist thought on the artist's prophetic vision.

of the war. Richardson's uncle, Alexander Askin, recorded in his diary the arrest of Westbrook and his imprisonment in the Niagara jail.[34] Eventually Westbrook escaped and joined the Americans. After the defeat of the British in the Battle of the Thames, Westbrook guided marauding parties of backwoodsmen and Indians on horseback along the Thames River, looting and plunging the district into great hardship. In 1826 when he was settled prosperously with a large family on land in Michigan on the banks of the St. Clair River, the United States Commissioner of Indian Affairs met him and left a description remarkably close to Richardson's characterization.

> . . . he has a quick-moving and intelligent eye. His form is good, with broad shoulders and chest, and excellent and well-finished limbs. He has no education, yet he talks well, and is precise and graphic in his descriptions. . .If he once resolves upon an accomplishment of any object, he is sure to realize it. The means are mere materials to be judged of by his conceptions of right; and these are generally made to obey the impulses of the moment,

[34] *John Askin Papers*, II, 713.

[35] Thomas L McKenney, *Sketches of a Tour to the Lakes, of the character and customs of the Chippeway Indians* and of incidents connected with the Treaty of Fond du Lac (Baltimore: Fielding Lucas Jr, 1827) pp.150-1. Incidentally, McKenney agreed with Richardson that R.M. Johnson killed Tecumseh, *vide* Thomas L McKenney, *Memoirs, official and personal...* (New York: Paine and Burgess, 1846), pp.180-3. Some of the incidents in the story were taken from life, for instance the attempt of one man to lure a regiment away from the command of Captain Stringer (i.e. Springer) *vide* C.O. Ermantinger, *The Talbot Regime* (St Thomas: Municipal World, 1904), p.74. Rist, Stringer's Lieutenant in the story, was the name of an English officer who married his sister Jane. Holmes was the leader of the American force which engaged the Canadian militia on the bank of a ravine near the Thames River on March 4, 1814 and fell back to Detroit (Ermantinger, p.73).

come from what quarter or involve what consequences they may.[35]

The sub-theme of love blossoming in a Montreal convent could be readily believed by the reading public owing to the *Awful Disclosures* about monks and nuns in a Montreal convent which had been sparking the Protestant Crusade in America for more than a decade. Richardson, however, made clear that he intended no insinuation against any church or creed: "Protestant clergymen are not, as all the world has had some reason to know in this glorious nineteenth century more Josephs than other men."[36] At a time when incendiary speakers were inciting mobs to attack Catholic cathedrals, Richardson found that he had to editorialize lest he be misunderstood.

No doubt his rather obsessive references to rape left him open to misunderstanding. But rape was the epitome of ugliness and depravity for this man who regarded the loveliness of women as God's greatest achievement. Its emphasis in *Westbrook* implies that a morbid pessimism was overtaking him; he seems to say that man could be destroyed by the evil innate within him.

His choice of theme may explain why no copy of *Westbrook, the Outlaw* could be found for over a century until July 1972;[37] the short novel was its own worst enemy owing to its graphic description of a subject which the leaders of American society regarded as morally subversive.

In a manner typical of his contempt for those who failed to appreciate the importance of his art, Richardson expressed his bitterness at Upper Canada by way of parenthesis in this, his last novel: ". . . that semi-barbarous province, which, even at the present day,

[36] *Westbrook*, p.33.

[37] *Sunday Mercury* (New York, Sept.14-Oct. 26, 1851) in seven consecutive issues; rpt. Montreal, Grant Woolmer Books, 1973.

when *affecting* a position among the nations of the earth, cannot boast in literature of three native authors, while it compels even those to court a strange soil for the harvest that awaits the man of talent and appreciation in every portion of the civilized world."[38] When the American officers express their relief that Westbrook is not an American, it is a tacit recognition by Richardson that one's allegiance to the American flag does not mean that one has been accepted by Americans. At that time Americans were becoming increasingly nativistic and hostile to immigrants, and, no doubt, Richardson, who understood their motivations from his years as a vociferous Canadian nativist, now encountered antipathy in his turn. Perhaps he felt that he, like Westbrook, was without a country.

In the same month that *Westbrook* was serialized, September 1851, Dewitt and Davenport brought out *Hardscrabble* and *Matilda Montgomerie* after publishing *Ecarté* in August. Griswold called *Ecarté* "a very brilliant novel"; many critics considered *Matilda Montgomerie* to be Richardson's masterpiece. Dewitt and Davenport purchased *Westbrook* for publication in book form but did not issue it until 1853.[39]

Although now a celebrated author, Richardson's pleasures were few. He spent much time in the lower town near Nassau Street, the publishing district, where there were inexpensive cafes frequented by many journalists as poor as he. Then there was the bath house placed between the Battery and the Castle Gardens overlooking New York Bay. Above the dressing rooms was a promenade with chairs and tables where one could sit after one's bath, smoke a cigar, take some wine, enjoy the cool breeze, and watch the games in the water. New York had an atmosphere of casualness. Lamplighters went about their business lighting the whale-oil or tallow candle street lamps only when the moon was not out, a decision made for them months in advance by the almanac. The Croton River water, which was brought to the city when Richardson first came to New York from England, serviced very few houses. Most people used the wells on every alternate corner, or if they were dry, the roof cisterns which caught the rain-water, breeding mosquitoes in summer and freezing over in winter. As for entertainment, there were plenty of theatres producing the usual farces and blood-and-thunder dramas like *Wacousta*. The Christie Minstrels were the musical sensation of the day, and the Fox Sisters conducted audiences through spiritualist meetings. But there were lonely nights in the city when he would have lain awake remembering his years with Maria and listening to a man sing out the hour from the roof of the police watch on Wooster Street and another pass through the streets with an "All is well."

Richardson still fostered his particular pantheistic philosophy — that the divinity of God is in every man in the measure to which he asserts his individuality. Strong individuals like Wacousta and the Monk Knight were superior in mind and soul to the hypocrites about them because the hypocrites blunted their spiritual development by falsifying their natures. Love alone was God's great gift, and through it man could attain the highest point of his individuality and spirituality. By chance there was a preacher, the Reverend William Augustus Muhlenberg, whose philosophy was similar to Richardson's and whose newly built Church of the Holy Communion Richardson attended. This tall, handsome, silver-haired man from a distinguished family could have had a lucrative post in the Episco-

---

[38] *Westbrook*, p.7.
[39] It was advertised for 25 cents in one octavo volume of a uniform set of Richardson's works, copyright 1856. The address of the printer, W.H. Tinson, is given as Spruce St on the flyleaf of the *Hardscarbble* volume which advertised *Westbrook*. The NYC directory lists him at that address only in 1853, at other addresses for other years. Also, if Richardson had sold *Westbrook* to Dewitt in 1852, the publisher would have issued it within a year.

palian Church, but he envisioned an "Evangelical Catholicism" proclaiming the universality of Christianity through all time.

Opposed to church doctrines which were devisive, Muhlenberg taught an active personal love. His Church which still stands on the corner of Sixth Avenue and 20th Street, served the poor from the alleys of low wooden tenements called "Horne's buildings" south of 20th Street, and many of the rich who came from lower Manhattan. The Church's stained glass windows were among the finest in America, and its boys' choir was the first in the country. Richardson, who admired simplicity and plainness in churches, would have liked the open, unchushioned benches. And he would have admired Muhlenberg's stand for the liberation of women (Muhlenberg began the first order of Episcopalian Nuns, who helped him in social work). Whether Muhlenberg would have agreed with Richardson that passion was "the most exquisite proof" of God's love, his pantheistic Christianity was in accord with the theme of spiritual love in *The Monk Knight of St. John.*

Muhlenberg's emphasis on the spiritual power of love seems to have brought Richardson to examine its quality in a short story, *Captain Leslie; or, the Generous Foe, A Tale of the Revolutionary War* which appeared at this time.[40] Richardson began his story by describing the location of Dog Watch Hollow and Chimney Rock in Somerset County New Jersey. A Delaware Indian, in despair over the white man's gradual encroachment of the entire continent, committed suicide at the Hollow which bears his name, and a squaw threw herself from Chimney Rock into the ravine below. During the Revolutionary War, General Washington's troops reconnoitered the British army under General Howe in this area and cut off the 17th British regiment at Princeton. Washington, remarking upon the valour of a young British Captain, puts the wounded officer under the

care of Mathilda Clarendon, a beautiful woman of refined accomplishments. They fall in love at first sight. This "secret intelligence" links their hearts and until he dies that night, the patient and his attentive nurse live in a sort of spiritual communion, which she never forgets.

> . . . she saw his memory floating in proud distinction over the fast-fading form that was once all beauty, and which, even in its decay, she looked upon as a sacred deposit confined to her superintending care and hand the flowers with which that ever-fresh and emerald mound was adorned.

Richardson leaves it to the reader to connect the spiritual depression of the Delaware brave and squaw, united in suicidal death, to the spiritual love of the British Captain and Mathilda Clarendon, who belong in some mystical way to the New Jersey country.

Although the story expressed Richardson's appreciation for the purity of spiritual love, he considered it as only one manifestation of love's mysterious power.

In his next story, *Criminal Love; or, the Thrilling Narrative of a Murderer,*[41] he seems to show that love arises from the peculiar nature of the human personality, and, therefore, it is not necessarily good or pure. The story tells of the court trial of a very handsome young man "accused of the murder of a married woman with whom he had for some time carried on a criminal intercourse" in the town of Tarbes in the French Pyrenees. Richardson sets the scene, and the mood of the story in a sentence: "Summer had thrown aside her glaring mantle, and disappeared with it, while autumn, in her varicoloured kaleidescopal robe, presented an aspect softened, calm and subdued." The young man escaping from an unsatisfactory love affair is seduced by the beautiful daughter of the household into

[40] *Sunday Mercury* (Nov. 16, 1851).

[41] *Sunday Mercury* (Nov. 23, 1851).

LOLA MONTES :

OR,

A Reply

TO THE

"PRIVATE HISTORY AND MEMOIRS"

OF

THAT CELEBRATED LADY,

Recently Published,

BY

THE MARQUIS PAPON,

FORMERLY SECRETARY TO

THE KING OF BAVARIA,

AND FOR A PERIOD

THE PROFESSED FRIEND AND ATTENDANT

OF

THE COUNTESS OF LANSFELDT.

"Nisi mentita muliere."
Juvenal.

Title page to *Lola Montes*, anonymously published by
Richardson (1851).

which he has just moved. When the affair is discovered
he has to leave, but consumed with passion tries to see
the girl. She now scorns his advances which maddens
him to kill her and attempts to take his own life. Moved
by this recital the court sentences him not to death, but
to five years imprisonment. Among the crowd of women spectators from the surrounding towns, Richardson remarks a voluptuous Spanish woman whose happiness at the light sentence seems particularly marked
and he notices "a parting glance of intelligence" pass
between the woman and the prisoner. Passionate love,
therefore, seems to be the destiny of this young man as
if it were the natural accompaniment to his attractiveness to women.

Richardson, who received enough money from
these stories to subsist upon, could sell stories only
rarely.[42] As for his novels, his publishers alone profited
from their sale. In November 1851, therefore, Griswold promised to help him in a publishing venture: a

booklet in defense of Lola Montes who was planning to
come to America.[43] The idea was promising. Foster had
set the example by successfully publishing *Memoir of
Jenny Lind* the previous year. Lola Montes was front
page news since the revolution in Bavaria. Though the
American press branded her a prostitute, Richardson
admired her spirit and resourcefulness; it was an opportunity for the lone knight to ride to a damsel's distress. The popularity of the subject would ensure the
book's financial success.

Entitled *Lola Montes; or, A Reply to the "Private
History and Memoirs" of That Celebrated Lady, Recently
Published by the Marquis Papon, Formerly Secretary to
the King of Bavaria, and for a Period the Professed Friend
and Attendant of the Countess of Lansfeldt*, this small book
was printed anonymously at Richardson's expense in
December and sold at all booksellers. Taking his theme
from Papon's mean little book replete with private
letters between Ludwig of Bavaria, a very old man, and
the young impelling Lola, Richardson belittles Papon
as a typical philistine courtier ready to turn any situation to his advantage; and he defends Lola's right to be
a courtesan, naming several that he knew in his youth
who were celebrated rather than scorned by society.
Quoting passages from the book and newspaper accounts of Lola, he slows his argument, in fact, belabours
it, for it is of small consequence to begin with, but his
scorn for Papon is amusing, and the few references to
himself are — as always — interesting. The opening
paragraph illustrates his mood at the time: "That this
world is made up of villany, hypocrisy, and selfishness,
none but the simple can doubt. The experience of each
day proves it, and the further we advance in the path of
what the world terms civilization, the more apparent
does it become."

---

[42] "...but here (New York) he found little occupation for
his pen..." *Sunday Mercury* (May 16, 1852).

[43] *The Pick* (May 22, 1852) established Richardson's authorship. From the *Sunday Mercury* (Nov. 16, 1851) it is
established that it was written in November 1851; Nichols
tried to boost its sales (*Sunday Mercury*, Dec. 21, 1851).

Richardson must have sunk his capital into the publication of his *Reply* as he sold *Wau-nan-gee* cheaply for publication in book form in December to H. Long and Brothers, publishers similar to Dewitt and Davenport.[44] Although widely known in Europe, Papon's *Memoir* was not translated into English; moreover, a New York magazine serialized "Memoires of Lola Montes" written by Lola herself. Thus Richardson's *Reply* sold badly. If his name had appeared on it, sales might have been better, but the ambiguous Griswold who had helped him finance it probably insisted that it appear anonymously. Disappointed in his own lack of creative ability, Griswold won a strange satisfaction from negating or usurping the personality of truly creative writers.[45] The critic left for Philadelphia. Richardson saw him again in New York in February 1852 when Griswold was organizing the Cooper Memorial meeting in honour of the author who had died several months previously. Griswold was very busy and likely had little time to become interested in Richardson's plight.

In mid-February, however, someone was concerned. A letter signed "Aborigine" was printed in a New York newspaper and reprinted by other newspapers and periodicals; it was headlined "Who Killed Tecumseh" and told of Major Richardson's connection with Tecumseh in the 1812 War and his knowledge of the circumstances surrounding the Chief's death.[46] A subtle way of advertising, it would only have been printed as it was without charge by those journal editors who knew the author of the letter personally. It called Richardson "perhaps the only man now living who knew well the unfortunate Chief" and continued:

> It is said that Major Richardson, by the earnest solicitation of many of our citizens, and military men in particular, will deliver a lecture at an early day, on the character and death of Tecumseh... A lecture on no other subject could scarcely afford the curious in the romantic history of our country more thrilling interest. An impartial essay by an officer then in arms against us, and made prisoner with the entire British force in that battle, by the gallantry of our arms, cannot but be interesting to all. The literary reputation as author of that celebrated novel, *Wacousta*, would of itself ensure a full attendance. Let the lecture be given in Tripler Hall.[47]

Griswold may have written the letter; if so, it was the last thing he could do for the knight whose paper on Tecumseh he had not published.

Since Tripler Hall seated five thousand people, it was found more practical for the lecture to be given in the New York Society Library Rooms on Broadway. Letters of the press from various claimants to the honour of shooting the Chieftain, had been currying interest in the subject of Tecumseh's death for some months. Richardson would tell who really did the deed, wrote the *Sunday Mercury* which announced that cards of admission, price 25 cents, could be had "at the principal hotels, and at the door, which will be open at half past seven, the reading commencing at 8 o'clock" on Friday,

---

[44] We can surmise that Richardson watched his publishers profit from the sale of his books and decided to risk making a profit on one of them. Unfortunately he chose *Lola Montes* for the experiment.

[45] Griswold's relationship with the young author Horace Binney Wallace is a case in point. Sam Nichols commented (*Sunday Mercury*, Sept. 28, 1851): "Some men are never happy but when they are basking under the sun of some great man's memory. If Mr. Griswold reminds us of any thing he reminds us of a sick kitten in everlasting search of a hot brick."

[46] *Courier and Enquirer* (New York, Feb. 13, 1852).

[47] *Evening Day Book* (New York, Feb. 13, 1852).

[48] *Sunday Mercury* (Feb. 15, 1852).

February 20.[48] Yet, in spite of the announcements, the attendance was disappointingly small. This was attributed by the *Sunday Mercury* "to the wretched manner in which the place was lighted up, and the absence of posters to attract the public eye." The organizers, however, hoped to renew the lecture soon "in a more favourable and attractive room."[49]

Who were the organizers? The pseudonym "Aborigine" on the letter to the press serves as a clue. In the late eighteen-forties there emerged a native American movement whose aim was to protect the American workingmen's jobs from the effects of cheap immigrant labour flooding the country. It fostered workingmen's associations and clubs. Out of it grew a secret society organized after the manner of an Indian tribal council with a Sachem or Chief at the head. Called the Order of United Americans, this society published periodicals which printed stories dealing with the early history of the country. Richardson was brought into its circle of writers about this time.

Robert Dewitt, Richardson's publisher, was a member of the Order, so that it was probably owing to his influence that Richardson found work on a newspaper, *The Sachem*, financed by the Order, but ironically staffed by English expatriates. Tom Picton ("the Colonel") was the chief editor, and Foster, Julie de Marguerittes, North, and Richardson were his assistants. Another ex-Englishman, William Henry Herbert, whom Foster called the greatest living novelist, was an editor.

Herbert is remembered for his hundreds of sporting articles under the pseudonym of Frank Forester — classics which were inspired by his trips into the Canadian wilds around Georgian Bay. He had a violent temper, distrusted everything British, and was continuously suspecting fellow literati of lampooning him. When he contributed an article on the British in Canada, both Richardson and North objected to his misrepresentation of the political facts. They argued heatedly over the matter until Herbert resigned from the paper rather than retract. That Richardson could have stuck to a journalistic task that required him to write ultra-nationalistic items for American patriots reveals how badly he needed money. His pride, however, made him draw the line at a deliberate defamation of Canada.

Since the staff prepared for the paper's continuous publication some months in advance of its first issue, due on June 5, 1852, the argument leading to Herbert's resignation probably took place in March or April. Picton referred to it in his biography of Herbert.[50] But it appears that he did not give the whole story. In a book [51] printed in the fall of 1852 Foster listed the staff on the *Sachem*; he reported Herbert and himself as assistant editors but he made no mention of North, (Richardson was dead then). Apparently the ultra-patriotic politics of the Order had caused Herbert to be reinstated and found the services of North and Richardson expendable. At any rate the Order eventually discovered to its horror that most of the editorial staff was British and closed the paper down. It then began another paper, *The True American*, with staff to match.

The market glutted with his works, the journalistic competition fierce, and with no other means of making an income, Richardson had to depend on the sale of *Lola Montes; or, A Reply* to keep alive. He made the rounds of the booksellers in hopes of collecting a bit here and there from copies sold, but the book was doing badly. He visited some editors of newspapers and periodicals asking them to advertise it. The editor of one newspaper, *Pick*, whose whimsicality and common sense made it extremely popular, reported that the Major called at his office with the book: ". . . he was

[49] *Sunday Mercury* (Feb. 22, 1852).

[50] Thomas Picton, *The Life and Writings of Frank Forester*, ed. David W. Judd, London [nd].

[51] George G. Foster, *New York Naked* (New York: Dewitt and Davenport, 1852), p.95.

quite sanguine that he should realize a great many thousands of dollars, if not more," but this editor, one of Lola's few supporters, felt that "it was a defence (over the left) as it replied to a hundred matters, that Lola, nor any person transpired ever heard or dreamed of having been made."[52]

Richardson may have been hoping to find an ally in Lola. When she arrived in the States in December at the time the book appeared in print, he gave it to the editor of *Pick* for him to draw to her attention. Lola was having a difficult time alone, and her future was too uncertain for her to accept aid from a romance-minded chevalier who might hamper her progress in a utilitarian America. In January she was ejected from a boarding house on Washington Square, the low point of her career (or was it dancing to a theatre audience of five ladies and one small girl that month?), but she quickly climbed back through a tour of sensational appearances in American cities, and five months later in New York drew an audience of over three thousand. Richardson's gallant offer of protection was misplaced — as if fate had cast him in a final Don Quixote posture.

Richardson was not alone in his poverty. Two-thirds of the literary men, like Richardson, were not listed in the city directory, in fact had no fixed living quarters; they drifted about principally as tenants-at-pleasure in boarding houses, or chance lodgers at third-rate hotels. Richardson, who enjoyed reading the *Pick* newspaper, would have seen an item in May 1 issue on "The Literary Hack" and had forebodings on his future:

Where the hack dines or sleeps, very few persons can tell; he is supposed, however, to pick up a portion of his sustenance at the "free lunches," and has been occasionally surprised snoring in a lofty garret, in some retired portion of the city. His purse is penury impersonified and cotton, and it rarely holds any of the great "root of all evil." The latter end of the literary hack is involved in profound mystery; he seems to gradually dissipate into the grave, but no one has ever witnessed his death, and his mortal remains rest in the grave, untombstoned and unknown.

Perhaps his last piece of writing was a short foreword to *Wau-nan-gee* dated March 30 in which he recalled the heroines of the Chicago massacre whom he had seen as a youth. To their courage and suffering he inscribed the book. Here he expressed an attitude about writing as idealistic as when he began to write thirty years before:

an author may gladly avail himself of the occasion to show that no common interest influenced the tracing of his pen — not the mere desire to make a book, but to establish on a high pedestal, and to circulate through the most attractive and popular medium, the merits of those whose deeds and sufferings have inspired him with the generous spirit of eulogistic comment.

[53] In this connection listen to Daniel Webster as chairman of the James Fenimore Cooper Memorial meeting speak to the assembled literati at Metropolitan Hall on Feb. 22, 1852. Richardson was undoubtedly in the audience, most of whom knew of his admiration for Cooper which he mentioned in his preface to the 1851 edition of *Wacousta*: "I should not be here tonight, ladies and gentlemen, to raise my feeble voice in honour of the memory of Fenimore Cooper, however distinguished by genius, talent, education and the art of popular writing, if in the character of his productions there was anything to be found calculated to undermine the principles of our religious faith, or debauch the morality of the country. Nothing of genius or talent can atone for an injury of this kind to the rising generation of the community." *Memorial of James Fenimore Cooper* (New York: Putman, 1852).

[52] *The Pick*, I, No. 14 (New York, May 22, 1852).

It was his last claim for his work to be judged as art; sadly, this novel was advertised with a flood of recent cheap publications, and from this moment, Richardson was typed as a maker of potboilers.[53] This was a convenient way for the bourgeoisie to disparage and ignore *The Monk Knight of St. John*.

Wau-nan-gee appeared the first week in May. In this week fine weather had returned after a cold spell. Pedestrians sank to their ankles in the juicy black mud of the main streets. Richardson was met in a bookstore by a little girl belonging to *Pick's* establishment. According to the editor of *Pick*:

> The Major was accompanied by "Hector," his favorite Newfoundland, and he observed, in a very melancholy tone, to the little girl, who was caressing the dog: "Ah! my poor Hector, we must part or starve," and we have heard that he was obliged to sell Hector to get food for himself.[54]

Although his friends knew that his fortunes were at a low ebb, none had guessed they were that low.

Richardson died penniless on May 12, 1852, of erysipilas, a poisoning brought about by undernourishment. Nicknamed St Anthony's Fire, it is accompanied by a burning fever causing a painful death, as if one were consumed in flames. Some of his friends contributed to his funeral expenses.

He was buried on Friday the 14th from the Church of the Holy Communion, but no tombstone marked his grave. A search for it was made in vain in 1900; an extensive enquiry in 1963 brought no better result. City death records reveal that his body was removed from the city limits, but do not specify to "potters fields." The Church of the Holy Communion arranged to bury its poor parishioners in unmarked graves in Flushing about 1852. Unfortunately the records for this small

54 *The Pick*, I, No.14 (New York, May 22, 1852).

196

area of what is now a gigantic cemetery ground were burnt.

The obituaries were merely announcements of the funeral, except for *Pick's* which was compassionate and fatalistic: "Such is the fate of genius."[55] In this obit-

55 *Ibid.* Nichols wrote in the *Sunday Mercury* (May 16, 1852) that he regretted to learn Richardson had died "under very distressing and melancholy circumstances. Verily, the way of literary men of the city is hard indeed!" Nichols knew the dire truth of this fact; he was probably the last to purchase a story from Richardson: "Ampata! A Tale of Lake George," which ran in three issues of the *Sunday Mercury* (March 28, April 4 and 11, 1852).

"Ampata!" relates the story of the unrequited love of an Indian girl for a British Major within the framework of the French and Indian War of 1755. Ampata's love blossoms during the Major's imprisonment in the Indian encampment. But the Major loves an English girl who awaits his return to the English camp. He can offer only his friendship to Ampata. Heartbroken, Ampata nevertheless helps him to escape. In the ensuing battle between the French and English forces, Ampata, throwing herself between the Major and a brave, takes the blow intended for the Major upon herself. The Major carries her into the camp where she dies but not before she sees the Major and his loved-one together and smiles her blessing upon them.

The point he seems to make in the story is that the Indian has a profound capacity for true friendship, which he dwells upon briefly, and in Ampata's case, her friendship led to sacrifice of self.

Richardson's authorship of the anonymous story is recognized in the sub-theme: that of General Lyman, a sensitive and brilliant soldier, over whom William Johnson has command owing to political influence.

> Johnson was an uneducated adventurer, suddenly raised to distinction by the aid of powerful friends, to whom he made himself convenient by his energy, shrewdness and activity, while Lyman was dignified in person, greatly beloved by the soldiers, and moreover was distinguished for learning and science. It is therefore not to be wondered at, that Johnson entertained

uary is found one of the rare personal descriptions of Richardson, which seems to have remained as true for those few literary scholars who have chanced on his works as for those of his contemporaries who barely knew him: "The Major was a queer fish in some respects, and a very eccentric Christian."

Afterword

SOME ATTEMPT should be made to explain why the first novelist of a nation should be unknown to the citizens of that nation. The entries about him in biographical dictionaries leave the immediate impression upon the curious that he was an unsavoury, dishonest character whose writings rose no higher than that of a scribbler of pot boilers. The *Dictionary of National Biography* even lists his dates of birth and death incorrectly.

The vilification which followed Richardson during his life pursued his name after his death. The Reformers never forgave Richardson his part in forming an opposition. Hincks and Daly went on to governorships and knighthoods,[1] yet in spite of their honours they would not forget the man whose intelligence and perserverance, whose extraordinary talent, showed him superior to them. The historian of the Canadian Reformers, J.C. Dent, wrote in 1881 that Richardson's novels were wooden and added: "it is difficult to understand how any writer possessed of true critical sagacity

towards Lyman an implacable jealousy. Not content with placing on his own brow the laurels he neither won nor merited, but in order to gratify the demon within his breast, he employed agents to calumniate his officer, who he felt was in every respect his superior.

could have found anything in them to admire."[2]

The Monk Knight of St. John was the unforgivable sin. By attacking the mores of the Establishment in the novel, Richardson gave critics the easy task of belittling him while posing as watchdogs for society. Dent is a case in point:

As for "The Monk Knight of St. John" it is simply beneath criticism, whether regarded from a moral or a literary point of view. The author had no faculty for drawing character, and he had knocked about in barrack-rooms so long that he seemed to have lost all perception of the eternal fitness of things.[3]

Dent called Richardson's *Eight Years in Canada* "unreliable." *The Cyclopedia of American Biography* wrote in a similar manner: "His novels are deficient in interest and his histories are inaccurate." Prof. Chester New, the biographer of Lord Durham, on the contrary, found *Eight Years in Canada* a valuable record of the time. The present author has checked Richardson's writings against many sources and has been convinced of Richardson's integrity, a sentiment which may have

[1] Hincks became Prime Minister of Canada 1851-1854, Governor of Barbados 1855-62, and Governor of British Guiana 1862-69. When the Tories lost power in the elections of 1848, the Reformers took revenge on Daly for his support of Metcalfe in 1843 by denying him a post with the Government. His unreasonable insistence that Lord Grey find him a top Government position as recompense for his service satisfied Grey "of his unfitness for a Government position even if any should become vacant." Eventually he was made Governor of Tobago 1851-54, Lieutenant Governor of Prince Edward Island 1854-57, and Governor of South Australia 1860-68.

[2] John Charles Dent, *The Last Forty Years; Canada since the Union of 1841* (Toronto: George Virtue, 1881), 2:547.

[3] *Ibid.*

become evident in the course of this biography. His writing is as fresh and exciting as when first published. Rather than belittling his fiction, critics should recognize his influence on the development of American realism.[4] Not every reader would agree with Casselman, writing in 1902, that in Richardson's writing "there are no carelessnesses, no crudities, no notable mannerisms . . . no straining after rhetorical effect, no attempt at fine writing" but all would agree that "interest is sustained to the end."[5] Certainly he pursued the meaning of life by faithfully recording it from all sides; and it is this dimension which serves as the foundation stone of Canadian literature to which Canadian writers may look back for guidance.

Richardson's individual struggle against the bureaucratic monoliths of army and government make him particularly significant in our day when bureaucratic conformity threatens to destroy the human race. And in this context we can appreciate the strength of his individuality.

The accepted version of Richardson's character, that of a quarrelsome liar, which was manufactured by his enemies with apparent success, had its counterpart in local gossip. An elderly resident of Niagara-on-the-Lake told the author of this work that she remembered as a small girl that her cousin, who was Charles Richardson's youngest daughter, burnt a packet of documents which referred to Richardson, rather than let other generations see them. When asked about him, she replied curtly: "He was one of the family but we'll let the dead past bury the dead."

The last of the family, Harvey McGregor Richardson, grandson of one of Richardson's half-brothers,

turned up in 1953 at the age of eighty-eight with a houseboat which he moored in the Detroit river at Windsor. He, in his poverty, believed that a trunkful of first editions of *Wacousta* existed somewhere in Windsor which would be worth a small fortune. During a spell of very cold weather that year the stove in his houseboat blew up and he died in the flames. The curse of Wacousta was merciless to the end.

A Check List of Richardson's Works

1825
Confessions of Julia Johnstone relative to herself and others. London, Benbow, March 25, 1825. In contradiction to the fables of Harriette Wilson, with a portrait of the author.

1826-1827
"A Canadian Campaign, by a British Officer," *New Monthly Magazine* 17 Pt 2 (1826) 541-548; 19 Pt 1 (1827) 162-170, 248-254, 449-457, 538-551. Philadelphia in *National Gazette and Literary Register*, 7, Nos 915, 942, 992, 993 (Jan. 30-Aug. 4, 1827).

1828
Tecumseh; or, The Warrior of the West: A Poem of Four Cantos with notes, by an English Officer. London, Printed for R. Glynn 1828.
1828: *Tecumseh; or, The Warrior of the West*: A Poem of Four Cantos and 188 Stanzas of Ottava Rima. London, James Moyes.
1842: in *The New Era, or Canadian Chronicle* (Brockville, Upper Canada) 2 Nos 15-18 (July 22-Aug. 19) abridged version.

1829
Ecarté; or, The Salons of Paris. London, Colburn 1829.

---

[4] The *Sunday Mercury* which carried Richardson's last writings adopted as a principle the encouragement of realism in literature until its demise in 1895.

[5] Alexander Clark Casselman, ed., *Richardson's War of 1812*, (Toronto: Historical pub., 1902), p.xliv.

1829: New York, G. Long; Philadelphia, Towar and Hogan; Baltimore, W. and J. Neal; Boston, Richardson and Lord.
1843: Kingston, in *Canadian Loyalist and Spirit of 1812* (Jan. 5-Aug. 10)
1851: New York, Dewitt and Davenport (Author's Revised Edition)
1856: New York, R.M. Dewitt
1888: New York, Pollard and Moss (Echo Series, No.31); New York, Pollard and Moss.

1830
Kensington Gardens in 1830; A Satirical Trifle by the Author of *Ecarté*. London, Marsh and Miller 1830.
Only known copy is in the British Museum.
1957: *Major Richardson's Kensington Gardens in 1830* ed and with an intro by Carl F. Klinck. Toronto, Bibliographical Society of Canada Bibliography Publication No.10.

Frascati's; or, Scenes In Paris. London, Colburn and Bentley, 1830. Philadelphia, Carey and Hart, 1836.

c1830
Recollections of the West Indies. London, 1830
Not extant.
1842: in *The New Era, or Canadian Chronicle* (Brockville) 2 Nos 1-12 (March 2-June 24).

1832
Wacousta; or, The Prophecy: A Tale of the Canadas, T. Cadell; Edinburgh, W. Blackwood 1832. 3 vols.
1833: London, Baldwin and Co.; Philadelphia, Key and Biddle (2 vols, first American edition); Philadelphia, in *Waldie's Select Circulating Library* 2 Nos 1-4 and *Waldie's* Circulating Library, new series, 1 Nos 14-17 (both serials running from April 16-May 7); Columbus Ohio, in *Columbus Journal and Gazette*.
1839: London, T. Cadell ("By Major Richardson"); Edinburgh, Blackwood.
1840: London, A. and R. Spottiswoode, Newstreet Square

(second edition).
1851: New York, Dewitt and Davenport (revised edition).
1857: New York, R.M. Dewitt (issued with other Richardson novels in "Uniform Octavo Volumes").
1858: *Wacousta, oder die Prophezeihung*. Eine indianische Geschichte von Major Richardson. Leipzig, Amerikanische Bibliothek 4 Bde Nos 338-341 (first German edition).
1868: Montreal, John Lovell (first Canadian edition).
187—: Montreal, in *The Transcript*
1875: New York, R.M. Dewitt.
1888: New York, Pollard and Moss (Echo Series, No.27).
1888: New York, Pollard and Moss.
1902: Toronto, in Toronto *Evening News* (March 22-July 26, 1902).
1906: Toronto, Historical Publishing Co. (with illus by C.W. Jeffreys) (second Canadian edition).
1906: Chicago, A.C. McClurg (reprinted 1912).
1923: Toronto, McClelland and Stewart (reprinted [1928-32])
1924: Toronto, Musson Book Co.
1924: Toronto, Ontario Book Co.
1925: New York, George Sully.
1925: Garden City, NY, Doran (reprinted 1927, 1928?).
1967: Toronto, McClelland and Stewart (abridged edition).

1836
Journal of the Movements of the British Legion. By an Officer Late of the Quarter-Master-General's Staff. London, Effingham-Wilson 1836.
1837: *Movements of the British Legion with Strictures on the Course of Conduct Pursued by Lieutenant-General Evans* By Major Richardson, K.S.F. Second Edition to Which Is Added with New Views A Continuation of the Operations from the 5th of May 1836 to the Close of March 1837. London, Simpkin, Marshall and Co, J. Macrone, and E. Wilson.
1847: *Kriegszüge in Spanien wahrend der Jahre 1835-1838* by R. von Stutterheim, Braunschweig, Meyer. (Said to be

trans. in part of the *Journal* with continuation through 1838. Baron Stutterheim entered 1st Cavalry Regiment "Reina Isabella" Lancers, as Lieut. on October 26, 1835).

1837
Peninsular War. London, 1837.
Not extant.

1838
"Inquisitor" dispatches in the London *Times*, March-Nov., 1838.

Personal Memoirs of Major Richardson; As Connected with the Singular Oppression of That Officer While in Spain By Lieutenant-General De Lacy Evans. Montreal, Armour and Ramsay; Quebec, W. Neilson; Toronto, R. Stanton; and Kingston, J. MacFarlane 1838.

1838-1839(?)
The Sentinel (Prescott, Upper Canada)
Richardson was said to be the editor of this weekly paper.

1839
Sketch of the Late Battle at the Wind Mill Near Prescott in November 1838 Prescott, Upper Canada, James Campbell, printer, Jan. 19, 1839 at the *Sentinel* Office.
Published anonymously.

1840
The Canadian Brothers; or, The Prophecy Fulfilled. A Tale of the Late American War. By Major Richardson, Knight of the Military Order of Saint Ferdinand. Montreal, A.H. Armour and H. Ramsay 1840.
1851: *Matilda Montgomerie; or, The Prophecy Fulfilled* New York, Dewitt and Davenport (Author's Revised Edition).
1856: New York, Dewitt and Davenport (rev. ed.) (reprinted 1875).

1888: New York, Pollard and Moss (rev. ed.).
1974: *The Canadian Brothers*. Toronto, Univ. of Toronto.

Major Richardson's Reply to Colonel Williams' Gasconade. Brockville n. pub. 1840.

1841
The Miser Outwitted. Brockville, n. pub.

1841-1842
The New Era, or Canadian Chronicle (Brockville) June 1841-Aug. 19, 1842.
A weekly literary newspaper of which Richardson was proprietor and editor.

1842
Jack Brag in Spain, by Mr Hardquill in *The New Era, or Canadian Chronicle* (Brockville) 1 Nos 1-34 (June 1841-Feb. 1842)
Toronto Public Library has 1 No. 31, only part of the novel known to be extant.

Operations of the Right Division of the Army of Upper Canada, During the American War of 1812 in *The New Era, or Canadian Chronicle* (Brockville) 2 Nos. 1-15 (March 2-July 22, 1842).
1842: *War of 1812; First Series; Containing a Full and Detailed Narrative of the Operations of the Right Division of the Canadian Army*. Brockville, n. pub. 1842.
1902: *Richardson's War of 1812; with Notes and a Life of the Author* by Alexander Clark Casselman. Toronto, Historical Publishing Co. 1902.

1843-1844
The Canadian Loyalist and Spirit of 1812 (Kingston) Jan. 5, 1843-July (?), 1844.
A weekly political newspaper of which Richardson was proprietor and editor.

1844

"Miller's Prophecy Fulfilled. In the Destruction of the Globe" *Canadian Loyalist and Spirit of 1812* (Kingston) 2 No.5 (Feb. 1, 1844).

A satirical poem.

1971: Toronto in *Papers of the Bibliographical Society of Canada* X, pp.21-28.

1846

Correspondence (submitted to Parliament) between Major Richardson, Late Superintendent of Police on the Welland Canal and the Honourable Dominick Daly, Provincial Secretary, also, between Major Richardson and Lieutenant-Colonel Elliot, Lately Commanding Niagara Frontier; Major Macpherson, Royal Canadian Rifles; Hamilton H. Killaly, Esq.; S. Power, Esq., Chief Engineer, Welland Canal. Montreal, Donoghue and Mantz 1846.

1846

"Eight Years in Canada; Embracing a Review of the Administrations of Lords Durham and Sydenham, Sir Charles Bagot and Lord Metcalfe" *The Weekly Expositor; or, Reformer of Public Abuses...* (Montreal) Aug.-Dec. 1846.

1847: Montreal, H.H. Cunningham; London, Simmonds and Ward.

1967: rpt. Wakefield, Eng. S.R. Publishers.

1846-1847(?)

The Weekly Expositor; or, Reformer of Public Abuses and Railway and Mining Intelligencer (Montreal) Aug. 20, 1846-Jan. 1847(?)

Richardson was proprietor and editor of this "anti-ministerial paper."

1848

The Guards in Canada; or, The Point of Honour; being a sequel to Major Richardson's *Eight Years in Canada*.

Montreal, H.H. Cunningham 1848.

1849

"A Trip to Walpole Island and Port Sarnia" *The Literary Garland* (Montreal) 9 (Jan. 1849).

Published anonymously.

1851: New York in *Copways's American Indian* (New York) July 10, 1851 (variant) "By Major Richardson, K.S.F."

1924: *Tecumseh and Richardson*; The Story of a Trip to Walpole Island and Port Sarnia with an Introduction and Biographical Sketch by A.H.U. Colquhoun. Toronto, Ontario Book Company.

1850

Hardscrabble; or, The Fall of Chicago. A Tale of Indian Warfare. *Sartain's Union Magazine* (Philadelphia) 6 (1850) Feb. 143, March 217, April 281, May 348, June 390.

1850 (1851?): New York, Dewitt and Davenport (Sold in August 1850 but perhaps not printed until October 1851).

1855: New York, R.M. Dewitt.

1856: New York, R.M. Dewitt.

1857: *Hardscrabble, oder Der Fall von Chicago*. Erzaehlung aus dem Indianerkriege von Major Richardson. Leipzig, Amerikanische Bibliothek 2 Bde Nos 261, 262.

1861: New York, R.M. Dewitt.

1868: Philadelphia, T.B. Peterson and Bros.

1875: New York, R.M. Dewitt.

1888: New York, Pollard and Moss.

The Monk Knight of St. John; A Tale of the Crusades, by Major Richardson. New York, Dewitt and Davenport 1850.

British Museum copy lacks 8 pages.

1850: New York, Published for the Trade.

"The Sunflower, A True Tale of the North-West" *Graham's Magazine* (New York) 37 No.5 (Nov. 1850)

"All Hail to the Land" (National Song) music by Nicholas Bochsa, lyrics by Major Richardson.
Not extant.

1851

"Since Thou Hast Robbed Me of My Heart" (Ballad) music by J.E. Gould, lyrics by Major Richardson.
Not extant.

Wau-nan-gee; or, The Massacre at Chicago in *Sunday Mercury* (New York) 13 Nos 22-34 (i.e. 35: No. 33 mistakenly repeated) June 1-Aug. 31 1851.
1852: New York, G. Long and Brother.
1856: New York, R.M. Dewitt.
1856: Philadelphia, T.B. Peterson and Brothers.

Westbrook, The Outlaw! or, The Avenging Wolf. An American Border Tale in *Sunday Mercury* (New York) Sept. 14-Oct. 26, 1851.
1853: New York, Dewitt and Davenport.
1973: rpt. Montreal, Woolmer.

"The North American Indian" in *Copway's American Indian* (New York) July 10, 1851.

"Captain Leslie; or, The Generous Foe. A Tale of the Revolutionary War" in *Sunday Mercury* (New York) Nov. 16, 1851.

Lola Montes; or, A Reply to the "Private History and Memoirs" of That Celebrated Lady, Recently Published by the Marquis Papon, Formerly Secretary to the King of Bavaria, and for a Period the Professed Friend and Attendant of the Countess of Lansfeldt. New York, "Sold by all Booksellers" 1851.
Published anonymously.

"Criminal Love; or, the thrilling narrative of a murderer" in *Sunday Mercury* (New York) Nov. 23, 1851.

1852
"Ampata! A Tale of Lake George" in *Sunday Mercury* (New York) March 28, April 4, 11 1852.
Anonymous.

Bibliography

This brief bibliography is in addition to the sources cited in the Notes and is intended to draw the reader's attention to background reading for the period.

The Americas — His Early Years
Askin, John. *The John Askin Papers* . . . edited by Milo M. Quaife, Detroit: Detroit Library Commission, 1928-31. 2 v.
Clift, G. Glenn. *Remember the Raisin*; Kentucky and Kentuckians in the Battles and Massacre at Frenchtown, Michigan Territory, in the War of 1812. Frankfort, Ky.: Kentucky Hist. Soc., 1961.
Davis, John. *History of the Second Queens Royal Regiment.* London: Eyre and Spottiswoode, 1906.
Humphrey, Helen H. "The Identity of Gladwin's Informant." *Mississippi Valley Historical Review*, v.21, no. 2 (Sept. 1934).
Klinck, Carl F. and James J. Talmon, eds. *The Journal of Major John Norton, 1809-1816.* Toronto: Champlain Soc., 1970. (Champlain Soc. Pub. 46).
Tucker, Glenn. *Tecumseh; vision of glory.* Indianapolis: Bobbs-Merrill, 1956.
Veritas (pseud., i.e. Honorable John Richardson). *The Letters of Veritas* republished from the Montreal Herald; containing a Succinct Narrative of the Military Administration of Sir George Prevost,

during his command in the Canadas; whereby it will appear manifest that the merit of preserving them from conquest belongs not to him. Montreal: W. Gray, July 1815.

Whitehorn, A.C. *History of the Welsh Regiment.* Cardiff: Western Mail and Echo, 1932.

Europe — His Middle Years

Chancellor, E. Beresford. *Life in Regency and Early Victorian Times;* an account of the days of Brummell and D'Orsay, 1800 to 1850. London: B.T. Batsford, 1926.

D'Almeras, Henri. *La vie parisienne sous la restauration.* Paris: Albion Michal, 1910.

Grant, James. *The Great Metropolis.* New York: Saunders and Otley, 1837.

Gronow, Rees Howell. *Reminiscences of Captain Gronow . . .* being anecdotes of the camp, the court and the clubs at the close of the last war with France. Related by himself . . . 2nd. ed. rev. London: Smith, Elder, 1862.

Praz, Mario. *The Romantic Agony.* Cleveland: World, 1951.

Redding, Cyrus. *Yesterday and Today.* London: T. Cautley Newby, 1863. 3 v.

Rosa, Matthew Whiting. *The Silver-Fork School;* novels of fashion preceding Vanity Fair. Ft. Washington, N.Y.: Kennikat, 1964.

Somerville, Alexander. *The History of the British Legion and War in Spain.* London: James Pattie, 1839.

Thirkwell, Angela. *The Fortunes of Harriette;* the surprising career of Harriette Wilson. London: H. Hamilton, 1936.

Viatte, Auguste. *Les Sources Occultes du Romantisme, 1770-1820.* Paris: H. Champion, 1928.

Westmacott, Charles. *The English Spy.* London: Sherwood and Jones, 1825-26. 2 v.

Wilson, Harriette. *The Memoirs of Harriette Wilson,* written by herself. London: Nash, 1909.

Paris lions and London tigers. London: Navarre Soc., 1935.

Young, Edward. *The Revenge;* a tragedy to which is prefixed the Life of the Author. Edinburgh: J. Robertson, 1774.

The Americas — His Later Years

Arthur, George. *The George Arthur Papers;* being the Canadian papers, mainly confidential, private, and demi-official, of Sir George Arthur in the manuscript collection of the Toronto Public libraries. Edited by Charles R. Sanderson. Toronto: Toronto Public libraries and Univ. of Toronto Press, 1957-59. 3 v. in 5.

Barrell, Joseph. *Shelley and the Thought of his Time,* a study in the history of ideas. New Haven: Yale Univ. Press, 1947.

Bayless, Joy. *Rufus Wilmot Griswold, Poe's Literary Executor.* Nashville, Tenn.: Vanderbilt Univ. Press, 1943.

Borthwick, J. Douglas. *History of the Montreal Prison.* Montreal: A. Periard, 1886.

Elgin, James Bruce. *The Elgin-Grey Papers, 1846-1852,* edited with notes and appendices by Sir Arthur G. Doughty. Ottawa: Patenaude, 1937. 4 v.

Green, Ernest. "Upper Canada's Black Defenders." *Ontario Historical Society Papers and Records,* v. 27, p. 365ff.

Morgan, Henry. *Sketches of celebrated Canadians* and persons connected with Canada from the earliest period in the history of the province down to the present time. Quebec: Hunter, Rose, 1862.

Neal, Frederick. *Township of Sandwich.* Windsor: Record Printing, 1909.

Pizer, Donald. *Realism and Naturalism in Nineteenth Century American Literature.* Carbondale, Ill.: Southern Illinois Univ., 1966.

Quaife, Milo. *Chicago and the Old Northwest 1673-1835.* Chicago: Univ. Press, 1913.

Ross, A.H.O. *Ottawa Past and Present*. Toronto: Musson, 1927.

Roy, James A. *Kingston; the King's Town*. Toronto: McClelland and Stewart, 1952.

Sartain, John. *The Reminiscences of a very old man, 1808-1897*. New York: Appleton, 1899.

Manuscripts

Manuscripts cited in the Notes are largely to be found in the Public Archives of Canada (Ottawa, Ont.) and the Ontario Archives (Toronto, Ont.); Viscount Harding's Papers are in the McGill University Library (Montreal, Quebec); General Chichester's Papers are in the County Record Office (Beverly, Yorkshire); the Rufus Griswold papers referred to are in the Boston Public Library (Boston, Mass.); George Villiers' papers are in the Bodleian Library, Oxford Univ. (Oxford, Eng.); Lord Durham's (Lambton) papers are in the Estate Office of the Durham Estate (Chester-le-sea, Durham Co.) and in the Public Archives of Canada; the Welland Canal papers are on microfilm in the Public Library, St. Catharines, Ont. The Public Record Office (London, Eng.) has the Muster Rolls of the British Army which include the Quarterly Pay Lists of the Queen's Own Regiment of Foot in Barbadoes, St. Vincent, and Grenada listing Lieutenant John Richardson from 1816 through June 24, 1818 (WO 12, 2030). (The War Office Monthly Returns of Officers, Windward and Leeward Islands (WO 17, 2507) lists Lt. G. (i.e. John) Richardson as obtaining leave of absence (to return to England) on Sept. 16, 1818.)

Previous writings about Richardson

Beasley, David. "Tempestuous Major: The Canadian Don Quixote." *Bulletin of the New York Public Library*. New York: v. 74, no. 1 (Jan. 1970), pp. 3-26; v. 74, no. 2 (Feb. 1970), pp. 95-106.

Burkholder, Mabel. "Gallant Major Our First Novelist." *Hamilton Spectator*. Hamilton, Ont.: Aug. 2, 1958.

Casselman, Alexander Clark, ed. *Richardson's War of 1812 with Notes and a Life of the Author*. Toronto: Historical Publishing Co., 1902; rpt. Toronto: Cole, 1974.

Colquhoun, A.H.U., ed. *Tecumseh and Richardson. The Story of a Trip to Walpole Island and Port Sarnia*. Toronto: Ontario Book Co., 1924.

Klinck, Carl F. "Major Richardson's 'Kensington Gardens in 1830'." *Ontario Historical Society Papers and Records*. Toronto: 1956. v. XLVIII, no. 3, pp. 101-107.

Lauriston, Victor. "Opening of John Richardson Library." *Windsor Daily Star*. Windsor, Ont.: Nov. 9, 1928.

"Wrecking Home of First Novelist." *Windsor Daily Star*. Windsor, Ont.: Oct. 26, 1929. "That house is memorable, not merely for its association with a man closely identified with the early history of the Detroit frontier, but as the cradle of Canadian literature."

Morley, William F.E. *A bibliographical study of Major John Richardson*. With an introd. by Derek F. Crawley. Toronto: Bibliog. Soc. of Canada, 1973.

Pacey, Desmond. "A Colonial Romantic, Major Richardson, Soldier and Novelist." *Canadian Literature*. Vancouver: "Part I: The Early Years" no. 2, Autumn 1959, pp. 20-31: "Part II: Return to America" no. 3, Winter 1960, pp. 47-56.

Riddell, William Renwick. *John Richardson*. Toronto: Ryerson, 1923.

Index